on Zaharias ● Rosa Kleberg ● Frances Farenthold ● Mary Maverick
g ● Sarah Weddington ● Mollie Goodnight ● Irma Rangel ●
Rogers ● Dorothy Scarborough ● Liz Carpenter ● Ima Hogg ●
Holley ● Miriam Ferguson ● Dilue Rose Harris ● Jane McCallum
rguson ● Dilue Rose Harris ● Jane McCallum ● Mary Rabb ●
on Zaharias ● Rosa Kleberg ● Frances Farenthold ● Mary Maverick
g ● Sarah Weddington ● Mollie Goodnight ● Irma Rangel ●
Rogers ● Dorothy Scarborough ● Liz Carpenter ● Ima Hogg ●
Holley ● Miriam Ferguson ● Dilue Rose Harris ● Jane McCallum
rguson ● Dilue Rose Harris ● Jane McCallum ● Mary Rabb ●
on Zaharias ● Rosa Kleberg ● Frances Farenthold ● Mary Maverick
g ● Sarah Weddington ● Mollie Goodnight ● Irma Rangel ●
Rogers ● Dorothy Scarborough ● Liz Carpenter ● Ima Hogg ●
Holley ● Miriam Ferguson ● Dilue Rose Harris ● Jane McCallum
rguson ● Dilue Rose Harris ● Jane McCallum ● Mary Rabb ●
on Zaharias ● Rosa Kleberg ● Frances Farenthold ● Mary Maverick
g ● Sarah Weddington ● Mollie Goodnight ● Irma Rangel ●
Rogers ● Dorothy Scarborough ● Liz Carpenter ● Ima Hogg ●
rguson ● Dilue Rose Harris ● Jane McCallum ● Mary Rabb ●
on Zaharias ● Rosa Kleberg ● Frances Farenthold ● Mary Maverick
g ● Sarah Weddington ● Mollie Goodnight ● Irma Rangel ●
Rogers ● Dorothy Scarborough ● Liz Carpenter ● Ima Hogg ●
Holley ● Miriam Ferguson ● Dilue Rose Harris ● Jane McCallum
rguson ● Dilue Rose Harris ● J   abb ●
on Zaharias ● Rosa Kleberg ● Fra   Maverick
g ● Sarah Weddington ● Molli   gel ●
Rogers ● Dorothy Scarborough ●   arpenter ● Ima Hogg ●
Holley ● Miriam Ferguson ● Dilue Rose Harris ● Jane McCallum
rguson ● Dilue Rose Harris ● Jane McCallum ● Mary Rabb ●
on Zaharias ● Rosa Kleberg ● Frances Farenthold ● Mary Maverick
g ● Sarah Weddington ● Mollie Goodnight ● Irma Rangel ●
Rogers ● Dorothy Scarborough ● Liz Carpenter ● Ima Hogg

for Benzee
in celebration of

Women
In
Texas

the best and most
wonderful friends
are your old friends
With love

Ann Fears Crawford

21 September 1982

Courtesy Austin-Travis County Collection, Austin Public Library

Women suffragists vote for the first time.

Women
In Texas

Their Lives
Their Experiences
Their Accomplishments

Ann Fears Crawford
And Crystal Sasse Ragsdale

EAKIN PRESS   ★   BURNET, TEXAS

Funding for research for WOMEN IN TEXAS
provided in part by a grant from the
American Association of University Women.

FIRST EDITION

Published in the United States of America
By Eakin Press, P.O. Drawer AG, Burnet, Texas 78611

ISBN 0-89015-305-1

for my grandmother, Dolly Conley Huey, throughout a
lifetime an East Texas woman

a.f.c.

for Paul C. Ragsdale, whose knowledge of history is
infinitely golden

c.s.r.

Contents

Acknowledgments

The authors wish to express their gratitude to the many people who shared ideas and interests concerning the research and writing of *Women in Texas: Their Lives — Their Experiences — Their Accomplishments.* To Valeska Linnartz Startz, Mrs. Herbert C. Acker, Jr. of New Braunfels, and the Seven Timmerman Sisters of Geronimo for supplying family stories of their great-grandmother, Louisa Ervendberg, to Ragsdale. Also Mrs. Walter Elbel, Sr. and the late Edna F. Faust, Ed Donaubauer, Oscar Haas, who gave generously of their Texas-German knowledge and especially of their interest in New Braunfels. Ragsdale also extends appreciation to the gathering of dedicated historians in Columbus, among whom are Miss Lee Nesbitt, Mrs. Robert E. Tait, Mary Elizabeth and James Hopkins, and the three Wilsons, "Miss" Sophila, Hattie Lee, and Ethe Lee.

Special help came from Esther Altgelt Riske with her remembrances of Texas Germans and their life in the new land and from Helen Spears Swanson and Lillian Duncan Jenkins, whose feel for Texas frontier families helped recreate the experience. To Nell Cox Shelton and Emmett Shelton, Sr., a debt of gratitude for bringing to life the legendary adventures of Lizzie Johnson Williams, whom they had both known firsthand. To E'Lane Carlisle Murray, who added the job of historical interviewer to her already full life by joining with Minerva King

Patch in taping the remembrances of Mrs. Patch's grandmother, Henrietta Chamberlain King. To Paul C. Ragsdale for information from his collection of early Texas maps and living knowledge of Bastrop history, its people, and geography. To Ragsdale's sons, Christopher Williams, for his photographic skill in reproducing illustrations and to Robert W. Williams for his sincere encouragement.

During years of researching the Ferguson era in Texas, Crawford interviewed a number of Texas politicians; their comments on this provocative era in Texas's political history proved invaluable in dealing with Miriam Amanda Ferguson. A number of people contributed comments and insights on the women portrayed, and Crawford wishes to extend sincere thanks to Suzanne Coleman, who shared her views on Frances Farenthold; to Dr. Martha Allen for her knowledge of women in the West; to the Honorable Edward Clark and Dr. Ira Iscoe for their comments on events surrounding the presidency of Dr. Lorene Rogers at The University of Texas at Austin.

In seminars that Crawford taught at The University of Texas at Austin, The University of Texas at San Antonio, and Southwestern University, a number of students explored women in Texas on the political, social, and business scene. For help with research and for enlightening discussions, Crawford wishes to extend her gratitude to those students, particularly to Janet Jette for her work on Barbara Jordan; Celeste Scalise for research on women on local political scenes; Maria Barriozobal for her comprehensive study of Mexican-American women in politics; Anna Galindo for following the career of Irma Rangel; and Andi Schermerhorn for her comments on Ima Hogg.

Many women politicians shared their insights and concerns concerning women in politics in Texas. A great debt of gratitude goes to them, especially to Carole McClellan, Sarah Weddington, Lupe Anguiano, and Ann Richards, who shared a wealth of wisdom and many good times.

Women in Texas could never have been written without the time and effort of a number of dedicated librarians and researchers. The authors are indebted to Audrey Bateman, Frances

Moore, Mary Jo Butler, and the staff of the Austin-Travis County Collection, Austin Public Library; Mary Beth Fleischer, Bill Richter, Ralph Elder, Jeanne Redrow Willson, and Sara Rambo of the Barker History Center, The University of Texas at Austin; Kathleen Gee and Mabrey Thompson of the Special Collections, Harry Ransom Center, The University of Texas at Austin; Martha Utterback of the Daughters of the Republic of Texas Library at the Alamo; Marie B. Berry, research librarian at the San Antonio Public Library; the staff of the Babe Didrikson Zaharias Museum, Beaumont; James D. Fisher, supervisor of community museums for the city of Austin; Frances Anna Barton of the staff of the *Texas Observer;* Byron Price, curator of the Panhandle-Plains Historical Museum, Canyon; and Kent Keeth, curator of the Texas Collection, Baylor University, Waco.

Special thanks goes to Kevin Brooks Crawford for his help with research. The greatest debt of gratitude goes to Marjorie Williams, faithful friend, intrepid editor, and Texas historian.

Preface

Women in Texas: Their Lives — Their Experiences — Their Accomplishments is the result of ten years of intensive research into the vivid and interesting legacy of the women who have helped to create the life, the literature, and the legend of the Lone Star State. These women's stories are tales of frontier ingenuity, pioneer spirit, and entrepreneurial skills woven into the rich tapestry of Texas history.

From nineteenth century to the twentieth, Texas women have created a history of lives well spent and talents explored. Success and accomplishment in Texas know no boundary lines, and the history of the state reflects an enduring legacy of women from a variety of backgrounds and ethnic groups. They rode the cattle trails, wrote the books, painted and sculpted, and helped to govern their state. They created a number of historic "firsts" — Mary Austin Holley, first woman to write a book about her adopted land; Miriam Amanda Ferguson, first woman governor elected in her own right; Irma Rangel, first Chicana to sit in the Texas legislature; Barbara Jordan, first black woman to sit in the Texas Senate and to represent her state in Congress; Lorene Rogers, first woman to serve as president of The University of Texas; Lady Bird Johnson, Texas's own First Lady.

Nineteenth-century Texas women joined without hesitation the fiercely active pioneers that probed a savage frontier; they witnessed its conquest. A philosophical eon now separates these women and their times from the twentieth century.

Changes in life patterns are irrevocable, but the female experience of the past is worthy of examination. We reclaim from memory the reality that created a civilization.

The lives of women in nineteenth-century Texas present a study in contrasts. Mary Rabb journeyed to Texas with her baby, accompanying her husband's family on its westering adventure. Rosa von Roeder Kleberg came from Germany as a bride with her aristocratic family and educated husband. Dilue Rose Harris grew up with Texas, watching it grow from colony, to republic, to state. Yet, women, from whatever culture, were bound by the singular inevitability of marriage followed by childbirth. Their spirits were all too often blighted by the cruel loss of their children. Years after their deaths, Mary Maverick could hardly bear to mention the names of her two young daughters.

Women on the frontier accepted a commitment to caring. Louisa Ervendberg provided a home for the bereft children of the community and then opened her doors to her own orphaned grandchildren. Some women turned their energies outward, as did Mary Austin Holley, writing her books about a Texas that forever remained a will-o'-the-wisp to her. Jane Long's buoyant good nature stands in sharp contrast to the snow-queen brittleness of Elisabet Ney's ambition.

Adina De Zavala and Clara Driscoll each transferred their remarkable Texas heritage into a productive obsession, while Lizzie Johnson nurtured her bookkeeper's training into a career in the cattle business. These special women did not choose their century nor the pattern of their lives. They, along with thousands of others, however, left their own permanent mark on the nineteenth century, never dreaming that they were closing a frontier on a rare, proud female experience.

Throughout the twentieth century women in Texas made good use of the heritage handed down to them by their pioneer ancestors. Frontier determination and adaptability were much in evidence, as Texas women began to break down the barriers and enter the traditional male worlds of business, athletics, and politics. Organizational skills developed as women worked for prohibition and campaigned for the right to vote.

With the passage of the Nineteenth Amendment on August 26, 1920, women across the United States gained the vote. Texas women flocked to the polls, helping to elect Annie Webb Blanton as the state's superintendent of public instruction, did battle against the Ku Klux Klan, and helped send Miriam Amanda Ferguson to the statehouse. A host of women suffragists, including Minnie Fisher Cunningham, Jessie Daniel Ames, and Jane McCallum, worked tirelessly to win the vote for Texas women, and McCallum later served as Texas's secretary of state. The male-dominated political arena would never again be the same.

Sarah Hughes served in the Texas House of Representatives and then made judicial history in Dallas; Frances Farenthold used her legislative experience to run for the governor's office; State Representative Sarah Weddington went from the Texas House to become a presidential adviser at the White House. In addition, numerous Texas women brought their skills and effectiveness to the Texas political scene, serving as both campaign workers and as candidates. Organization became their byword, and groups ranging from the Texas Woman Suffrage Association to the Texas Women's Political Caucus promoted Texas women into the political limelight. They serve on schoolboards, on city councils, in the legislature, and on countless boards and commissions. By 1982 the women of the state could point with pride to three women as mayors of major cities.

Texas history books may continue to concentrate on the deeds and actions of the heroes of Texas, but Texas heroines recorded their own unique and valuable "herstory." From the memoirs of the state's frontier women to the novels and folklore of Dorothy Scarborough to the wise and witty comments of Liz Carpenter, Texas women have created their own legends. This is their story.

Ann Fears Crawford
Crystal Sasse Ragsdale
Austin, Texas
15 January 1982

Kemp Collection, Courtesy Barker Texas History Center,
The University of Texas at Austin.

"Mother of Texas"

Jane Wilkinson Long

No pioneer woman led a more adventurous and exciting life in early Texas than did Jane Wilkinson Long, whose destiny brought her to Texas in October 1819, following her husband, the filibustering romantic, Dr. James Long. James Long's dreams of carving out an empire in frontier Texas led to his tragic death before the age of thirty, but Jane continued living in the republic of Texas, participating in a long series of adventures, from holding off attacking Indians to becoming the sweetheart of Texas hero Ben Milam. She lived to see Texas grow from a wilderness populated only by Indians, a few settlers, and bands of horse traders to a fledgling state in the nation. She was honored by having the romantic poet-politician of the republic, Mirabeau B. Lamar, write a poem called "Serenade," containing an allusion to "bonnie Jane."

Jane Herbert Wilkinsons's life was destined for adventure and romance from the day of her birth on July 23, 1798. She was born the tenth and last child of Captain William Mackall Wilkinson and his wife, Anne Herbert Dent Wilkinson, on their plantation in Charles County, Maryland. Jane's uncle, the illustrious and sometimes notorious General James Wilkinson, became one of her earliest romantic heroes and exerted a decided influence on the young girl during the most impressionable years of her life.

Wilkinson's military exploits dated from the Revolutionary

War, and as a swashbuckling businessman and politician in frontier Kentucky he attempted to get the settlers to align their loyalties with Spain and to secede from the United States. Despite Wilkinson's traitorous activities, President Thomas Jefferson recognized his cleverness and designated him as one of the men to take possession of the lands stipulated as part of the Louisiana Purchase. He was named governor of the provinces above the 33rd parallel and commanded U.S. troops stationed along the eastern boundary of Texas. Although Wilkinson collaborated with Aaron Burr in an attempt to invade Mexico and to establish an independent republic, the wily general became disenchanted with Burr and betrayed the plans to Jefferson. Then he signed an agreement with Spain to establish a neutral ground along the Sabine River, bordering the United States. Later he succeeded in capturing Burr and his accomplices.

Burr's intrigues became well known throughout the United States, and rumors circulated that Wilkinson was in reality the main figure behind the conspiracy. Ever mindful of his own welfare, Wilkinson served as the prosecution's main witness against Burr. Later, charged with complicity and court-martialed, Wilkinson was cleared of all charges.

Westward expansion and dreams of empire, however, continued to consume Wilkinson, and he sent his son to establish a fort on the Platte River, later commissioning the explorer Zebulon Pike to undertake a second expedition up the Mississippi River in search of the headwaters of the Red River deep in Spanish territory.

When Jane's father died her mother moved the family to Mississippi to be close to the dashing general, and Jane soon became the pampered darling of her captivating "Uncle James." She was still a schoolgirl of sixteen when she met handsome Dr. James Long, who had been cited for bravery fighting against the British at the battle of New Orleans. When Dr. Long came to the plantation of Jane's aunt to treat a wounded soldier, Kian, Jane's black maid, persuaded her mistress to postpone leaving for school in order to meet the gallant lieutenant.

The young couple played backgammon, wagering a pair of

gloves as forfeit. When Dr. Long lost, he presented the gloves to Jane, offering his hand along with them. Reared in the aura of romance and swashbuckling adventure that surrounded Wilkinson, Jane was quickly fascinated with Long. However, when the young doctor asked the general for Jane's hand, her indulgent Uncle James refused, no doubt sensing in Long many of the impulsive, adventurous, often dangerous qualities that he himself possessed. Jane pouted and pled, and then, taking matters into her own hands, named Long her guardian and married him on May 14, 1815.

Long had resigned his commission in order to gain Jane's promise of marriage, and he immediately set up a medical practice in nearby Port Gibson, Mississippi. When smalltown life began to bore Jane, Long gave up his practice, moved to Walnut Hills Plantation, and quickly became immersed in the life of a Mississippi planter. On November 26, 1816, the couple's first child, Ann Herbert, was born. Tiring of life on a plantation, Long sold their property and embarked on a mercantile venture with W. W. Walker in Natchez.

Controversy continued to ferment in the neutral ground that Wilkinson had established on the Texas border, where opportunists and filibusterers engaged in thievery and banditry. The ratification of the Adams-Onis treaty and the establishment of the United States boundary giving Texas to Spain caused turmoil. In Natchez, a town bordering on the frontier, opposition to the treaty swelled, and a meeting was held to organize an invasion to free Texas from Spanish rule. Long joined the financiers who subscribed some $500,000 to mount an expedition, and recruits, promised a league of land in Texas for service in the campaign, quickly signed up to fight for Texas's freedom. Dr. James Long was chosen to head the expedition.

True to the bold, reckless spirit of the Wilkinsons, Jane became feverish with excitement to accompany her husband. Long, however, prevailed on her to remain behind until after the birth of their second child. Dr. Long then left Natchez with an army of seventy-five men, whose ranks had swelled to three hundred by the time he reached Nacogdoches, Texas. With him he carried a fringed flag of white silk, decorated with red stripes and a white star on a red background, dutifully stitched by his wife.

Arriving in Nacogdoches Long proclaimed the independence of Texas and flew Jane's red and white flag from atop the Old Stone Fort. The dissidents under his command elected a Supreme Council and named Long president of the republic and commander of the armed forces. Long, however, made a tactical error that was to prove costly later. He scattered his forces along the frontier, instead of concentrating them to protect Nacogdoches from possible attack.

Meanwhile Jane gave birth to a daughter Rebecca and set out for Texas to join her husband. Traveling by carriage and on mules, over mud-clogged roads and through rain-swollen streams, she and her escorts arrived exhausted in Nacogdoches in mid-October 1819. Soon after his wife's arrival Long left for Galveston to plead with the buccaneer Jean Lafitte for supplies and aid in his campaign against the Spanish.

Reaching the Trinity River Long received news of the advancing Spanish army too late to summon all his forces to aid the settlers at Nacogdoches. With Indians attacking, soldiers deserting, and the Spaniards on the march, Jane and the other settlers hurried across the Sabine River. On October 26 Long joined her in time to console her when news arrived of the death of their daughter Rebecca, left in the care of Jane's sister. Jane traveled back to Louisiana, while her husband departed for Bolivar Point on Galveston Bay to survey his forces.

Then Long returned to Louisiana to raise funds for his army before sailing back to Texas. Jane, her maid Kian, and baby Ann arrived at Bolivar Point in December 1820. When Long marched off to storm the Spanish fort at La Bahia, Jane, pregnant once again, stayed at Bolivar with only a handful of soldiers for protection. When the other residents evacuated the fort Jane remained, saying, "My husband left me here to wait for him and I shall stay until he returns."

Winter came, and a devastating storm hit Galveston Bay. Jane and Kian fished through holes in the ice and shot birds to provide food. On December 21, 1821, lying in a makeshift tent on a pallet covered with snow, Jane Long gave birth to another baby girl, Mary James, one of the first Anglo-American children born in Texas. With Kian ill with fever, Jane and young Ann collected frozen fish from the beach for their Christmas dinner.

Kian recovered and once again was able to help. She and Jane fished and gathered oysters, with their eyes ever watchful on the campfires of the warlike Karankawa Indians at nearby Galveston Island. Then one day Kian spotted a Karankawa canoe headed toward Bolivar Point. While the young black girl pointed their one cannon toward the approaching Indians, Jane hoisted her red flannel petticoat over the fort to serve as a warning to the savages. Jane loaded and fired the cannon, and miraculously the Indians turned back. The red flag, however, continued to fly defiantly over Fort Bolivar, and from time to time Jane fired the cannon to frighten the Indians. Kian also donned a soldier's uniform when she went to gather oysters.

With the coming of the new year the women were desperate for food, when immigrants heading for Austin's new colony discovered them and provided them with cornmeal and venison. Captain James Smith persuaded Jane to sail with him to meet her husband in Mexico City, but before they could undertake the voyage Smith died. Randal and James Jones helped build Jane's family a cabin at Atascosita Crossing on the Trinity River, and there Jane received the news that her husband had been killed in Mexico City under highly suspicious circumstances. Reports reached Texas that Long, having received his passport, was on his way to freedom when he was shot in the back by a Mexican soldier.

Jane, now the sole support of her small family, set out for San Antonio in the company of the Jones family. With Jane's children and the Jones's servants, the small party camped at La Bahia near Goliad, where Jane was accorded a celebration in honor of her husband. Although Jane had time to rest and regain her vitality in the warm San Antonio climate, she was disappointed when the Mexican government refused to grant her a pension for Dr. Long's service in the revolution. While she was on a short visit to Louisiana, her baby Mary James died. Nevertheless, Jane set out once again for Texas, where she met Ben Milam, who returned to her Dr. Long's papers, along with his blood-stained clothing.

Jane and her daughter Ann rested for the summer at the plantation of the wealthy planter Jared Groce on the Brazos River, and then continued their journey to San Felipe de Austin, the capital of Austin's colony. There Jane became involved in civic affairs, while waiting for Austin to confirm her title to a headright league of land near Fort Bend. By her thirtieth birthday, J. C. Clopper, a visitor to the colony, described her as

> . . . tall . . . with a beautiful figure . . . with the energies of masculine vigor yet moving with a grace that is truly and wholly feminine — her countenance tho' not expressive of the fire of genius . . . is highly interesting — her features are regular — her aspect smiling — her eyes sparkling, her tongue not too pliant for a female . . . very engaging in all her conversation . . .

While Jane was at Austin's colony, Milam became her ardent suitor, but she persuaded him that she could never love another man but James Long. Jane also became close friends with Stephen F. Austin, who tried in vain to persuade the Mexican government to award her a pension for James Long's service.

When Ann Long married Edward Winston in 1831, Jane took her growing family to Brazoria and opened a boarding house that became famous throughout Austin's colony. There she often entertained that flamboyant young attorney William Barret Travis, who not only enjoyed the good food that Jane provided but often helped her in collecting her business accounts.

One of the more interesting visitors at Mrs. Long's boarding house was charming and gallant Colonel Juan Almonte, sent by the Mexican government to investigate affairs in the colony of Texas. While Almonte dined at Jane's excellent table and made the surveys that convinced him that the Texians were not preparing for war, members of the Texas war party cautiously stored gunpowder at Mrs. Long's in anticipation of the fight. Soon the boarding house was the central focus of the war party activities; and when Austin returned from negotiations in Mexico City, the colonists held an elaborate dinner and ball in his honor at Mrs. Long's on September 8, 1835. There, with some one thousand colonists in attendance, Austin delivered an impassioned address that called the Texians to war.

While the Texians were arming for the coming conflict, Jane met the fascinating General Sam Houston and, legend has it, presented him with Jean Lafitte's powderhorn as a good-luck token. Later Houston, supposedly presented the horn to one of Santa Anna's guards after the battle of San Jacinto. Like many of the settlers in Austin's colony, Jane and her family headed toward the Sabine River during the Runaway Scrape, when word reached them that Santa Anna's armies were on the march.

When the battle of San Jacinto had been won and the Texians set about establishing a republic, Houston was rumored to be one of her suitors. So widespread was talk of their marriage that Houston protested to his confidant and admirer Anna Raguet:

> . . . Bye the bye I am told that it is reported I am married to Mrs. Long! I never saw her but twice and I don't think she would marry me, and besides she has one or two pretty grandchildren, which would argue she was older than I am.

Despite his protests, Houston continued to see Jane at many state functions during the early years of the republic, and the young widow, who was actually five years younger than Houston, danced with him frequently at state balls and was seen riding with him in his carriage.

Houston was not the only official of the republic whom Jane Long fascinated. The artistic and sensitive vice president of the republic, Mirabeau B. Lamar, met Jane at a celebration at her hotel in honor of the New Orleans Greys before the revolution. When Lamar began his march to meet Houston at Harrisburg, he wrote his brother, "In the event of my falling in battle, you will find my trunks, papers, etc. in possession of Mrs. Jane Long." Evidently he proposed marriage to Mrs. Long and then wrote the poem, "Serenade," containing the lines:

> O bonnie Jane, thou art to me
> Whate'er in both is best —
> Thou art the moonbeam to mine eye
> The sunbeam to my breast.

When Lamar campaigned for the presidency of the republic of Texas in 1837, he set up headquarters in Jane's new hotel in Richmond, and at the same time continued his work on compiling biographical material concerning James Long, with Jane his willing helper. Jane's fortunes prospered, and she became the owner of several town lots, acres of land, slaves, and horses. Lamar continued to court her until the death of his sixteen-year-old daughter in 1843, when he resolved to travel to forget his sorrow. In 1851 he married Henrietta Maffitt in New Orleans and returned to Texas the following year.

Lamar soon resumed his friendship with Jane Long, and the wealthy widow provided needed capital to expand Lamar's plantation, with the stipulation that her family be allowed to occupy part of the premises. The plan never came to fruition, and Lamar soon dissolved the partnership. He also changed the names in his poem "Serenade," to read "O bonnie Ann," and rededicated it to Anna Truesdell. When he wrote "The Daughter of Mendoza" in 1858, however, certain lines seem to speak of his lost love for Jane Long.

When the Civil War broke out, Jane was a well-established woman in Richmond, described by one of her friends as

> . . . a remarkably handsome old lady, tall and erect,
> with bright dark eyes, an abundance of dark hair just
> sprinkled with grey, and a mouth and chin in which
> sweetness and firmness are singularly blended.

She was fiercely loyal to the Southern cause and refused to wear any clothing made outside the South. She attended meetings of the Texas Veterans Association, and one writer noted that

> . . . Her presence was considered an event and she was treated by those venerable and venerated men with distinguished and affectionate consideration. A common sympathy united her to them in bonds of the strongest friendship. Her place among them was that of a heroine . . .

Feeling the advances of old age, Mrs. Long, in November 1880, made a farewell visit around the town of Richmond, calling on her physician, her friends, and her relatives. Then she went to the local ice-cream parlor and had a dish of the confection before going home. There she spent her last Christmas among her family, and died peacefully on December 30, 1880. Crowds of admirers flocked to her funeral, and she was buried in the Richmond cemetery among a number of Texas heroes including Mirabeau B. Lamar, her once courtly beau. Newspapers across the state of Texas eulogized the heroic frontier woman whose fortunes reflected those of the state, and who had well won the accolade, "Mother of Texas."

REFERENCES

Baylor, Mary. *Mary Baylor Reminiscences, 1827-1840.* (typescript). Barker Texas History Center, The University of Texas at Austin.

Bell, Alexander. *The Daughter of Maryland Was The Mother of Texas.* Washington, D.C.: The Law Reporter Printing Company, 1935.

Brindley, Anne A. "Jane Long." *Southwestern Historical Quarterly.* LVI (October 1952).

Briscoe, Mary Jane and Adele B. Looscan. *Sketch of the Life of Mrs. Jane Long.* (typescript). Barker Texas History Center, The University of Texas at Austin.

George, Mrs. Albert. *The Mother of Texas, Mrs. Jane Long.* (reprint). Houston: The Union National Bank, 1937.

Hatcher, Mattie Austin. *Letters of an Early American Traveller.* Dallas: Southwest Press, 1933.

Hogan, William Ransom. *The Texas Republic.* Norman: University of Oklahoma, 1954.

Moore, Effie Missouria. *Alone by the Sea.* San Antonio: The Naylor Company, 1951.

Turner, Martha Anne. *The Life and Times of Jane Long.* Waco: The Texian Press, 1969.

Warren, Harris Gaylord. *The Sword Was Their Passport.* Baton Rouge: Louisiana State University Press, 1943.

Courtesy Fort Bend County Museum, Richmond

Jane Long

Courtesy Lillian Rabb

Mary and John Rabb

"Trials and Troubles" in Texas

Mary Crownover Rabb

One of the few firsthand accounts of early Texas life was written by a pioneer woman, Mary Crownover Rabb, who came to Texas "about the 15 of december " 1823. Wanting her children and grandchildren to have authentic documentation of her and her husband, John Rabb's, experiences in early Texas, she turned out an earnest narrative, replete with phonetic spelling and quaint sayings, that stands as a monument to frontier women. In her lively account of Texas life she captured the hearty vernacular of her Anglo-American friends and neighbors in early nineteenth-century Texas. Written over one hundred years ago, Mary Rabb's *Reminiscences* remain a testament to the Texas frontierswoman who helped to build a state in spite of the numerous perils of wilderness life.

Born in Buncombe County, North Carolina, on April 8, 1805, Mary Crownover was the daughter of an important hat manufacturer who dreamed of a life in the West. Following the frontier, Crownover moved his family to the Arkansas Territory in early 1820, and there Mary, age sixteen, met and married John Rabb, twenty-three, at Jonesboro in 1821. John's father, William Rabb, was such a frontier mover that he had made a trip to Spanish Texas in 1819. With his son Thomas he explored the river valleys along the Guadalupe and Colorado rivers and had planted one of the first corn crops to be raised by a white man in Central Texas. After this remarkable accomplishment, he returned to his family with a new dream of "westering" — they would soon be moving to Texas. One more exploratory trip to Texas in 1821 determined him to move, and the Rabbs were bound for Texas, just as word came that the Mexican government had granted colonization permits to Stephen F. Austin.

The Rabbs traveled as a group, as many pioneering families did, and William Rabb brought his three sons, John, Thomas, and Andrew with their families, along with John's sister Peggy, her husband Joseph Newman, and their seven children. The thick forests were turning red and gold as the Rabbs began their trek south, and Mary opened her memorable account of life in Texas with the straightforward observation that on October 1, 1823 she left Jonesboro, Red River, Miller County, Arkansas, with her husband and "little Babe to coum to Texas."

On their wilderness adventure the Rabb party must have stretched for a considerable distance; but on the frontier trail, the more hands the better. Men were needed to drive the wagons and manage the livestock, and women were important in cooking the meals and tending the children. The Rabbs brought along their own cattle, and John and Mary took along fifteen or eighteen head of "small cattle" — two grown cows and three or four "tollerable large ones that would make oxen." In addition to their cattle and six horses, the young couple owned little else. Along the way, however, they added the fifteen-year-old orphan, John Ingram, to their party. Ingram had already been to Texas and was returning to make a life on the frontier.

The Rabbs traveled for two-and-one-half months before they reached the Colorado River near present-day La Grange. Mary was astounded to find that "thar was no haus thar then nore nothing but a wilderness not eaven a tree cut down to marke this plais." Riding sidesaddle on a tall gray horse, Tormenter, she reached the other side of the Colorado without having to lift her feet above the water. South of the river the

Rabbs headed upstream, traveling six or seven miles to the house William Rabb had built on his second trip. There waited John's mother and another brother Ulysses, who had stayed behind when Rabb returned to Arkansas to collect the family.

Mary had little time to enjoy the fragile paradise along the Colorado River, where wild oats and rye grew in great luxuriance along the river bottom. She was busy settling into the house that John and young Ingram had built. That primitive dwelling, built of rough-hewn logs and complete with chimney and "earthing" floor, was her first home in Texas, and soon Mary was busily spinning thread for her family on a spinning wheel, a gift from her brother-in-law Andrew.

John Rabb and young Ingram cleared six acres for a corn-field near the river bottom below Indian Hill. As they worked, Indians crept through the forest, watching the white men. During the night they stole Rabb's tools and the wooden rails destined to be used for a horse corral. Only Tormenter, pad-locked to the house, remained.

Frustrated in his first attempt at wilderness farming, Rabb resolved to move where the Indians would not harass his family, but the savages had left him with only one horse. He stubbornly refused his father's offer of a second horse; taking Tormenter would have left Mary alone with no means of communication with the Rabb family. Knowing his son's pride and in-dependence, William Rabb brought the pony Nickety Poly to John and Mary's house. Seeing his grandson sitting in the door, William "put the bridle in his hand and said he gave the pony to the Babe." The present was accepted and John set out on "Poly" to find another home for his family.

With John gone for ten days, Mary remained alone and defenseless in Indian territory, but household chores kept her busy from dawn to dusk. The baby had to be watched closely, and there were always the dry corn kernels to be pounded into meal for bread. Mary kept her spinning wheel whirring and whistling, sitting outside during the day. When dark came she moved the wheel inside and kept at her spinning, for the roar-ing of the wheel "drownded" out the sounds of the Indians "walking around and hunting mischief." When Mary became too sleepy to spin, she followed another comforting routine. She scattered dry corn under her bed and let in the young pigs anxiously waiting under the house. The pigs proved good company, and the cracking of the dry corn was a comforting sound as she drifted off to sleep.

Riding along the Brazos River John Rabb located a league of land fifteen miles below where the town of Richmond now stands, and registered his headright at Stephen F. Austin's capital at San Felipe on July 8, 1824. He returned to Mary, bringing the good news of their new homesite. Her safety from the savages, had come as an answer to his prayers, "although," as Mary commented wryly, "he was not a religious man then." During the next few years Mary and John were constantly on the move from one homesite to another, for, as Mary discovered, John Rabb's choice of sites always seemed to be wrong.

John brought back the additional news that Mary's parents and her brother John had arrived in Texas and set up camp near their headright, and John Crownover came along to help the Rabbs move, bringing an extra horse to carry household goods. Although they made "quick hast and got ready to pack up," it must have taken a good part of the day from first light before they were ready to leave Indian Hill. They loaded the horse and oxen with an intricate puzzle of household supplies. On the packhorse Flacus the clothes were placed first; then the iron kettle. Next the skillet and lid were piled, and last the spinning wheel, which rode along on top. The wheelbench was tied to the "necking stick," or yoke of the oxen.

The little party made a colorful caravan as it headed down country toward the Brazos. First came the cattle and pigs, with Mary and the baby following on Tormenter. John followed on Nickety Poly; and last came John Crownover on his horse Shurk, leading Flacus. All went well for the first two days; then one of the pigs wandered under a cow's hoof and was lamed. John made the unfortunate decision not to abandon the pig, but to fasten it on the packhorse under the spinning wheel. The pig's squealing and squirming caused Flacus to bolt, scattering his pack on the ground and killing the pig, and Mary bemoaned the loss of her cooking pot, which was "broke all to bits."

Five days later, however, everyone in the party, with the exception of the ill-fated pig, arrived at the Crownover camp. Mary's family welcomed her with open arms and a hearty feast of bear meat, venison, cornbread, butter, and honey — with plenty of fresh milk to wash it down. While the campsite seemed perfect for a permanent home, the Crownovers and Rabbs soon found the mosquitos on the coast unbearable. Mary could neither spin nor weave unless she sat under the mosquito bar, and the flies rapidly began disturbing the horses and cattle.

Soon the party was on the move again, settling near the Brazos, where John Rabb set up camp with a tent made from a quilt and a sheet. In this makeshift home Mary was soon busily spinning again, with the head of the wheel under the tent. It was some time before she would have another real home. During good weather, however, the Rabbs' camp became a gathering place, where Texians from miles around came to hear the famed Methodist preacher Henry Stevenson. Despite Mary's urging, however, it was another four years before John Rabb became a member of the church.

During these years the Rabbs were constantly on the move. First they camped on an island in the Brazos River, where the mosquitos and flies were annoying, and where Mary feared the alligators might rise up out of the river and snatch her children. On a visit to the Newmans in Wharton County Mary awoke one night to the sound of moving water, put out her hand, and found that "the river had rose and was nerely level with the bed plais." All she could think of was that her children would drown before she could reach them.

In March 1825 the Rabbs settled on the San Bernard River, and John built his family a home, trading a "nise heffer" for three hundred feet of planking for the floor. Then John was off to the Colorado River bottom, where he chose fertile land, burned off a canebrake, and planted his first corn crop. Having no fence around the field, he camped near it all spring and summer to protect his crop.

Mary remained with the children and livestock at their home, spending her time spinning thread from cotton lint that she plucked from the seeds herself. She and the children lived on milk, cottage cheese, and dried meat, and the pigs soon ran away as Mary had no dry corn to feed them. By midsummer when John had harvested his corn crop, Mary loaded up the children and followed the livestock to the Colorado River to join her husband. There the Rabbs lived in a shed that John built for them.

With the coming of spring the prairie was once again covered with a patchwork of vivid flowers. Then the Rabbs, like migrating birds, headed north, returning to John's headright league on the Brazos River. Mary sorrowfully recorded the injury John received when he was pinned between an ox-drawn cart and a tree, remembering for her children that, ''As soon as your Pa was ready to travel we went to our plais ouer leag of land ouer headright that we got for coming to Texas poor things how bad that was for us.''

Mary was not usually such a recorder of hard times, and took great pride and pleasure in her growing family of children, Zebulon Montgomery Pike Rabb, known in the family as ''Gum''; Melissa or ''Lissa''; and George Washington, lovingly known as ''Washai.'' Amid a tumble of children and a clutter of household goods Mary survived in a rough camp, spinning enough thread for forty-six yards of ''muscato baring.'' While John was in a building mood, Mary had him build her a loom, then a twenty-foot-square house, and a shed for the loom. With enough to eat for both family and livestock, it seemed that the Rabbs had finally settled into a home on the frontier.

Still Mary recalled that John ''had a nocien that he could not stay there,'' and in the fall of 1827 they abandoned the site and moved to Egypt, where Andrew and Peggy Rabb lived. Not realizing the danger from the Indians, John set up camp too far from his brother's house, and soon they were threatened by primitive coastal Karankawas and the Tonkawas. ''So trummelson'' did the Indians become that the Rabb brothers and their neighbors drove them even ''further in the frunteer.''

Five years later Andrew and John moved their families back to the first settling place and made their homes at Rabb's Prairie, the river valley on the north side of the Colorado several miles upstream from Moore's Fort, which marked present-day La Grange. Old William Rabb was delighted to have his family around him, and in 1831 the family erected a gristmill for grinding corn for their neighbors and a sawmill for cutting boards from the forests that surrounded the prairie.

Here John was to have his first direct communication with God. When a fire broke out in refuse beside the sawmill, he fell to his knees and begged the Lord to save his mill. He made a promise that one-tenth of the mill's output would go to building churches, if the mill was spared. As he uttered his final "Amen," he opened his eyes to find that the wind had shifted and now was blowing the flames in the opposite direction.

The Rabb mill was spared from fire, only to be destroyed in 1833 by high water from the Colorado River that swept it away and caused all the families on the prairie to flee for their lives. After moving his family to safety, John and a neighboring Frenchman named Batiste returned to the Rabb home for clothing and bedding. John made a hole in the roof and managed to salvage the butter churn still filled with cream. The water had risen so high, however, that the men were forced to spend the night just out of the flood's reach. Wrapped in his cloak and clinging to the churn, John shivered on the roof, while the Frenchmen hung precariously nearby in a cedar tree. The next morning John Castleman, another neighbor, brought his boat and rescued the two men.

John Rabb chose another homesite for his family on high land above the prairie, but relinquished it to his brother Andrew and then chose another place. When Andrew spotted the new site, he decided he would rather have that one, but John refused to move and Andrew contented himself with building a home several hundred yards from the John Rabbs. At last Mary thought she might have a permanent home, but the Indians continued to plague the settlers, stealing tools and livestock and destroying crops. When two of their neighbors were killed by the Indians the Rabbs moved to Moore's Fort, but they returned home in the fall of 1835 to mend their fences so they could begin their spring planting.

Then word reached them that Santa Anna's troops were on the move through Texas in pursuit of General Sam Houston's straggling band of Texian soldiers. Immediately there was a scramble of terrified women and children, old men and slaves heading toward safety across the Sabine River, driving their livestock before them. The Runaway Scrape spelled tragedy for the Rabbs, for Mary recalled, "We were all drove out of ouer houses with ouer little ones to suffer with cold and hungry." Mary's infant child Lorenzo died during the trip, and Thomas Rabb's wife died from the effects of the journey soon after they returned home.

While the settlers rejoiced at the news of the Texian victory at San Jacinto, they returned to their homes to find that the Mexican army had stolen or burned everything of value. The livestock had been driven off and the wild game frightened from the prairies. Those settlers who could find seed corn put in a late June planting, but the crop failed. Once again hard times came to the Texians, and once again they began home building on the frontier. Only now it was safe from Mexican armies.

Within several years times improved, and the Rabbs became important landholders and active members of the community. Andrew became the first county judge in Fayette County, and John Rabb served on juries and road maintenance crews. In a burst of camp-meeting fervor John joined the Methodist church, and soon became one of the church's chief benefactors. He helped found Rutersville College, the first college in Texas, generously supporting it with both land and money, and seven of Mary and John's children attended the school. Then John got the wanderlust again, and the couple made their last move, following the Colorado River upstream to settle in a log house near Austin's Barton Springs.

Mary and John Rabb were an integral part of early Texas history as members of Stephen F. Austin's settlement. With their friends and neighbors they shared a common risk and fortune, watching Texas win its independence and become an independent republic. They witnessed Texas's becoming a part of the United States and saw their state leave the Union to join the Confederate States of America.

John Rabb did not live to see the end of the Civil War. He died in the summer of 1862, proclaiming the glory of God in a loud voice that rang through the pecan and cypress trees, telling the world that John Rabb was "going home."

Mary lived out her life on her homestead, and in 1867 she tried her own hand at building, letting the contract for a fine, limestone house built near the site of the old log house. From the second-story porches she could look out toward the hills while remaining safely above the flowing creek waters. She continued to maintain the cattle John had left her, and her cattle brand, the bow and arrow, became a well-known mark in Central Texas. She remained an active member of her beloved Methodist church, and took great pleasure in her grandchildren. She mourned the four children she had lost, young Marion and Lorenzo; Washington, who had become a Methodist preacher before his death; and Melissa, the talented singer who died in 1867. Being a religious woman, however, she looked with pride on the survivors — the soldier sons, Montgomery, who fought in the Mexican war, and Virgil Sullivan and John Wesley, who served the Confederacy. Mary Elizabeth Rabb Croft lived with her family on a Fayette County plantation, while Gail Texas, the youngest son, remained at home.

When Mary Crownover Rabb died on October 15, 1882 she was buried beside her husband John in Austin's Oakwood Cemetery, high above the unpredictable waters of the Colorado River that had so often threatened her early years in Texas. Her *Reminiscences*, written for her children and grandchildren, testify to the strength and fortitude of that Texas frontier woman, who endured the "tryals and trubles" of an untamed Texas.

As members of Stephen F. Austin's settlement, Mary and John Rabb were an integral part of early Texas history.

REFERENCES

Bailey, Ernest Emory. *Texas Historical and Biographical Record.* Austin: n.p., n.d.

Dewees, William B. *Letters from an Early Settler in Texas.* (compiled by Cara Cardelle, pseud.). Louisville: n.p., 1852.

Kemp, Louis Wiltz. *Biographical Notebooks.* Louis Wiltz Kemp Papers. Barker Texas History Center, The University of Texas at Austin.

Kuykendall, J. H. "Reminiscences of Early Texas." *Quarterly of the Texas State Historical Association,* VI, January 1903; VII, July 1903.

Lotto, P. *Fayette County, Her History and Her People.* Schulenberg, Texas: n.p., 1902.

"Mrs. John Rabb." Austin *Statesman,* October 17, 1882.

Pickrell, Annie Doom. *Pioneer Women in Texas.* Austin: E. L. Steck Company, 1929.

Rabb, Mary C. Biographical folder, Austin-Travis County Collection, Austin Public Library, Austin, Texas.

Rabb, Mary C. *Family papers, 1823-1922.* Barker Texas History Center. The University of Texas at Austin.

Rabb, Mary Crownover. *Travels and Adventures in Texas in the 1820s.* Waco, Texas: W. M. Morrison, 1962.

Robert E. Lee Road. Austin-Travis County Collection. Austin Public Library, Austin, Texas.

Sinks, Julia Lee. *Chronicles of Fayette, The Reminiscences of Julia Lee Sinks* (edited by Walter P. Freytag). La Grange, Texas: n.p., 1975.

Thrall, Homer S. *A Brief History of Methodism in Texas.* Nashville: n.p., 1889.

Ulmer, Mary Lewis (ed.). *An Abstract of the Original Titles of Record In The General Land Office.* Austin: Pemberton Press, 1964.

Weyand, Leonie Rummel and Houston Wade. *An Early History of Fayette County.* La Grange, Texas: La Grange *Journal,* 1936.

White, Gifford (ed.). *The 1840 Census of the Republic of Texas.* Austin: Pemberton Press, 1966.

Williams, Marjorie L. (ed.). *Fayette County: Past and Present.* La Grange, Texas: n.p., 1976.

Mary Rabb Home — Rabb Road Austin, Texas

Courtesy Sophienburg Memorial Museum Assn., Inc.,
New Braunfels, Texas.

Foster Mother To
A Community

Louisa Ervendberg

How could seventeen-year-old Maria Sophie Dorothea Louisa Muench, newly immigrated to Chicago from Germany in 1837, have dreamed that her life would encompass a frontier adventure in far-off Texas, or that she would spend part of her life caring for orphan children amid hardships on the frontier. Her destiny was sealed, however, when she married the young German Protestant minister, Louis Cachand Ervendberg, soon after arriving in Illinois. The couple lived at Ervendberg's pastorate at Salt Creek near Chicago, where Louis devoted his efforts to his growing congregation of German immigrants, and there their first child, a son, was born and died within a month.

Sorrow and poverty engulfed the young couple, for the young pastor's salary was barely enough for them to exist in the depression years that swept the United States during the 1830s. Together Louisa and Louis compared their present situation with their future possibilities and resolved to adventure westward to the frontier republic of Texas, where land was cheap and ministers of the gospel were in short supply.

After selling their few possessions the Ervendbergs booked passage down the Mississippi, the first leg on their journey westward. Their traveling companions, the gamblers, hunters, trappers, land speculators, and slave traders far outnumbered the pioneer families. When they reached New Orleans they crowded into a small sailing boat to make the trip to Galveston Island. There the passengers transferred to a steamboat to make the trip to the inland town of Houston City.

Moving up the narrow San Jacinto River, its banks crowded with tall magnolia trees, tropical vegetation, and wild grapevines, the steamboat passed the historic San Jacinto battleground, where the Texians had two years earlier defeated the Mexican army and won their independence. Then it was on to Houston City, the hub of business activity for the republic of Texas. There the Ervendbergs found themselves among many Germans, all living in tent camps and log cabins amid the tall pines and tree stumps.

Luckily there was no pastor, and the Ervendbergs decided to remain in Houston, with Louisa resolving to help her husband to raise and sell vegetables, and with Louis pursuing his ministry as pastor of the German First Protestant Church. His congregation soon numbered almost one hundred members counting the fifty-eight "souls," as those who had not joined the church were called.

After two years of devoted work, however, the pastorate had not flourished, and the Ervendbergs decided to move inland to a healthier and more peaceful location. They traveled west to Colorado County to live among the German farmers in the well-established settlement of Blumenthal. Soon Louis was well known among the settlers, for he could read Greek and Latin and discuss history and the classics with the well-read Germans who had migrated to Texas. Ervendberg joined a group of friends from nearby counties to sign a memorial to incorporate Hermann's University in Colorado County, a testament to his belief in education. Louisa spent her time caring for their small daughter, Auguste, born a year after the death of another baby girl.

Ervendberg soon extended his pastorate to Columbus, and then eastward to Industry and Cat Spring in Austin County. Riding into Fayette County, he baptized settlers and preached sermons in La Grange, stopping at Biegel's Settlement, where he gained additional members for his church from the French, Germans, and Swiss in the colony. Even with a growing church Ervendberg looked to new fields and decided to take the challenge of moving ever westward in the republic of Texas.

Word of the boundless lands of Texas, selling at cheap prices, had circulated in letters, newspapers, books, and land advertisements in both the United States and in Europe; and in the years following Texas's fight for independence, immigration had increased to such an extent that few settlers could find farms along the coastal plains. Far to the west and north of San Antonio between the Colorado and the Llano rivers, however, lay a vast tract of land known as the Fisher-Miller grant. Located deep within the Comanche hunting grounds, it was being advertised by promoters, who by 1844 had arranged with a group of German noblemen to establish a colony on the grant. These Rhinelanders formed a joint stock company officially named The Society for the Protection of German Immigrants in Texas; however, it soon became known as the *Adelsverein,* or simply the *Verein.* The group's director, who came to Texas to arrange for the colonists's arrival, was the enthusiastic minor nobleman, Prince Carl von Solms-Braunfels. A chance meeting with Louis Ervendberg led Prince Carl to offer the pastorate of the Texas-German colony to the young minister.

The Ervendbergs embraced the chance of Louis's developing his church following into a full-fledged congregation, and Louis left Blumenthal before Christmas 1844 to establish a temporary pastorate among the newly arrived immigrants encamped on the shores of Lavaca Bay. Louisa remained behind to await the birth of another child. In the spring Louisa with her newborn son and little Auguste left Blumenthal in a horse-drawn wagon with the couple's valuable milk cows tied behind. With no other companions she set out, passing through the settled areas until she reached the Colorado River crossing at La Grange.

Traveling at a tediously slow pace, the horses pulled the wagon through ruts worn by the hooves of thousands of horses, buffalo, oxen, and cattle that had traveled the road for centuries. What fears Louisa had of Indians or bandits were swept away by the chores of caring for her children, making camp each evening, hobbling the horses, and milking the cows. The nights were lonely, however, and Louisa realized with pangs of sadness that she was leaving further behind each day everyone she had known in Texas. Finally, after days of bone-weary traveling, she reached the ford on the Guadalupe River and gazed over the tops of the trees bordering the river. Searching in vain for the tents of the settlers, she saw no smoke rising from campfires, heard no voices. The only sounds were the river's rushing over the shallows, and the wind's whistling through the cypress trees. Standing alone above the Guadalupe River, Louisa Ervendberg was the first German woman to glimpse the future site of the town of New Braunfels.

Fortunately, before too many days passed men on horseback, riding ahead of ox-drawn wagons filled with German immigrants, joined a puzzled and relieved Louisa. Reunited with Louis, together they made friends among the settlers, and when the last stragglers arrived, they made the historic crossing of the Guadalupe on Good Friday, April 21, 1845. Prince Carl, whom Louisa's fellow countrywoman Rosa Kleberg described as an impractical and autocratic fool, led the way. Following him in aristocratic, Old-World fashion came his uniformed and mounted attendants. Then, assisted by a troop of twenty-five men, the German immigrants, who were to make the dream of settlement a reality, crossed.

In a flurry of activity the settlers began their lives. Tents were erected so that orderly living could proceed; soon the town was surveyed, and a public square and marketplace laid out. Then men drew numbered slips for the homesteads and business plots that were laid out in half-acre lots. Located on the main street were the lots for the First Protestant Church, but it would be a year before Louis's dream of a church became a reality. First a home must be completed for the pastor and his wife, and in May Louisa moved her family into the first home in New Braunfels.

Serving as the wife of the settlement's pastor was a fulltime job for Louisa. Her home served that first year as both church and parsonage, and in cold or rainy weather, the couple's living room was used for church services. Louisa, in typical German fashion, gathered green boughs to decorate the improvised altar. Life in the fledgling colony was even harder for the Ervendbergs than it had been in Houston. For quite a meager salary Louis preached on Sundays, taught school during the week, and cultivated his corn field and garden in his spare time.

Louisa's lot was just as demanding, for she, as an experienced frontier Texan, had to sympathize and console the bewildered German *hausfrauen*. They were querulous and uncomfortable in their dark European dresses and heavy stockings, much too thick for the strong Texas sun. They bemoaned the state of their family linens that had molded while packed in damp, wooden sea chests. But by far the most serious problem was the lack of *kartoffel* — the white potato — for the staples of the German diet: potato soup, potato dumplings, and steaming boiled potatoes. To the Germans the Texans lived on strange uncivilized food — venison, sweet potatoes, and the corn they considered fit only for livestock. Louisa helped the women adjust as best she could, measuring out milk from the Ervendberg cows and dividing the vegetables from their garden to supply needy families. Added to the difficulties of their lives was the sorrow over the death of the baby who had been born before Louisa left Blumenthal.

Before the year 1846 was over a series of events occurred that changed the lives of the New Braunfelsers and of the Ervendbergs most of all. During the winter and spring of 1846 a second group of over five thousand colonists arrived at Galveston and Indianola. These immigrants came ashore to a vastly different Texas than their fellow Germans experienced only a year before. Texas had become part of the United States, and war with Mexico had erupted. In the rush to transport soldiers from the Texas coast to the Rio Grande border, the United States army commandeered every available wagon and horse. Unfortunately, these included the teams and wagons hired to take the immigrants to New Braunfels.

For many of these people stranded on the coast the grim weeks of waiting were to be their only Texas experience. The few huts available were needed for soldiers, so colonists lived in dugouts on the beach. Added to the desolate conditions was the fact that the *Adelsverein* was bankrupt and could provide the colonists with only a little food. With spring came days of soaking rain followed by days of burning sun. Then fever broke out, and many of the immigrants perished without ever seeing the promised land of New Braunfels.

As conditions became intolerable many families began to walk inland, abandoning their possessions and carrying their children. Day by day the line of fresh graves marking the camping sites along the route increased, and many more died within sight of the flooding river that separated them from New Braunfels. The New Braunfelsers, consumed with compassion for their fellow immigrants' lot, built a brush arbor where the sick were cared for. Then when the fever subsided, a tragic count was made. Sixty children remained orphaned and homeless in the new land.

They were watched over for by a hired woman and housed in a tent next to the First Protestant Church, with Louis and Louisa supervising their care. Relatives and friends claimed most of the orphans, until only nineteen remained—eleven boys and eight girls, "who were left entirely alone in the world and had to be provided for," as Auguste Ervendberg remembered years later. "After thinking the matter over carefully, my mother and father decided to take over the responsibility of these orphans themselves," she added, describing her parents' momentous and heroic decision.

The unselfish act seemed natural to the Ervendbergs, for Louis was pastor and Louisa the pastor's wife. Nevertheless, providing a home for twenty-three persons was a monumental task in New Braunfels, and no house could be found to hold them all. Louis managed to secure several acres of land three miles north of town along the Guadalupe River, and he named the home of his burgeoning family of foster children "New Wied."

In 1848 the Ervendbergs' West Texas Orphan Asylum was incorporated.

Less than three years after the tragic epidemic the orphanage was securely established in a part-Texan, part-German style frame house. The central room became the dining room and a place for presenting plays and musicals, with the orphans' rooms and a schoolroom in the north wing. When warm weather came everyone pitched in to clear out the brush for a park for plays and masquerades, and on the fourth of July everyone celebrated with "games and general merrymaking in addition to a dance." Soon the park became a popular retreat for people from the town.

Louis Ervendberg realized a longtime dream in 1850, when the West Texas University at New Wied was chartered, with Louis the only professor. Weekdays were filled with teaching practical agriculture, as well as academic subjects. In addition, Louis was an amateur botanist, and with his students he experimented with raising Egyptian cotton, growing mulberry trees, and breeding silkworms. The tobacco which they raised and cured was smoked by the German men in their long pipes. The little farm was coaxed to produce bushels of corn and vegetables to suppy the orphanage, and the orphan boys cared for the cows that supplied meat for the table, as well as milk and butter. Hogs were raised and killed, and the pork made into winter sausage. The farm was largely self-sustaining, and only staples such as unrefined sugar, coffee, vinegar, oil, and wheat flour were purchased in town.

Louisa was up at dawn, supervising the kitchen tasks. Aided by the orphan girls and her own daughters she made some twenty loaves of bread each day, an arduous task as they had only three Dutch ovens, each holding only one loaf of the good German bread. Disliking the grainy Texas cornbread, the German women devised a recipe for cornmeal sour dough, more pleasant to the appetite, but more complicated to prepare. Everyone pitched in to make home and farm prosperous, and Auguste recalled years later that there was so much activity at the *Weisenfarm* that the children were always happy and busy.

The Christmas season was a magical time in all German communities, and beginning in early November the women and girls began making traditional cookies and sweets. The homey scent of honey, molasses, butter, and spices filled the old-fashioned kitchen and seeped into the classroom. In December the boys scouted the pastures for a Texas juniper for their Christmas tree. When it was set up in the schoolroom all the children hung the tree with paper ornaments and ginger-cookie stars. Under the tree a snow city, a miniature Jerusalem, was assembled, complete with a tiny Christ child, shepherds, animals, and a hovering angel.

Christmas morning dawned to the enchantment of a flickering, candlelit Christmas tree. Gifts were a surprise — caps for the boys; homemade aprons for the girls. Often the boys made little plaited whips for each other. The Germans thought Christmas too magical to last only one day, and they heralded a second Christmas day with homemade cookies and wild grape wine, served to visitors who rode out from town.

Still, life in a wilderness settlement held many terrors for Louisa. On one occasion Indians came out of the woods, watched the children silently, and begged food which the orphanage could ill afford to share. One of the small boys died of a rattlesnake bite, which occurred while he was playing in the hay stored in the barn. She also had to cope with many strange problems that often required all her tact. Once a Comanche chief brought Dr. Ferdinand Herff a strange gift in payment for medical services. The chief presented the German doctor, who lived in a colony on the Llano River, with a Mexican girl, captured during an Indian raid into Mexico. It was unseemly for the bachelor doctor to keep the young girl, so he rode into New Braunfels and arranged for her to live with families there. Lina, as she was called, after a time found herself one of the orphans under Louisa's care, and romance bloomed between the young girl and Hermann Spiess, one of the directors of the orphanage.

There was other causes for fear and concern. The day came when Louisa felt she had to face Louis concerning the state of their marriage. Although the orphanage was self-sustaining the

Ervendbergs had little to show for seven years of grueling struggle. Their worldly possessions were few, and Louis had made a
tragic mistake by falling in love with the oldest of the orphan
girls. When she had first come to the orphanage she had been
twelve years old, but now she was nineteen, and Louisa knew
there would be talk. She and Louis met by the river to talk over
the situation. Some said later that Louis asked Louisa's
forgiveness and help and that the couple reconciled; but
whatever was said between the two, they had made a plan by
the time they returned to the house.

They made a decision that the boys and girls at the *Weisen-*
farm were to be placed with families throughout the community. Then Louisa was to take their own three girls, Auguste,
Bertha, and little Thusnelda to Illinois to stay with her family.
When Louis had taken care of the final affairs at the orphanage,
he was to follow with the couple's two boys, Otto, now seven,
and Rudolf, five. Then Louis and Louisa planned to open
another school somewhere, far from the temptations of New
Wied.

Louisa packed bags for herself and the girls, and Louis took
them to New Braunfels to catch the stage for the long trip north.
Louisa waved to the boys until they were no longer in view. She
was never to see them again. As soon as Louisa departed, Louis
and the young orphan girl planned to leave for Mexico, and by
1855 they had gone, taking the Ervendberg boys with them.
They left the *Weisenhaus* unattended, and a lawyer in charge of
the *Weisenfarm* property. Louisa was never to hear from any of
them again.

When Louisa learned of Louis's flight, she returned to
Texas and filed suit for divorce and for possession of the *Weisen-*
farm property. Gossip circulated throughout the community,
and harsh words were spoken against Louis, the once revered
pastor and teacher. Still, when her divorce was granted Louisa
and her girls returned to live in the old orphanage, and she soon
married again, this time a man ten years younger then herself,
the Prussian farmer, Balthazar Preiss.

Once again the orphanage rang with the laughter of young

children — Louisa's son and daughter by Preiss, and the six orphan children of her daughter, Bertha. Preiss became a prosperous farmer and owner of a livery stable in New Braunfels, but in 1886 Louisa filed for a second divorce, claiming that Preiss had abandoned her after twenty-three years of marriage and that he had become a "man of violent passions and ungovernable temper." Awarded her divorce, Louisa lived out her life at the old orphanage, and her children and grandchildren recalled that she never forgot the once happy days when the *Weisenfarm* rang with the bright, young voices of the immigrant children.

Nor did she ever forget her first love, Louis Ervendberg. She allowed no one to use Louis's silver soup spoon, always setting it lovingly at her own place. Often on warm summer evenings when a breeze rustled through the cypresses along the Guadalupe River, she would stand on the old porch, looking sadly down the road. Was Louis finally returning to the home they had built when Texas was a young state? She never seemed to accept the fact that Louis had been shot and killed by a bandit in a Mexican mining town soon after he fled Texas.

It was most fitting that at the end of her life Louisa Ervendberg died during the Christmas season, when the green boughs were again being hung in the old orphanage for the children's Christmas. She was buried in the New Braunfels cemetery on a snowy Christmas Eve in 1887. Descendants of the Preiss family continue to live at the orphanage, and each Christmas the old German cookie cutters are brought out, and spicy molasses and sugar cookies in the shape of the rocking horse, the star, and the tree are baked and stored in round lard cans. A hardy mountain cedar tree is still brought in from the pasture and decorated with real candles and familiar paper decorations. The little Jerusalem village is once again arranged at the foot of the tree, and the high point of the German Christmas is when the candles are lighted on Christmas Eve.

Each year in late spring Louisa's descendants and family friends gather at the orphanage to remember the pioneer couple who came to Texas so long ago — Louis, the pastor and teacher, whose love of humanity drew him westward to Texas; and Louisa, the caring German woman who became the foster mother of the orphaned children of her community.

REFERENCES

Biesele, Rudolph Leopold. *The History of the German Settlements in Texas, 1831-1861.* Austin: n.p., 1930.

Delong, David G. *Historic American Buildings: Texas.* Volume I. New York: Garland Publishing Company, 1980.

"Descendants gather for spring picnic." New Braunfels *Herald-Zeitung* (May 8, 1980): 2.

Ervendberg, Louisa M. and Louis C. *Legal Papers.* In possession of Mrs. Herbert C. Acker, Jr. The Orphanage, New Braunfels, Texas.

Geiser, Samuel Wood. *Naturalists of the Frontier.* Dallas: Southern Methodist University, 1948.

Haas, Oscar. *The First Protestant Church, Its History and Its People, 1845-1855.* New Braunfels: n.p., 1955.

Haas, Oscar. *The History of New Braunfels and Comal County, Texas, 1844-1946.* New Braunfels: n.p., 1968.

"Historic Building Plaque." New Braunfels *Herald-Zeitung* (May 24, 1973): 1.

"History Is Read." San Antonio *Express-News* (May 27, 1973): 16.

McKeller, Sarah S. "Pioneer Times in New Braunfels." San Antonio *Express* (September 8, 1935): 16.

Pinkard, Tommie. "Seven Sisters Celebrate Christmas at the Orphanage." *Texas Highways* (December 1981): 22.

Ragsdale, Crystal Sasse. *The Golden Free Land.* Austin: Landmark Press, 1976.

Roemer, Ferdinand von. *Texas.* (translated by Oswald Mueller). San Antonio: n.p., 1935.

Seele, Hermann. *The Cypress.* (translated by Edward C. Breitenkampt). Austin: The University of Texas Press, 1979.

Seele, Hermann. "In Memory of A German Wife." (translated by Edna Faust). New Braunfels *Zietung* (January 12, 1888): 2.

17 May Day Picnic at The Orphanage. Program (May 4, 1980). New Braunfels Archives, New Braunfels, Texas.

INTERVIEWS

Mrs. Herbert C. Acker Jr. and Crystal Sasse Ragsdale. The Orphanage, New Braunfels, May, June, July, August, 1980.

Valeska Linnartz Startz and Crystal Sasse Ragsdale. New Braunfels, June 1981.

The Timmermann Sisters and Crystal Sasse Ragsdale. The Orphanage, New Braunfels, May 1980 and Geronimo, December 1980; December 1981.

Courtesy Mrs. Herbert C. Acker, Jr., New Braunfels

Louisa Ervendberg's grandchildren stand in front of the old Orphanage near New Braunfels where their parents were reared in the 1870s.

Courtesy Miss Lee Nesbitt, Columbus

Texas's Girl

Dilue Rose Harris

To many Texans Dilue Rose Harris remains forever a little girl, living out her life in those adventurous days when Texas was a frontier territory and independence from Mexico was uppermost in the minds of the Texians. Dilue Rose arrived in Texas on April 28, 1833. That day was her eighth birthday, and her memoirs, many of them based on the detailed journal of her father, Dr. Pleasant Rose, focus on her childhood years and the hardships her family endured. Both Dr. Rose and his daughter were keen observers, and the frontier physician began his journal when his family left St. Louis to make the arduous journey to Texas. Dilue Rose Harris's recollections form a careful weaving of her own memories with the factual account her father recorded in his journal, which is now lost.

The Rose family group that left St. Louis for the wilds of Texas included Dr. Rose, his wife Margaret Wells Rose, Margaret's brother James Wells, and the Rose children, Granville, Ella, and Dilue. The Texas they came to in 1833 was a world of the unexpected and the feared. Indian raids and lack of food were common. Dr. Rose chose to farm on the Texas coast near the Brazos River, where the great cotton and sugar plantations were located, and although the Roses brought no slaves with them, they were constantly aware of both slave smuggling and illegal slave trading among their Texas neighbors.

The stories that Dilue Rose heard were tales of Texas in turmoil. Texas was part of Mexico, and the Anglo-Americans living in the area had to obey Mexican laws. The constant threat of punitive laws enforced by Mexican soldiers was always with the settlers, along with the dread specter of the Indians, who still ranged from the High Plains to the Gulf Coast.

The stormy two-weeks passage across the Gulf of Mexico from New Orleans to Texas was an exceedingly rough voyage. During the uncertain days and nights, the small sailing boat often remained still in the water or stuck on a sandbar. Most fearful of all to young Dilue were the hours spent in darkness huddled down in the tiny, airless hold when high winds pushed threatening waves over the small schooner. All of the passengers were terribly seasick, and when the schooner docked at Galveston Island, Dr. Rose had to be lifted off the boat and carried to shore. Wet and cold, the passengers stood around for several hours waiting to be fed; Dilue recalled that she was exceedingly hungry.

Soon a boat carried the weary settlers up Buffalo Bayou to Harrisburg, the bustling, new Texas settlement laid out amid the pine stumps. It was hard for the Rose family to imagine a settlement without one church, preacher, schoolhouse, or courthouse. Harrisburg, however did have two general merchandise stores which sold most of the supplies needed by the settlers — groceries, dry goods, gunpowder, and farm implements. The ships that kept Harrisburg supplied sailed from New Orleans, and they came to Texas only when there were cotton and hides to be shipped back. Often the settlers went without flour, coffee, and sugar for months at a time.

Dr. Rose decided to move his family to a rented farm at Stafford's Point on the Brazos some fifteen miles from Harrisburg. With all their belongings loaded in a cumbersome cart and on a sleigh, the family followed as best they could the bridgeless, muddy roads, often mere trails through water. It took them two days to cover the distance.

Dr. Rose had been a physician during the War of 1812, but he lacked experience as a farmer. The economy of the Texas he came to, however, was based on agriculture, and here the settlers depended entirely on two crops — cotton for cash money and corn for food. Corn was the survival crop, and farmers saved back one bushel of dry corn for spring planting and then divided it in half in case frost killed the first planting. Dry and hard corn were made into cornmeal and hominy, as well as being fed to horses, oxen, and barnyard fowls.

Fortunately, Margaret Rose had been reared in the country and understood the hardships farm life involved. She had brought the cards to prepare raw cotton for spinning, and she had a spinning wheel and a loom to make sheets and towels, as well as plough lines when there were no ropes on the farm.

Dr. Rose built a two-story house of rough logs. Cracks between the logs, however, often let in the icy winds and blowing rains. A chimney at one end of the main room provided warmth and a fireplace for cooking. A ladder served as access to the second floor; the two doors were of heavy timber held together with wooden pins reinforced by iron bars, and the window openings were fastened inside with heavy wooden shutters.

Several months after the Roses moved into their home Margaret Rose glimpsed a large group of people coming toward the house. Fearing an Indian raid, she sent young Granville running to the cornfield for Dr. Rose and James Wells. Soon the anxious family realized that the strangers were a motley group of slaves off a ship at Galveston. Following their owner, Benjamin Fort Smith, and two other white men, they were lost and hungry. Smith bought two beeves from Dr. Rose, killed and skinned them, and cooked the meat for the starving men. The blacks spoke no English, and the Rose children stood in silent awe of them.

Despite the long days of drudgery on the farm, the Rose girls found their existence enlivened by the dances or "balls." While parents and children visited with friends, the young people's feet flew over the puncheon floors, shuffling and stomping, making the splinters fly to "Monkey Musk," "Piney Woods," and "Molly Cotton-Tail," tunes played by a black fiddler from one of the neighboring plantations. Long winter days brought quilting bees, where all the women gathered round to help a neighbor complete a quilt.

On the fourth of July 1834 the settlers gathered at the Stafford Plantation for an enormous feast, camping under the live oaks for the occasion. Dilue recalled an array of barbecued beef, chicken, and venison plus honey, cornbread, and hot coffee. There were no cakes for the celebration, as the settlement had been without flour for several months.

Margaret Rose missed her church services, as settlers in Mexican Texas were prohibited from establishing Protestant churches. Public schools were also barred, but Dr. Rose hired a teacher for his own children and those from the neighboring farms. School opened in June and ended in August, with the onset of the corn harvest and cotton picking. When Dr. Rose was away from home Margaret was uneasy and afraid, and Dr. Rose told Dilue that she must be her mother's "right-hand," helping to care for Ella and the new baby girl, Missouri. Once when Dr. Rose had gone to Brazoria with bales of cotton and pelts, the family woke to find a tribe of Indians had set up their tents between them and their neighbors. Later an Indian woman who spoke English came to buy corn for their horses, and the Roses were relieved to find them peaceable Wacos, traveling from their village on the Brazos to Harrisburg with dry buffalo hides and bearskins to sell. They camped among the settlers for three months, exchanging beaded moccasins and woven baskets for food.

Then one morning when the wild flowers began to appear on the prairies, the Wacos left, moving in an orderly procession into the pine woods. First, the men with their guns led off; then the women, their papooses strapped to their backs, drove the pack ponies, loaded with a strange assortment of buffalo robes, blankets, bearskins, pots, and kettles. The children rode in baskets tied to each side of the heavily laden ponies.

Another problem arose to replace that of the Indians. Relations between the settlers in Texas and the Mexican government had worsened, and the young men began to talk of fighting. The settlers expected trouble in 1835 when Mexican soldiers arrived in Anahuac, the customs port at the head of Galveston Bay. One disturbance had already occurred, and in late June, fifty men led by William Barret Travis demanded the surrender of the garrison. General Antonio Tenorio agreed to abandon the post on June 30, but Travis, not trusting the commander, brought the Mexican soldiers to Harrisburg, where the settlers were celebrating the fourth of July.

The Texians were dismayed when the soldiers played cards, indifferent to the Texian forces they had recently fought, and Tenorio joined in the festivities as if he were the special guest. While the Mexican officers attended the ball, none knew the country dances. Caroline Kokernot, wife of settler David Kokernot, knew the waltz, and enlivened the occasion by waltzing with General Tenorio, carrying on a lively conversation with him in French. Dilue noted that they made a fine-looking couple on the dance floor and that they "attracted a great deal of attention."

The summer corn crop was in, but the cotton was still to be picked, when news reached the colony that the Mexican army under General Cós was marching toward Bexar. Dilue recalled that nearly every man and boy who had a gun and a horse went to the army, joining with other volunteers in the siege of Bexar. The women and children were left to pick the cotton remaining in the fields.

In mid-December the settlers received the news that the Texian forces had subdued the Mexicans and that Cós had surrendered, evacuating Bexar and promising never to return to Texas again. They were confident that fighting with Mexico had ended, and the men soon returned to their farms with a new sense of peace. They had plowed their fields, preparing for planting, when they received word that General Santa Anna, joined by the defeated General Cós and a horde of Mexican soldiers, was marching toward Bexar. Again the men rushed off, this time to join Sam Houston's army at Gonzales. Eleven-year-old Dilue remembered helping her Uncle James prepare to join the volunteers. While her mother made her brother two striped hickory shirts, and bags to carry his provisions in, Dilue spent the day "melting lead in a pot and dipping it with a spoon to mold bullets."

Settlers began fleeing their homes, heading for the Sabine River in advance of Santa Anna's troops. Dr. Rose, too old to join the army, planted his corn and helped his wife pack provisions for their family, planning to leave at a moment's notice should word arrive that the Mexicans had crossed the Colorado River. With the announcement that the Alamo had fallen, Sam Houston urged Texians to flee their farms and homes. Soon the Roses were hurtling through the events that young Dilue described as "the horrors of the Runaway Scrape."

Margaret Rose and the children set off on a sleigh with one yoke of oxen to meet a man who had promised the family a cart, while Dr. Rose gathered in his cattle. When the family was united, Dilue and her mother rode Dr. Rose's horse, while Dr. Rose took the little children with him as he drove the team of oxen. They joined the caravan of carts, wagons, people on foot, and livestock that hurried toward the Sabine, following a course over almost trackless and rain-soaked prairies and swollen streams.

On the second night, the Roses camped near Harrisburg and the next day crossed Vince's bridge over the flooded bayou. When they arrived at the San Jacinto River, Dilue saw what seemed to be "five thousand people waiting at the ferry." Planters and slaves gathered from nearby plantations, waiting their chance to cross the river. Tempers were short and often angry words exploded between desperate settlers. There was nothing for the Roses to eat but the cold cornbread and boiled beef that Margaret Rose had hurriedly packed.

Crossing the flooded Trinity was beyond Dilue's power to describe. Illness broke out in the wake of chilling rains and sharp April winds. Adults and children alike suffered from measles, sore throat, and whooping cough, and Missouri, Dilue's sister, died and was buried in the cemetery at Liberty. Margaret Rose was so ill that the family remained with her even after word arrived that Santa Anna had crossed the Brazos.

On Thursday afternoon, April 21, 1836, the Texians heard

a sound like distant thunder. Dr. Rose explained that it was cannon fire, and that surely the Texian forces had lost or the cannon would not have ceased firing so quickly. Hurriedly, the families fled, traveling all day on boggy and muddy roads. Suddenly a horseback rider caught up with them to deliver his unbelievable, yet wonderful message: "Turn back! Turn back! The Texian army has whipped the Mexicans! Turn back!"

The refugees stopped momentarily to consider their sudden change of fortune; then like some giant, clumsy animal, the line reversed. All headed back toward the Trinity to security and freedom. To escape the rush, Dr. Rose took a dangerous route along the bay, sailing in a little boat just offshore. Fortunately, the only casualty was Dilue's sunbonnet, which blew off her head and into the water. Rose offered to swim for it, but her mother prudently substituted a tablecloth to protect Dilue's white skin from the sun and elements. When the family passed the San Jacinto battleground, still not cleared of the Mexican dead, Margaret Rose declined an introduction to the captured Santa Anna, feeling that after weeks of almost constant traveling and illness she was "not dressed for visiting."

The Roses and the other families of the Runaway Scrape heard tales of a devastated land. San Felipe, the capital of a now independent Texas, had been burned, as had Harrisburg. General Cós had burned the Stafford plantation to the ground, and the settlers were now deprived of its cotton gin, gristmill, and blacksmith shop. Some of the stored corn had been overlooked, however, and it could be used for food and seed. Ten days of constant traveling saw the Roses at their home. Amazingly, it was still intact. Only the floors had been ripped up by wily Mexican soldiers searching for hens' nests with eggs.

Hogs had rooted through the rooms, and Dr. Rose's books and medicines lay scattered outside on the ground. Even though it was Sunday, Dr. Rose headed for his cornfield, located his plow and set to work cultivating the crop he had planted earlier. Margaret Rose found her wash pot and soon was boiling the pitiful clothes that remained to her family.

School began again for the Rose children, when a young

survivor of the battle of San Jacinto appeared at the door, offering to trade instruction for his room and board. For months the men of the family worked at rebuilding fences, replacing tools, and trading for new livestock. Dr. Rose went to the new capital of Texas at Houston the following March to serve on the grand jury and returned with tales of jury service being held "on a log under an arbor of pine bushes." He also brought home even more exciting news, an invitation for the Roses to attend a grand ball to be held on April 21, 1837, to commemorate the first anniversary of the battle of San Jacinto. Women were in great demand, Dilue was glad to note; and if the town of Houston could not make up a "sufficient number of ladies" there was a "general beating of the bushes along the Brazos, Oyster, and Caney creeks to make up the necessary complement." Unfortunately, the needs of an ill neighbor kept the Rose girls from attending the ball, and they were further upset when those who had gone to Houston for the festivities stopped by to recount what a grand affair it had been.

Dilue had little time, however, to lament missing one ball, for Dr. Rose had determined to move his family to Houston. He located a farm on Bray's Bayou, five miles from Houston, and there Margaret Rose could attend the church services and prayer meetings she had so ardently longed for, and Dilue could attend a new two-room school. Here the boys sat on one side and the girls on another, and Dilue recalled that the boys's side had "no shutter to the door, nor glass to the window." Seats and desks were simple, rough planks placed on barrels and nail kegs, and Dilue was much chagrined at one pretty girl from New York who criticized the school, Houston, and Texas to such an extent that the students nicknamed her "Texas."

Houston was a boom town, considered the "El Dorado of the West," and by the time the 1838 San Jacinto ball came around Dilue was a young lady of fourteen, alert and aware of her surroundings and priding herself on taking part in every social occasion in the grand city of Houston. Twice she was to be in close proximity to General Sam Houston, but both times pretty young widows usurped her place, much to Dilue's annoyance. She was supposed to march with Houston at the grand ball in 1838, but a young widow changed places with her. Once more, at an elaborate wedding held in Pamela Mann's famed Houston Mansion Hotel, Houston was to serve as best man and Dilue as first bridesmaid, but another young widow claimed that Dilue was "too young and timid," and marched off on General Houston's arm. The occasion still remained a special one for Dilue, for here she met young Ira A. Harris, and "as there was no pretty widow to interfere," they soon became friends.

With her eye ever on the social affairs of the republic, Dilue recorded a most memorable excursion to a play, presented as the crowning finish to the day honoring Sam Houston as the retiring president of the republic. Although it was the rainy season and the streets of Houston were deep in mud and water, the pupils of Mrs. Robertson's School, including Dilue, gathered at the schoolhouse. Then they marched to the theatre, only to find that their seats on the first row had been taken by a group of local gamblers.

Houston entered, and the band played a salute to the retiring chief. But there was no place for the president to sit, and when the gamblers were asked to relinquish their seats, they refused. They fired on the police who came to oust them, and neither the sheriff nor the local soldiers could move them. Houston stood on a chair, demanded silence, and stated that he, the ladies, and the children would move to the back of the hall. Immediately the gamblers offered to vacate the theatre, if the management would refund their money. The play resumed, and at the conclusion, Houston gave a farewell speech, reminding the children to be "diligent in their studies" and obedient.

Sleet and snow ushered in the year 1839, and Houston was building. While the capital moved to Austin, new settlers continued to arrive at the town on Buffalo Bayou. The year was a memorable one for Dilue Rose, as on February 20 in a log house on Brazos Bayou, amidst a host of relatives and friends, she married young Ira Harris.

The year was also marked by the death of Dr. Rose, who had labored beyond his strength on behalf of his patients when a yellow fever epidemic raged through the summer. Little could be done for those who were struck down by the dread disease except to prescribe doses of calomel, bleed the patient, and induce vomiting.

Dilue and Ira continued to live on their farm until 1845, when they moved to the old settlement of Columbus on the Colorado River. They became the parents of nine children, all of whom were living in 1899 when Dilue, at age seventy-four, began writing the reminiscences which give us such a perceptive view of Texas during the revolutionary days and the years of the republic. Two of their sons fought in the Civil War on the Confederate side and returned safely. Ira died in 1869, during the difficult years following the war when farming was not profitable and there was little money in business.

Through the remaining years of her widowhood Dilue lived among her children, working on her memoirs even while visiting one of her sons at Purcell, Indian Territory, before Oklahoma became a state. Nevertheless, she always claimed "dear old Texas" as her home, and she was always in demand to recount her experiences in early Texas, contributing articles to the Eagle Lake *Headlight* and the *Quarterly of the Texas State Historical Association.*

Dilue Rose Harris died at age eighty-nine on April 2, 1914, at her home in Eagle Lake, a woman who had lived to see Texas turn from a frontier wilderness to a struggling republic to a great state moving onward with the twentieth century. Her memoirs capture the spirit of the early days of Texas's independence as well as the spirit of a young girl who lived through great moments in the Lone Star State's history.

REFERENCES

DeShields, James T. *Tall Men with Long Rifles.* San Antonio: The Naylor Company, 1971.

Gardien, Kent. "Kokernot and His Tory." *Texana* VIII, 1970.

Harris, Dilue Rose. "The Reminiscences of Mrs. Dilue Harris." (In three parts). *Quarterly of the Texas State Historical Association* (October 1900; IV, January 1901; VII, January 1904).

Hauser, Vincent. "Texas Tabby." *Perspective* IX, December 1980.

Hogan, William Ransom. *The Texas Republic*. Norman: University of Oklahoma Press, 1946.

James, Marquis. *The Raven*. New York: Blue Ribbon Books, Inc., 1929.

Muir, Andrew Forest (ed.). *Texas in 1834*. Austin: The University of Texas Press, 1958.

Nesbitt, Lee. *Letter* to Crystal Sasse Ragsdale. January 10, 1981.

Nesbitt, Lee. *Letter* to Crystal Sasse Ragsdale. January 25, 1981.

Weems, John Edward. *Dream of Empire*. New York: Simon and Schuster, 1971.

Lady Ambassador
For Texas

Mary Austin Holley

The annals of nineteenth-century literature are filled with the writings of lady ''scribblers and scribes'' who wrote pleasant verses and travel narratives detailing the life and times of the places they lived and visited. No woman's writings were to have a greater influence on the growth of Texas than did those of Mary Austin Holley, cousin of Texas's colonizer, Stephen F. Austin. After Austin arranged for her to visit his colony in 1831, she wrote the book that made her reputation as a writer, *Texas Observations, Historical, Geographical, and Descriptive in a Series of Letters Written during a visit to Austin's Colony, with a View to a Permanent Settlement in that Country in the Autumn of 1831.*

Despite its lengthy title, her book was an immediate success, giving a valuable picture of life in early frontier Texas, and, along with the popular emigrant guides, helped create a picture of Texas as a land of promise, where each settler could realize a fortune. Immigrants flocked to the colony, no doubt lured by Holley's words:

> It is impossible to imagine the beauty of a Texas prairie when, in the vernal season, its rich luxuriant herbage, adorned with its thousand flowers, of every size and hue, seems to realize the vision of a terrestrial paradise. None but those who have seen it can

form an idea of its surpassing loveliness, and pen and pencil alike would fail in its delineation.

Born on October 30, 1789, in New Haven, Connecticut, daughter of Elijah Austin, an important merchant in the China trade, and his wife, Esther Phelps Austin, Mary grew up amid a large family of relatives, who lived in and around New Haven. She counted among her relatives her father's brother, the adventurous Moses Austin, who soon left New Haven to travel to Spanish Missouri on a lead mining venture, and who eventually obtained an empresario grant to settle three hundred families in Spanish Texas.

When Mary's father died of yellow fever, the family found themselves impoverished, and Timothy Phelps, her uncle, and his wife took the young girl to live with them. Mary Austin had the best education then possible for a young girl, studying music, drawing, writing, painting, English, and French. Unfortunately, she was never allowed to study mathematics, as women were not supposed to have anything to do with business. Her ignorance of money matters caused her great hardship during the nineteen years of her widowhood.

Mary was taught all kinds of needlework, and throughout her life she designed and stitched her own dresses, petticoats, and underwear. Music was also an important part of her life, and she often sang, accompanying herself on her guitar. The instrument went with her on her innumerable travels, and a silhouette made of her in 1827 pictures an elegantly and fashionably dressed woman standing with her guitar and holding a sheet of music.

Although Mary early demonstrated a remarkable mind and quick wit and Yale College was located in New Haven, she could not attend, as women were prohibited from studying in institutions of higher learning. She did, however, continue to read widely and to practice her music, so that her conversation was both intelligent and spritely, and she was sought after as an entertainer at many social gatherings.

The sixteen-year-old Mary Austin met young Horace

Holley, a Yale divinity student, and at twenty-one, married him and moved to western Connecticut for his first ministerial assignment. Soon the young couple moved to Boston, where Holley served as minister to the Hollis Street Church for nine years. There, amidst a growing social circle of women friends, Mary studied botany and wrote poetry. In the evenings the ladies joined their husbands to discuss books and affairs of public interest.

During the Holleys' years in Boston, Mary began a life of traveling that was unusual for her time. Few women journeyed so continuously or as far. She never minded traveling alone, if there was no member of her family to accompany her; and during her lifetime she was to travel across the expanding United States several times, journeying from New England to the frontiers of Mexican Texas. Early in her travels she began keeping journals and notes of her experiences, as well as writing wonderful letters describing her travels. Inveterate land traveler that she was, often riding sidesaddle or bumping along in wagons, stagecoaches, and carriages over rough roads and trails, she was inevitably seasick on the various ships and sailboats on which she journeyed to Texas.

Horace Holley became a popular speaker in Boston, and it is almost certain that his wife helped him polish his speeches. Mary had a good deal of time to devote to her studies, as her family, including their young daughter Harriette, lived in an apartment and took their meals out. She seldom found time for nor was interested in the endless chores of domesticity that plagued the nineteenth-century woman.

Although her uncles and her brother Henry had left the Atlantic coast to explore opportunities on the expanding American frontier, Mary was reluctant to leave the refinements of Boston when her husband was elected to the presidency of the newly established Transylvania University in Lexington, Kentucky. In 1818 the journey across the United States to her new home in the West was a long, slow one, and with two young children to provide for, undoubtedly, a tiring one. Mary took along her guitar, shipped her pianoforte and a generous supply of books and pictures, and once settled, the Holleys became leaders in the social and academic life of Lexington.

When General Lafayette, the French hero of the American Revolution, was an honored guest in the city, two of Mary Austin Holley's poems, signed only with her initials, were published in local newspapers and in the literary journal, *Western Review.* During these years as wife of the president of Transylvania University Mary became known as a writer of unusual talents.

Horace Holley's term as president of the university, however, was plagued with religious misunderstandings between the president and the trustees, and finally he was forced to resign. Plans to begin a college in New Orleans also failed, and on the voyage from New Orleans to New York, the couple fell ill with yellow fever. Dr. Holley died and was buried at sea, and Mary, still weak from fever, and their young son Horace, continued the journey to Boston.

Immediately Mary began plans for a book about her husband's life and work. With the help of a college professor in Lexington she completed her first full-length book. In a bold move for a woman, she traveled to Washington and sold a number of subscriptions for her book at sessions of Congress. As she had agreed to use the name of the college professor as the author, her name did not appear and the book was called Caldwell's *Discourses*.

At the age of forty-five, widowed with a son to support, Mary Austin Holley became a teacher at Good Hope Plantation in Louisiana, and with the French-American family she worked for often traveled to their town house in New Orleans. There she heard much talk of land available in the Mexican state of Texas. She had met her cousin, Stephen Fuller Austin, during his college days in Connecticut, and news of his colonization efforts along the Brazos and Colorado rivers had reached her family in the United States. Henry Austin had already settled on a large tract of land on the Brazos, and Stephen F. Austin wrote Mary that he had set aside a league of land for her. Brother Henry wrote also, encouraging Mary to come to Texas to settle on her grant.

Thus began the great adventure, and Mary Austin Holley immediately began contemplating a book about Texas from the viewpoint of a potential settler. In October 1831 she began her voyage from New Orleans, and arrived at Brazoria at the mouth of the Brazos River, where Henry met her and took her upriver to his log house in the newly laid-out town of Bolivar. She immediately began gathering information for her book on the ample opportunities for a better life offered in Texas. Henry knew that the London Geographical Society had recently written Stephen F. Austin about material relative to Texas. Immediately the brother and sister realized the potential for a travel book answering questions about immigration to the Mexican state. With a detailed journal and bulging notebooks Mary began writing.

Her work intensified when Stephen F. Austin came down the Brazos from his capital, San Felipe, and talked to her at great length about his plans for the colony and the troubles between the colonists and the Mexican government. Perhaps two such intelligent people as Mary Austin Holley and Stephen F. Austin were destined to fall in love, and in the ten days they spent together, talking and planning, they determined that they would marry when Austin had settled affairs between his Texas colony and Mexico.

Austin's Christmas visit with Mary and with Henry's family at Bolivar House was a time for rejoicing, and the group sang the lyrics of the song Mary had written on her arrival in Texas. She termed "The Brazos Boat Song" a rallying cry for the family that had journeyed westward:

Come whistle, my boys, to the good San Antonio,
Whistle, my boys, that fav'ring gales blow.
Spread wide the swelling sheet,
Make fast the oaken sprit,
And steer to our forest home.
　　　Far o'er the wave.

The last days of 1831 Mary spent finishing the book with Austin's helpful suggestions and corrections. She left Texas for Louisiana soon thereafter, and on a later trip to Lexington, she readied the book for publication. *Texas* was published in 1833, dedicated to the man who was destined to be "The Father of Texas."

No one could have approved more of *Texas* than her cousin. With its idyllic portrait of the land and its romantic elegies to nature, her book lured many an immigrant searching for a new life to the wilderness that was the Mexican province in the 1830s. The ending of her final chapter reflects the tone of her hymn of praise for Austin's colony:

> One's feelings in Texas are unique and original, and very like a dream or youthful vision realized. Here, as in Eden, man feels alone with the God of nature, and seems, in a peculiar manner, to enjoy the rich bounties of heaven, in common with all created things. The animals, which do not fly from him; the profound stillness; the genial sun and soft air — all are impressive, and are calculated both to delight the imagination, and to fill the heart with religious emotions.

While she was in Lexington, word came from Henry that his wife had died. Mary took his five motherless children to Kentucky so that she could care for them. Once in Kentucky, she rented a large house and tried to sell part of her Texas lands to meet expenses for her adopted family. On a second, but very short, trip to Texas in the spring of 1835, Mary found that much had changed. Austin was in Mexico City, held prisoner by Santa Anna. The settlers were openly talking rebellion, making plans to free Texas from Mexican rule. She spent her time sketching and outlining a second book on Texas.

By midsummer Mary had received a letter from Stephen F. Austin written from New Orleans, telling her that he had reached the United States after his long imprisonment and was at last on his way to Texas. For the first time the Texas leader was in agreement with other Texians that only war could settle the growing difficulties between Texas and Mexico. As news reached her by letter and newspaper, Mary immediately began cataloging the events that would lead to the Texas revolution.

Traveling throughout the United States to gather support for the Texas revolution, Austin visited with Mary in Lexington. The two discussed the events that had led to revolution and to the siege of Bexar. Nothing is known concerning what the two discussed of their own private feelings, but Austin was consumed with events in Texas and the imminent peril of his adopted land. Not until he had left did the news of the fall of the Alamo reach Kentucky. Several weeks later, when the reports of the Texian victory at San Jacinto was brought up the river from New Orleans, Mary immediately wrote lyrics which she set to a Scottish tune to commemorate the stunning battle. A short time later a German composer set ''The Texas Song of Liberty'' to original music.

By July 1836 *Mrs. Holley's Texas,* a much larger book than her first, was printed and ready for sale. With her intense loyalty to Texas and to Austin, Mary lobbied the Kentucky legislature for the recognition of the newly formed republic of Texas. Then she wrote Austin that she would be returning to Texas to oversee the development and sale of her land on Galveston Bay. Unfortunately, the two friends were never to know happiness together, nor to ever meet again. Stephen F. Austin never received her letter; he died on December 27, 1836. Once again Mary lost the man she loved, and as she had written out her anguish over the loss of Horace Holley, she immediately wrote a loving poem to Austin's memory.

With expenses increasing, Mary Austin Holley traveled to New Orleans to sell some of her Texas land. Then she returned once more to Texas to observe firsthand life in the new republic and to sell even more of her property. At the new capital at Houston, Mary Holley was introduced to President Sam Houston and Vice-President Mirabeau B.Lamar. Finances were an ever-increasing burden, and Mary soon returned to Lexington, living on what little money Henry sent her together with the help of her more affluent son-in-law. Her purpose was to oversee the settling of Henry's children, sending the boys to boarding schools and establishing the girls with relatives.

With her two nephews as companions she traveled once again to New Orleans and then to Texas. Continuing down Galveston Island, she saw for the first time the land grant that Austin had established in her name. She spent several months at the new settlement on San Luis Island below Galveston and sent articles and poems to the local newspaper. Perhaps she might have written pungent essays and lively columns, but even in the new republic of Texas, no woman wrote in that style for publication. Still, ever musical, she composed the lyrics for a song, "Invitation."

Expenses forced her to return to her daughter's home in Lexington for a year, but as soon as she was able, she returned to Texas. The spring of 1843 saw her once again in Galveston. Still worried about poor finances and even poorer land sales, she busily began filling notebooks with observations concerning Austin's life for a projected biography of "The Father of Texas." Although Austin's sister and her family refused her permission to write the official biography of the colonizer, and word reached her that Austin's nephew, Guy Bryan, was also collecting material, she never abandoned the project.

Faced again with the familiar pattern of exhausted finances, Mary Holley went back to Lexington, where she continued her work on Austin's life as she watched with high interest the politics that swirled around the admission of Texas into the Union. Forced to leave Harriette's home because of unpleasantness between young Horace and her son-in-law, Mary once again took her son and sailed down the Mississippi. This time she stopped at Good Hope Plantation to teach yet another generation of children. Several months later she moved to New Orleans as companion and teacher to the children of her first pupil at Good Hope. There, during the yellow fever epidemic of 1846, she died, only a few months after her beloved Texas had ceased to be a republic and was admitted as the twenty-eighth state in the United States.

The legacy she left was a generous one. Her books, poems, and observations form one of the most astute pictures of life in frontier Texas and during the years of the republic. Her letters and newspaper articles informed people throughout the United States and Europe of Texas, and her writings portrayed for thousands of immigrants the land that they would settle. Her letters brought sympathy for the colonists during the Texas revolution, and her enthusiasm assisted in bringing aid to the beleaguered fighters for independence. Her collected works. including her writings to Stephen F. Austin, form a valuable background of firsthand information on early Texas.

REFERENCES

Austin, Henry. *Letter* to Mary Austin Holley (May 16, 1831). Henry Austin Papers. Barker Texas History Center, The University of Texas at Austin.

Austin, Henry. *Letter* to Mary Austin Holley (September 19, 1831.) Henry Austin Papers. Barker Texas History Center, The University of Texas at Austin.

Austin, Stephen F. *Memorandum Relation to the Heirship of Stephen Fuller Austin.* (typescript). Hallie Bryan Perry Papers. Barker Texas History Center, The University of Texas at Austin.

Bryan, J.P. "Mary Austin Holley: The Texas Diary, 1835-1838." *Texas Quarterly.* VIII (Summer 1965).

Casteneda, Carlos E. and Early Martin, Jr. *Three Manuscript Maps of Texas By Stephen F. Austin.* Austin, n.p., 1930.

Hatcher, Mattie Austin. *Letters of an Early American Traveler: Mary Austin Holley, Her Life and Her Works, 1784-1846.* Dallas: Southwest Press, 1933.

Holley, Mary Austin. *Letter* to Emily Austin Bryan Perry (March 23, 1844). Mary Austin Holley Papers. Barker Texas History Center, The University of Texas at Austin.

Holley, Mary Austin. *Letter* to Emily Austin Bryan Perry (April 12, 1844). Mary Austin Holley Papers. Barker Texas History Center, The University of Texas.

Holley, Mary Austin. *Letter* to Harriette Holley Brand (March 6, 1838). Mary Austin Holley Papers. Barker Texas History Center, The University of Texas at Austin.

Holley, Mary Austin. *Letter* to Harriette Holley Brand (November 12, 1840). Mary Austin Holley Papers. Barker Texas History Center, The University of Texas at Austin.

Holley, Mary Austin. *Letter* to Harriette Holley Brand (July 10, 1846). Mary Austin Holley Papers. Barker Texas History Center, The University of Texas at Austin.

Holley, Mary Austin. *Texas* (reprint). Austin: The Steck Company, 1935.

Lee, Rebecca Smith. *Mary Austin Holley, A Biography.* Austin: The University of Texas Press, 1962.

Meinig, D. W. *Imperial Texas.* Austin: The University of Texas Press, 1975.

Mary Austin Holley poses with her guitar and sheet music.

Courtesy Jean Houston Daniel.

The Woman Who Gentled A General

Margaret Lea Houston

When Margaret Lea Houston was an older woman, she often reflected on how fateful the month of May had been in her life. It was in May 1836 that she first glimpsed the hero of San Jacinto, who was to become her husband and lead her to frontier Texas. Three years later—again in the month of May—she was visiting in Mobile, Alabama, and by chance met the tall, blue-eyed man she had seen on the New Orleans docks. A year later in May she married her general. The tall, older man from Texas and the serious, young woman from Alabama fell in love soon after their first meeting at a garden party at her sister's home. As Margaret said later, "He won my heart!"

Margaret Moffette Lea was merely a schoolgirl when she first saw General Sam Houston. The daughter of Temple and Nancy Moffette Lea, she was born on April 11, 1819 near Marion, Alabama. When her husband died Nancy Lea brought her two young daughters to live with her son Henry then an Alabama state senator, in order to receive an education in the town schools.

Still grieving for her father, young Margaret enrolled in Judson Female Institute. Intelligent and pious, Margaret as a schoolgirl was described by the Baptist preacher William Carey

Crane as winning in manner, and fascinating in appearance. She was tall, with a fair complexion. Her most compelling features were her large, intense, violet eyes, framed by her wavy, brown hair, parted in the middle and drawn back in long loops.

While her classmates visited New Orleans they greeted the hero of the celebrated battle of San Jacinto, and Margaret witnessed a scene she would never forget. The docks were crowded when General Sam Houston's ship arrived. Wounded and ill, he had come to New Orleans seeking treatment for the ankle shattered during his advance against Santa Anna's troops on the plains of San Jacinto. Houston looked the romantic figure to move a young girl's heart. His clothes were in tatters; part of his shirt had been torn away to serve as a blood-stained bandage for his ankle. Houston fainted from pain as he was lifted onto a stretcher.

When he journeyed to Alabama three years later to publicize a townsite company in Texas, however, Houston was indeed the compelling, gallant figure that legend had made of him. At forty-six years of age, he was just completing his first term as president of the republic of Texas. His life had been an adventurous one, a romantic fantasy that would appeal to a twenty-year old girl. Houston was already a famous man when he became the leader of the Texian forces in their fight for independence.

Congressman and governor of his home state of Tennessee, Houston claimed the close friendship of President Andrew Jackson. He was headed for a distinguished political career when in 1824, in a highly dramatic incident, he resigned the office of governor and abandoned a new marriage to live in Arkansas among his old friends, the Cherokee Indians. Marrying Tiana Rogers, the daughter of an Indian chief, in a tribal ceremony, Houston lived the ways of the civilized Cherokee for six years. During this time he used his legal training and his political connections to represent the Cherokees in diplomatic and business affairs.

Frontier Texas, however, was the place where Houston was destined to fulfill his leadership role. He had made the acquaintance of settlers in Nacogdoches and kept abreast of relations between the colonists and the Mexican government that soon led to the revolution. In the spring of 1835, when Houston moved to Texas, Tiana chose to remain with the Cherokees, and, according to tribal custom, their marriage was dissolved. Soon Houston was involved in the trouble brewing between the Anglo-American settlers and the Mexican authorities. Amidst much controversy concerning his command, he led the Texians in the historic confrontation at San Jacinto on April 21, 1836, and emerged a hero to the nation and president of the newly formed republic.

Hero he might be to a nation, but to Margaret Lea's family he was much too old for the young girl. With all his prestige, past and present, the Leas insisted that his reputation was not what they had expected of the man who would be Margaret's husband. Sam Houston, however, was used to getting what he wanted and pressed his suit, begging Margaret to marry him at once. For her part, Margaret had never been seriously in love before, and she naively wrote to her fiance´ that he was the first gentleman she had ever "addressed."

Houston returned to Texas without his prize, but he gave Margaret a fine, carved cameo portrait of himself, which the young woman promptly fastened onto a green ribbon and wore proudly around her neck. A year later, after their marriage, Margaret wrote a poem about her treasured gift, which she called "To My Husband's Picture." Throughout her married life, she manifested her romantic nature through dozens of love poems which she composed and tucked into the letters she sent her general.

From the time she told Sam Houston goodbye as he journeyed back to Texas, Margaret began corresponding with him. Her letters, on delicately tinted writing paper written in her regular, even handwriting, line after line with postscripts and notes crowding the margins, along with Houston's replies, continued throughout the twenty-three years of their lives together. Fortunately, much of their correspondence has endured, forming a rare record of the couple's lasting devotion to one another.

Houston's letters contained impassioned pleas for Margaret to sail at once for Texas and become his wife. Margaret continually refused, insisting that her general come to Alabama to claim her. Finally, in May 1840 Houston arrived in Marion, and he and Margaret were married at her brother's house among the Lea family and friends, just as Margaret had desired.

The woman that Sam Houston brought with him to frontier Texas had an intelligence and education that many of her fellow settlers could have envied. She was a serious reader and eager student, and coupled with daily Bible study, her reading of novels and poems remained a part of her life in Texas. In addition, she had studied music and she sang, accompanying herself on the guitar or the piano. When her mahogany furniture, purchased as part of her trousseau, arrived in Texas, among the most treasured pieces was her rosewood piano.

In addition, Margaret brought with her from Alabama trunks and boxes of household linens and china, plus dozens of brass candlesticks to start her new home. But more important than any of the treasures that made the memorable trip across the Gulf of Mexico was her beloved Eliza. This understanding and capable young black woman was through the years to manage the various Houston households, wherever they lived; and, as she had been in Alabama, Eliza remained Margaret's constant companion and friend.

The trip to Texas must have been a hazardous one for Margaret, for throughout her life she remained a poor traveler over long distances, and despite Eliza's care, she usually became ill. Sam Houston, however, was constantly traveling on his annual trips to Washington, D.C., serving as the U.S. senator from Texas. But Margaret left Texas only twice, making journeys out of state only at the beginning of her marriage when she had only one child. When Houston was elected president of the republic of Texas for a second term, the couple lived a few months in Houston City, as Houston was then called, and at Washington-on-the-Brazos, for Austin, the capital of Texas, was not considered safe as it was constantly endangered by Indian raiding parties.

Although Sam Houston, immersed in the politics of the annexation of Texas to the United States, was away more than he was at home, Margaret's feelings for her husband never changed. She remained totally devoted to him. At the same time she steadfastly held no interest in politics, her husband's main concern. Her life as a married woman in frontier Texas was in many ways the same as that of most married women of the Victorian era. She made a home for her husband and their children, wherever her husband chose for them to live.

After three years of marriage the Houstons' first child Sam Houston, Jr., was born. He was soon the older brother to four sisters, Nannie, Nettie, Maggie, and Mary William, before the brothers he kept asking for rounded out the family of eight children. Temple Lea, Andrew Jackson Houston, and Willie Rogers were the last children born to the Houstons. The young Houstons grew up eagerly anticipating their father's arrival from Washington or from one of his political speaking tours.

Often when Houston arrived home he would pack up the family and move them to yet another of the Houston homes. Margaret, Eliza, and the children traveled in the famous yellow coach that Houston had purchased for Margaret during the first years of their marriage. The luggage wagons followed the family coach, and Sam Houston rode horseback alongside. The homes the Houstons traveled to for many years were plain, rugged log houses built dogtrot style with open chinks in the walls and with uneven floors. They were all kept well furnished, however, so that whenever the family moved in life could begin almost immediately.

The old town of Independence came to have increasing importance as a place where the hero of San Jacinto and his family lived. It was a well-known center of education in Texas, and soon the Houston children were attending school there. The Houstons and the Leas, for Margaret's mother and sisters were living in Texas, enthusiastically joined the Baptist church and faithfully attended services with all their servants. To Margaret, her membership in the church was an important matter. In the Houston household, Bible reading and prayer service with family, servants, and visitors followed breakfast and supper as part of each day's schedule.

Margaret had taken on the job of converting her husband to the Baptist faith soon after their marriage. She found, however, that she had to wait on the Lord. Family and friends alike praised her efforts that had resulted in Sam Houston's giving up drinking strong spirits. Although he attended church services with some degree of regularity, baptism was quite another matter. Margaret enlisted the aid of the Reverend Rufus Burleson, president of Baylor College, but it still took fourteen years to lead the hero of San Jacinto to the baptismal pool. When her husband was baptized, an exuberant Margaret memorialized the baptism site in nearby Rocky Creek in her poem, "Farewell to Independence."

With her husband absent from home much of the time, Margaret depended on Eliza to run the Houston household and on a friend of Sam's to attend to finances. Neither Margaret nor Sam Houston concerned themselves overly much with business affairs. Sam was involved with politics, and Margaret had little training in practical matters. Although Nancy Lea had been a businesswoman long before she came to Texas to buy and sell land, she had little influence on the Houstons' finances. While Sam Houston owned considerable land, he and Margaret never managed to have enough cash to meet their family needs. Early in their marriage, Sam borrowed a hundred dollars from Nancy Lea to help pay household expenses, writing to his young wife, "I regret that I cannot send you a million in gold."

When Houston went to Washington as the senator from Texas, he dreamed of following in the footsteps of his political mentor Andrew Jackson, and of being elected president of the United States. His national political dreams died with the politics of annexation and slavery, and he suffered another political defeat in 1857, when he lost the election for Texas governor. In 1859, however, he was elected governor, and Margaret, Eliza, and the smaller children climbed into the old yellow coach once again, while the other children rode horseback. The Houstons were off to Austin to live in the new, two-story, yellow-brick governor's mansion.

The second floor of the mansion was living quarters for the family with Margaret's bedroom serving as the family living room. During the hot summer nights, with young Sam enrolled in Allen's Military Academy in nearby Bastrop, the Houston children slept on the long, upstairs gallery. Temple Lea, Margaret and Sam's last child, was born at the mansion in early August 1860, and Margaret entertained a steady stream of visitors, including plump, dignified old Nancy Lea, as well as Margaret's two sisters and their families.

One picture of Margaret taken during the mansion years shows a sweet, gentle-looking woman. She still wore her hair parted in the middle, much as she had as a bride. It was somewhat puffed over the ears, and now she used the stylish silver or tortoise shell "tucking" combs to gather her hair into long curls.

Despite the excitement of state politics, the Houstons' two-year stay in Austin was not a pleasant one, for Sam Houston had taken an unpopular political stand in regard to the slavery issue. Even before he had left the United States Senate, Houston had made it clear that he would never favor the concept that states could secede from the Union. With the Southern states talking secession to preserve the institution of slavery, Houston warned Texans that at the same time the North was prepared to fight to preserve the Union.

Tempers flared and feelings ran high among Texans, and Margaret had to watch with sadness as her husband fought his final political battle. Angry mobs often gathered at the capitol, and one night a group turned its rage against "Old Sam." They overran the fence and poured into the yard of the mansion, trampling Margaret's flowers. They had come to convince Governor Houston that he must change his mind on the subject of secession and advance the cause of Texas's separating from the Union.

The new year brought the time for decision. One day in mid-January 1861 Margaret was sitting with her husband on the mansion porch when loud shouts echoed from the capitol.

In his most serious manner, Houston took Margaret's hand in his saying "Texas is dead." Texans had voted to secede from the Union and to join the new Confederate States of America. When the oath of allegiance to the Confederacy was taken by all public officials in March, however, Sam Houston refused. The Houstons packed their belongings and left the capital for the last time. After twenty-five years as the pivotal leader in Texas's time of destiny, Sam Houston was forced to retire from public life.

The Houstons first stayed at Cedar Point on the coast. Young Sam marched off to join the Confederate forces and to fight in Tennessee, the oldest girls attended school in Independence, and Margaret kept the younger children at home. Before winter came the family moved to a rented home in Huntsville, called the Steamboat House. There, on March 2, 1863 seventy-year-old Sam Houston celebrated his birthday. Few visitors came now to the Houston home, for Sam's political views kept him out of favor in Texas. The old hero was also in poor health; his war wounds bothered him, and he had difficulty walking.

With sadness, Margaret watched her husband's hopes of a return to political life fade and regretted his sadness at being passed over for leadership roles in favor of younger men. With the onset of summer his health declined noticeably, and on July 26, 1863, after a few weeks's illness, he died. His last words were the watchwords of his life: "Texas! Margaret! Margaret!"

Margaret was shattered by her husband's death and soon after decided to return to Independence to be near her mother and sisters. At forty-four, for the first time she had to take full responsibility for her own life and those of her children. She moved the family to a two-story house near her mother's and began to adjust to life during the trying days in Texas after the Civil War. Times were hard, but at least the family had vegetables from the garden and fruit from the orchard. Still, like most Texans, the Houstons had little money.

Margaret found herself surrounded by her children who were rapidly becoming adults and making their lives in a new

Texas. Young Sam returned from the army to try his future in a rapidly expanding cattle industry, while Nannie and Maggie married and moved away. With Texas growing into a more populous state, Margaret was even more determined that Texas should not forget her husband. Working with historian William Carey Crane, she compiled Houston's papers, letters, and documents, and although Carey completed the manuscript and sent it to numerous publishers, no one was interested in the man who had once been a legendary frontier hero.

Discouraged, Margaret began to burn many of the historic documents. The heat from the fireplace, however, was so intense during the summer days that she had to leave the task to sit in the hall, and so she never completed the job. Long years of neglect almost finished the job she had begun, and many of Houston's valuable papers were later destroyed. Margaret also began to change. She now wore her hair swept back and up, smooth and plain. Her bright-eyed liveliness, so much a part of the young girl Sam Houston had loved, was replaced by her humorless and rather gaunt appearance.

Suddenly, in early September 1867, the pattern of living at Independence changed. The dread yellow fever, epidemic in its death toll, moved inland from the coast, and Margaret moved her family to nearby Labadie Prairie to wait for a norther to blow the dreaded fever away. As soon as cool weather came and the fever abated, Margaret returned home with her children to prepare for Christmas in Georgetown at her daughter Nannie's home. Before she could leave Independence, however, she fell ill with the fever.

Within only a few days, Margaret Lea Houston was dead at forty-eight. That night Nettie and Mary William followed the cart bearing the homemade coffin down the dark street to their grandmother's burial plot across the street from the Baptist church. In addition to her two children, only Dingley, the Houstons' black man-of-all-work and the Houstons' longtime friend, Major Eber W. Cave, attended Margaret's last rites. With Margaret gone, the Houston children, the two youngest boys and their two older sisters, went to live with Nannie in

Georgetown. Eliza accompanied them and spent her remaining days with the Houstons, as they married and began their own families. When she died, she was taken back to Independence. There she was buried in a simple plot adjoining that of Nancy Lea and her loyal friend, Margaret Lea Houston.

REFERENCES

Alexander, Drury Blakely. *Texas Homes of the Nineteenth Century.* Austin: University of Texas Press, 1966.

Bracken, Dorothy Kendall and Maurine Whorton Redway. *Early Texas Homes.* Dallas: Southern Methodist University Press, 1956.

Crane, William Carey. *Life and Select Literary Remains of Sam Houston of Texas* (2 vols. in 1), Philadelphia: Lippincott and Company, 1884.

Flanagan, Sue. *Sam Houston's Texas.* Austin: University of Texas Press, 1965.

Friend, Llerena B. *Sam Houston: The Great Designer.* Austin: University of Texas Press, 1956.

Hollon, W. Eugene and Ruth L. Butler. *William Bolleart's Texas.* Norman: University of Oklahoma Press, 1956.

James, Marquis. *The Raven: A Biography of Sam Houston.* Indianapolis: Bobbs-Merrill Company, 1929.

Pickrell, Annie Doom. *Pioneer Women in Texas* (reprint). Austin: Jenkins Publishing Company, 1970.

Seale, William. *Sam Houston's Wife.* Norman: University of Oklahoma Press, 1970.

Shuffler, R. Henderson. *The Houstons at Independence.* Waco: Texian Press, 1966.

Turner, Martha Anne. *Sam Houston and His Twelve Women.* Austin: Pemberton Press, 1966.

Williamson, Roxanne Kuter. *Austin, Texas, An American Architectural History.* San Antonio: Trinity University Press, 1973.

Courtesy Barker Texas History Center, The University of Texas at Austin.

Margaret Lea Houston in later life.

Painted by J. T. McCann, 1915. Courtesy the King Ranch

Rosa von Roeder Kleberg and her son Robert

Founder Of A Dynasty

Rosa von Roeder Kleberg

The motto of the aristocratic von Roeder family of Prussia is translated "God helps those who help themselves," and no woman's life more completely embodies that maxim than does that of Rose von Roeder Kleberg. Energetic and imaginative, she personified the work ethic inherent on the Texas frontier and proved a helpmate to her husband and an inspiration to her children and grandchildren, causing her husband to comment that marrying Rosa was the best act of his life.

Rosa's life of productivity and service began in 1813 on a feudal estate in Brendenborn, Prussia, where Rosalie, or "Rosa" as she was called by her family, was born, the ninth of eleven children of Ludwig Siegismund Anton von Roeder and his wife, Caroline Louise Sack. She grew up on her father's estate until he fell from political favor, and the family was forced to move into a smaller house. The younger children were sent to live with an aunt in town, and the older boys enrolled in the University of Göttingen, but Rosa stayed in the country with her parents, performing household chores, caring for livestock, and selling embroidery to make extra money. This practical training stood her in good stead when she left Germany for the rigorous frontier life of Texas.

Through her brothers she met their college friend, the young lawyer Robert Justus Kleberg. A cultured man who read and spoke three modern languages, Kleberg wished to escape the structured political and social order of Prussian society, and he joined the von Roeders, who were making arrangements to move to faroff Texas. When Kleberg proposed marriage, Rosa accepted his offer with the stipulation that they accompany her family in their daring adventure. Then practical Rosa paid their passage with her dowry money.

The couple was married the morning the family sailed for America; Rosa wore a short-sleeved, low-cut party dress of white mull, a small hat with a long veil, and dancing slippers. When the family walked down the street on the way to the ship, people thought them strolling players, for although Rosa had changed her dress, she still wore her hat, veil, and slippers. So she was married "without wedding dress, wreath, ring, or love," but 'Kleberg,' as she always called him, told her she would never regret the step and she didn't.

The ship which took them from New Orleans to Texas was wrecked in the shallow waters off Galveston Island, and Kleberg, the only member of the group who could speak English, set off with his brother to find the von Roeder party who had come earlier. Luckily they met friendly Indians, who told them of the death of Rosa's brother and sister. Kleberg managed to rescue her two remaining brothers, who were starving and ill. Then he hired a boat to bring all the waiting passengers up the San Jacinto River to the village of Harrisburg. There the von Roeder women and Rosa's father waited while Robert Kleberg and the von Roeder sons built a log house on their land at Cat Spring in Austin County.

In Harrisburg Rosa had her first experience with Indians, for Kickapoos and Coushattas roamed freely in and around the little settlement. One day as she was carrying bundles into the house, she found an Indian standing in her kitchen, looking at several loaves of Rosa's freshly baked bread. In an instant trade, he quickly threw down two venison hams, picked up the bread, and yelled "Swap! Swap!" to the astonished Rosa. Soon she learned not to fear the friendly Indians, and in the spirit of "Swap! Swap!" she made clothes for them in exchange for leather moccasins.

In the fall of 1835 Rosa and Robert moved to their home in Cat Spring, below San Felipe, the capital of Austin's colony. No doubt Rosa's new home was a surprise to her, for there was only one large room with a fireplace. But there was no floor and no ceiling. Soon, however, her husband and brothers built another house for their parents with both floor and ceiling. The young Klebergs and von Roeders quickly made friends with the Austin colonists and soon found a strong feeling among the early Texas settlers to be free and independent from the restraining control of Mexico.

When war broke out Kleberg, his brother, and Rosa's brother Louis joined the Texian armies. After the fall of the Alamo on March 6, 1836, Rosa fled with her parents, her baby girl Clara, her sisters-in-law, and young brother, in the mad scramble of the Runaway Scrape. They joined thousands of Texians, old men, women, children, and slaves, who, driving their cattle ahead of them, headed toward the Sabine River in advance of the Mexican army marching toward Harrisburg. Rosa rode on horseback, carrying her child in front of her, and, ever mindful of her family's comfort, she soon learned to take the Spanish moss from the trees to fashion mattresses for them. Her mother was midwife to daughter-in-law Pauline when she gave birth to a baby boy in a corn crib along the way.

While the terrified settlers hurried pell-mell toward Louisiana, General Sam Houston raced his army toward Harrisburg, and on April 21, 1836, his small force of Texians defeated the Mexican troops at the battle of San Jacinto. After the battle Rosa and the von Roeders settled in Galveston, and there Robert, having left the victorious army, found them, the women sick from exposure to the elements, poor food, and brackish water.

Captive Mexican prisoners worked for the party, gathered oysters, and made fires for cooking. They helped Robert and Otto von Roeder clean and prepare deer the men had killed, but the survivors had very little else. They lacked even the basic staples, cornmeal, sugar, and coffee. When Pauline von Roeder died, she was buried on high ground, beside the landmark trees, and Rosa took her little son to rear.

The desolate pioneers returned home to find their houses had been burned, and their precious books that they had buried secretly had been discovered and destroyed. They learned that when the Mexican troops burned Harrisburg on their way to the San Jacinto River, all the family's belongings stored there were lost. Their corn and vegetable crops were gone, and the fences around their fields had been torn down and burned. Of all their livestock, only one lame ox and a pig were to be found.

Desperate for food, they formed a partnership with a neighbor to replace fences and to plant the all-important corn crop for food. With all the men racked by chills and fever, the work of cutting down trees, splitting rails, and rebuilding the needed enclosures went slowly. Robert rode for two days and a night from Cat Spring to Bastrop to get seed corn that a man had hidden in an underground cistern to keep it from Mexican troops.

The hardships of frontier Texas after the revolution were very real to Rosa, who wrote:

> There was no ready money in the country in 1837; at any rate, we had none of it. A cow and a calf cost ten dollars, and if you took them to a store they were accepted as if it was ten dollars cash. What was worse, we were in want of provisions. We had no coffee and I sold my fine linen tablecloth which I had brought from Germany for rice and flour. We could not afford to buy meal; we had no corn and had to substitute hard curd [cottage cheese] for bread.

While Robert traded one labor of land [177 acres] for a work horse to pull the plow, Rosa and her sisters worked making candles and lye soap, and washed their clothes in an iron pot. Hours were spent taking care of the children, bending over the hot fire in the fireplace hearth, cooking the meals, caring for the chickens, and milking the cows.

Although she believed fiercely that ''the man is the head of the house,'' Rosa's sense of individuality shone through in all of her life. Wearing her own style of garments and headdress, she planted her gardens in crooked rows and built log-cabin-style houses for her chickens — all of which disturbed her methodical husband.

Life during the republic of Texas was not all hardship and deprivation. Two years after the revolution a number of Texans gathered to celebrate the battle of San Jacinto at the old capital of San Felipe. Settlers came in wagons and on horseback, bringing their best clothes to wear to celebrate the great victory at a grand ball. That evening the courthouse was ablaze with candles as reels were called to the music of a single violin, all unusual entertainment to the amazed Germans, who were used to more restrained dancing and more refined music.

Persuaded to move west, Rosa and Robert, along with a number of their neighbors, moved to DeWitt County in 1847, settling in Meyersville. When the community built the first school building, Robert and Rosa saw that their seven children began their education. In fact, in the small community the von Roeders and the Klebergs were known as "lateiners," or intellectuals, a class apart from the uneducated German farmers and craftsmen who had immigrated to Texas at the same time.

Three of the Kleberg sons, Rudolph, Marcellus E., and Robert Justus, Jr., became lawyers and two of them served in public life. Rudolph, a newspaper editor in Cuero, was a state senator during the Eighteenth and Nineteenth Sessions of the Texas legislature, and then became a member of the United States Congress. Marcellus, a civic leader in Galveston, served in the Thirteenth Texas legislature and as a member of The University of Texas Board of Regents.

A third son, Robert Justus, attended the University of Virginia. He practiced law first in Cuero and then in Corpus Christi, where one of his clients was Richard King, founder of the King Ranch. When her husband died in 1885, Henrietta King asked Kleberg to take over the administration of the ranch, and afterwards Kleberg married their daughter Alice Gertrudis. Kleberg's direction of the ranch led to great expansion, including the drilling of artesian wells, the introduction of Hereford, Shorthorn, and Brahman cattle, and the acquisition of more land.

Alice and Robert Kleberg's son Richard served in the United States Congress, while their other son Robert became the manager of the gigantic King Ranch holdings when his father was stricken with paralysis. Robert continued the agricultural experimental work begun by his father, including the further development of Santa Gertrudis cattle, a breed suitable to the warm Texas climate and grasses, such as the KR Bluestem and Kleberg grass. Under his direction the King Ranch became known throughout the world as the prototype of South Texas ranch development and cattle raising.

Rosa von Roeder Kleberg's gift to the state of Texas was children who served their state and led as productive lives as she had done. Her strong sense of German industry combined with her devotion to the work ethic made her a successful and adaptable frontier daughter, wife, and mother. Her belief in productive work of all kinds found in the rigorous life of early Texas a challenge to her creative, intelligent energies. When she died in 1907, nineteen years after her husband, she was buried beside him. The headstone on their grave carried the von Roeder motto, the symbol of Rosa's life on the Texas frontier: "God helps those who help themselves."

REFERENCES

Biesele, Rudolph Leopold. *The History of the German Settlements in Texas 1831-1861.* Austin: n.p., 1930.

Kleberg, Robert Justus. *Papers.* Archives, Barker Texas History Center, The University of Texas at Austin.

Kleberg, Rosa von Roeder. "Some of My Early Experiences in Texas," *Texas State Historical Association Quarterly,* I, II (April, 1898; October, 1898).

Lea, Tom. *The King Ranch,* Volume II (reprint). Boston: Little, Brown and Company, 1974.

Ragsdale, Crystal Sasse. *The Golden Free Land.* Austin: Landmark Press, 1976.

INTERVIEWS

Carol Hoff and Crystal Sasse Ragsdale. Seguin, October 1976.

Rosalie Hoff Osbourne and Crystal Sasse Ragsdale. Seguin, October 1976.

Rosa von Roeder Kleberg with her three sons: Robert with his wife Alice Gertrudis King in back; Rudolph with his wife Mathilde Eckhardt at her left; Marcellus at her right; and grandson Rudolph II in the background.

Courtesy Daughters of the Republic Library, the Alamo, San Antonio

Mary Maverick and the Maverick clan

Recorder of
Texas Life

Mary Adams Maverick

When Samuel Augustus Maverick met Mary Ann Adams by chance the couple began a companionable romance that led to the founding of one of Texas's most influential pioneer families. Thirty-three-year-old Sam, a lawyer of some distinction, had left Alabama some years before to journey to Texas, arriving just at the time the Texians were revolting against Mexico. Serving as one of the guides for Ben Milam's men at the siege of Bexar, Maverick distinguished himself, and later was one of the signers of the Texas Declaration of Independence.

On a return trip to Alabama he was riding down a country road when he glimpsed "a lovely blue-eyed blonde young woman in a green muslin dress; [a] tall fair girl whose feminine air hid a will and compulsion for activity" which would meet that of her husband. Mary was eighteen at the time, and the couple's meeting kindled a devotion that would last a lifetime. They were married on August 4, 1836 after what must have been a whirlwind romance by nineteenth-century standards. Sam Maverick was a man always in a hurry, and as soon as he and Mary were wed he was eager to return to Texas and the future that it held for him. In the years ahead he realized his potential, taking an active part in the historic events surrounding the republic of Texas, surveying the lands he bought and sold, becoming active in a booming business of buying land certificates, and serving as mayor of San Antonio.

Because of the unsettled conditions in San Antonio following the siege of Bexar and the battle of the Alamo, Sam wisely chose to wait a year before bringing his bride to his adopted city. But the year was hardly a wasted one. From the beginning of her married life Mary Maverick kept a diary, a timely record of the happenings concerning her family and events. In 1881 she collected her notes in *Memoirs,* intended for her children and grandchildren. The remarkable record with her comments and notes forms a perceptive view of Texas, written during a time when few pioneer women had the time, inclination, or education to record the events and affairs of a world outside their own families and homes.

The woman Samuel Maverick married had a sense of pride and family as strong as his. The daughter of William Lewis Adams and his wife, Agatha Strother Adams, Mary Ann Adams was descended from pioneer families such as the Lewises, the Madisons, and the Strothers. Samuel Maverick's family had come to pre-Revolutionary America, settled in Boston, and then migrated as Mary's family did to frontier Alabama. From Mary's widowed mother's home the young Mavericks set off for Texas in December 1837. They left with a caravan that included Sam, Mary, their young son, Samuel Augustus or "Gus," and the baby's nurse Rachel. Following the carriage in a Kentucky wagon loaded with tents and provisions for the journey were the black servant Joe Griffin, the cook Jinny Anderson, and her four children. Mary's young brother Robert and three black men rode alongside, accompanied by three extra saddle horses and a blooded filly that Sam hoped to breed in Texas.

The journey was a long one, and Mary did not see her new home until June 1838. What a strange place it seemed in contrast to the Alabama plantation! San Antonio with its Spanish and Mexican ambience was a village of adobe and stone houses, with adobe walls enclosing the buildings and picket fences surrounding vegetable gardens and fruit trees. Water flowed through *acequias,* that crisscrossed through the center of the town, where Mexican women washed clothes on the low banks and bathed in the running streams. Other citizens bathed in curtained bathhouses at the water's edge.

Samuel Maverick had purchased property for his family on Main and Soledad streets, and the couple quickly set about adding other buildings to supplement the stone house, building a "homely pickett fence around the garden" with its sixteen fig trees and rows of pomegranates. Their land reached down to the river, where Sam built a bathhouse and wash place under a "grand, old cypress." Mary and Sam's second son, Lewis Antonio, was born in their new home in March 1839; he was the first Anglo-American child born and reared in San Antonio.

Romantic as old San Antonio seemed to Mary, there were still dangers from Indian raids and Mexican invasions. When Griffin and Wiley, part of the Maverick "people," were cultivating a labor of corn north and east of the Alamo, the Indians surprised them, cutting the traces and stealing the work animals. The two black men jumped into the river to save their lives. Mary's two brothers attempted to farm land near Mission San Francisco de Espada, but the Indians stole their mules so many times that they finally gave up their venture.

In March 1840 Mary described a "Day of Horrors," the Council House Fight that took place at the San Antonio courthouse. Sixty-five Comanche warriors with their women and children rode into town with fifteen-year-old Matilda Lockhart, an Anglo girl they had kidnapped in 1838. It was the third time the Comanches had come trading, demanding gunpowder, flannel blankets, and paint in exchange for Matilda and their other prisoners. Not trusting the Indians, the Texians announced that they would hold the Indians in the courthouse until the Anglo captives were released.

When the Indians immediately shot arrows into the crowded room, killing several people, the Texians retaliated by firing on the Comanches, who raced wildly toward the river. Three stumbled into the Maverick kitchen, and when one approached the Maverick children, Jinny raised a rock and threatened to "mash his head." Fearing for his life, he bolted for the river and safety. Matilda Lockhart was freed and spent some time in San Antonio recovering from her ordeal, cared for by the women there.

With more Anglo-Americans choosing to settle in San Antonio, the Mavericks found that life in the city was becoming a social whirl with dinners and balls given to celebrate special occasions. Mary especially remembered a ball at the Yturri home in June 1841 that General Mirabeau B. Lamar attended. She took special notice of his dress, for Texians were used to the flamboyant style of dress that General Sam Houston affected, a quality noticeably lacking in the old-fashioned dress of Lamar.

The women of San Antonio, "all young, healthy, happy, and contented," spent the warm afternoons leading "a lazy life of ease," according to Mary. During that last peaceful summer the women, children, and their nurses swam and picnicked under the trees. The bathhouse on the San Antonio River was not far from the center of business along Commerce Street, and Mary remembered those lazy summer days as "a grand, good time . . . we joked and laughed away the time, for we were free from care and happy."

No matter how peaceful the times might seem, Texians lived in constant fear. Although the Texians had defeated the Mexicans, won their independence and established a republic, there remained the continued threat of enemy troops recapturing their lost province. In March 1842 the Mexican army was once again headed for San Antonio. The citizens quickly organized to leave the city in what became known as the "Runaway of '42," and Samuel Maverick and a number of other men accompanied their families part of the way to safety. Sam, Mary, Griffin, and Wiley set out on horseback, while Granville, another of the Maverick "people," drove the wooden cart piled high with provisions and carrying the children, both black and white. Mary carried her baby girl Agatha.

The old Gonzales road northeast toward La Grange proved

dangerous as spring rains had caused the creeks to rise, and the rocky fords were flooded. The group traveled slowly, camping along the way or resting when they could in sheds and barns. As soon as his family was safely beyond the area threatened by the Mexican army, Sam sailed for New Orleans, and then proceeded to Alabama to see to his business interests.

When Sam Maverick returned the Mexicans had marched back across the Rio Grande without harming the inhabitants of San Antonio. Nevertheless, Samuel did not want to bring his family back to San Antonio until the Mexican threat had been quelled, so he bought several acres of land across the Colorado River from La Grange. He immediately made plans for what Mary hoped to be a temporary home, providing cabins for the slaves who were a permanent part of the Maverick household. Sam decided to return to San Antonio in time for the fall term of court. Overcome by sadness at her husband's imminent departure, Mary begged him so eloquently to stay that Maverick commented, "You almost persuaded me not to go!"

Mary's fears were justified, for she was not to see her husband again for almost a year. In September 1842 General Adrian Woll and his troops stormed San Antonio, capturing the town and taking prisoner fifty Americans, including Maverick. Woll headed back to Mexico with his captives, and Griffin fled to La Grange to tell Mary of her husband's plight. He begged to be allowed to follow Woll's troops and joined Captain Nicholas Dawson and a group from La Grange who marched after the Mexicans. Unfortunately, Mexican forces surrounded Dawson's handful of men near Cibolo Creek, and in the battle that followed Griffin and most of the group were massacred.

On October 6, 1842 Maverick wrote to Mary from San Fernando, forty miles southwest of the old Presidio Crossing on the Rio Grande. Having heard of Griffin's death, he wrote to comfort Mary and all of "his people," saying of the young black man who had traveled with him to Texas,

> God knows I felt his death as the hardest piece of fortune we have suffered in Texas. Poor faithful, brave

boy! I owe thee a monument and a bitter tear of
regret for thy fall. I mourn thee as a true and faithful
friend and a brother, a worthy dear brother in arms!

Sam Maverick and the other Texian prisoners were marched
deep into Mexico to the infamous Perote prison, 150 miles east
of Mexico City. There the men suffered unbelievable hardships,
hunger, and forced labor waiting for Santa Anna to release
them. Maverick's father wrote letter after letter to people in the
United States government trying to secure his son's freedom,
and on March 30, 1843 Sam was released. On the same day Mary
and Sam's second daughter was born and named Augusta for
her father.

Maverick returned to Texas an important citizen, for he had
been elected to represent Bexar County in the Eighth Congress
of the Republic, meeting in Washington-on-the-Brazos. Then
hurriedly he returned to San Antonio for the March term of the
district court. While Sam was in Mexico Mary had busied herself
with enlarging her home by building another cabin connected
to the main house by a breezeway. The river bottom, however,
proved to be an unhealthy spot, and the Maverick children were
ill much of the time. As San Antonio continued under threat of
Mexican attack, the Mavericks moved to Decrows Point across
the bay from the town of Matagorda which Mary noted "had
probably the most cultivated society in Texas" at the time.

Several wealthy families had plantations on nearby Caney
Creek and spent their summers near Matagorda, while the German empresario Prince Carl of Solms-Braunfels established the
port of Carlshafen, or "Dutch Town," as the Texans called it,
across the bay from Decrows Point. The prince spent a day and a
night with the Mavericks, and one evening he and a group of his
attendants came near shore in a little boat and serenaded them.
Ever observant, Mary found the prince courteous and polite, but
also noted that he and his entourage wore "cocked feathers in
their hats," and their tight riding trousers, "did not appear
quite fitted to frontier life."

Peace and tranquility reigned temporarily on the Gulf

coast, for in July 1845 Texas was annexed to the United States, and in early September Sam and Mary's fifth child, George Madison, was born at Decrows Point. When land became available on the peninsula Sam bought the Tilton ranch and four hundred head of cattle at three dollars a head. With a sizeable investment in country property, the Mavericks began building a home in the settlement. This time, however, Mary's sixth sense failed to warn her of danger. Sam tripped on a loose step at the new house, fell twelve feet to the ground, and was knocked senseless. He suffered a sprained shoulder, developed a high fever, and remained in bed six weeks before he was able to walk again.

Work on the house continued despite Sam's illness, and in April the Mavericks moved into their new home. From the tall, three-story house they had a "fine view of both the bay and the gulf." There was always plenty of food, for the ranch supplied the family and the "people" with chickens, turkeys, beef, eggs, butter, and a generous supply of vegetables in season. They were near enough to the port of Indianola to receive fresh fruit shipped to Texas from New Orleans.

Life on the peninsula was pleasant for the Mavericks, but hurricanes threatened and Sam was constantly on the road to San Antonio, attending to his business there as land agent and lawyer. When the aftermath of the revolution and the threat of Mexican invasion subsided, the Mavericks returned home again where Mary found a good deal of damage to their home. The picket fence had disappeared, the cement on the floors had been worn away, and a walnut mantel in the main room had been carried off. Luckily she had stored her bureau with Mrs. Soto, a neighbor, and there she found her treasured wedding dress, silver, books, and a number of keepsakes.

The Mavericks were at home, content and at peace, and on Christmas Eve 1847 their sixth child Willie was born. Mary's existence was filled with the endless, time-consuming tasks of caring for her household and children. Illness was prevalent and there were constant dangers to the children. Open fires were numerous, and one day four-year-old Agatha's clothes caught fire. The child would have been badly burned had not one of the "people" thrown a bucket of water over her. She was not seriously injured, but Mary noted in her diary that Agatha was quite sore for several weeks.

Three years later the little girl was dead, a victim of bilious fever, one of the numerous diseases that plagued the city. Agatha was her father's favorite, and Sam was away on a surveying trip to Moras Creek at the time the child became ill. When he returned to San Antonio and heard of her death, he threw himself on her grave and grieved so that Mary commented that he was "ever after a sad, changed man." In 1880 Mary wrote of her child's death, "Even now . . . after thirty-two years, I cannot dwell on that horrible bereavement. [Agatha] possessed such a glad and joyous disposition that her very presence was a flood of sunshine." Mary grieved so that she had no milk for baby Willie, and the child became ill with dysentery. Nursed back to health with pomegranate-root tea, young Willie was soon thriving on goat's milk and hoarhound tea. Sam, however, remained in such a low state of mind that friends became concerned for his mental well-being. When Colonel John Coffee Hays organized an expedition to open a trade route to Chihuahua, he persuaded Mary to convince her husband to accompany him. Traveling thirteen hundred miles over incredibly hard terrain, often without food and water, Samuel Maverick returned to his family in good health, and more cheerful and hopeful than he had been in months.

The year 1850, however, brought the chilling news that cholera had spread through New Orleans, and during the winter months measles, scarletina, smallpox, and influenza swept San Antonio. The Mavericks and several other families began preparations for taking their children to the country. Chilling winds, rain, and fog prevented their leaving, and by April twenty-one San Antonians had died. Then six-year-old Augusta became ill, died the same day that her two older brothers were stricken with cholera, and was buried beside her sister. "O world of grief!" Mary lamented. "I could not go."

The cholera epidemic lasted six weeks, and so many

members of the family became ill that Sam and Mary resolved to move from the river to a new home near Alamo Plaza, on what is now Houston Street. While their new home was being built the family lived in an old adobe house on the grounds, and early in 1850 Mary gave birth to their seventh child, named John Hays after the well-known ranger scout. This delicate infant died of cholera five months later.

Mary's sadness over the deaths of her children was partly alleviated by the excitement of the new two-story stone house completed in December. From the front porch the Mavericks could look across the plaza to the ruins of the Alamo where so many of Sam's friends had died for Texas only fourteen years before. Mary was "glad and thankful" in June 1851 when another daughter was born. She was named Mary Brown for Sam's Quaker great-grandmother.

Sam continued to spend a good deal of time away from home surveying and attending to state business, as he had been elected to the state legislature to represent Bexar and Medina counties in 1852. When Maverick County was created from Kinney County in 1856 it was named in honor of the Texas hero and statesman, Samuel Maverick.

From time to time while Sam was at the state capital Mary and the children spent time with friends and relatives. In 1855 when the Mavericks were visiting the Houstons near Seguin the alarm went out that the Indians were on the warpath. The two oldest Maverick boys joined in pursuit of the savages, and neighbors crowded into the house frenziedly fortifying the flat-roofed structure and keeping watch through the night. Although the Indians never attacked, the Texans named the fortress-like house "Sebastopol," in honor of the Russian city so important in the Crimean War.

The years before the Civil War were ones of change for the Mavericks. Mary welcomed their ninth child Albert on May 7, 1854, and in June 1856 she kissed young Lewis goodbye when he left home to attend college in Vermont, noting that his departure was as if "some dear one had died." Accidents and illnesses continued to plague the young Mavericks. George was bitten by a rattlesnake while swimming in the San Antonio River. Young Sam cut the wound and sucked out the poison, while Mary sent for Dr. Ferdinand Herff to treat the boy. Then Willie ran a nail through the heel of his foot, recovering in time to say goodbye to his older brother Sam, off to study at the University of Edinburgh in Scotland.

One of the more far-reaching events of the Maverick saga in Texas concerns Sam's adventures in the cattle business that led to his becoming a part of international cattle lore. In 1854 Sam bought the Conquista Ranch, forty-five miles below San Antonio and brought his cattle up from Matagorda, putting Jack, one of the "people," in charge of the ranching operations. From this venture Sam learned much about branded and unbranded calves and the realities of the Texas cattle business. Being somewhat lax in keeping close tab on his yearly calf crop, Sam was open to neighboring ranchers branding Maverick calves with their own marks.

Maverick was somewhat distressed to find that his herd never increased, but a rancher friend, who signed his letter "a friend of Justice," wrote Mary that the Maverick calves and yearlings wore the brand of some "highly respectable citizens" on adjoining ranches, and that Sam was in peril of soon having the unheard-of ratio of one calf to ten cows. When Maverick sold his stock he had so little idea of the number of cattle he owned that he had to rely on the honesty of the buyer. While the sale was being completed he wrote Sam that the hardest work he had ever done was rounding up the unbranded Maverick calves. The local ranchers used the term "maverick" for any unbranded calf, and in time the name came to be applied to any animal or unconventional human who failed to bear the brand of the herd.

In 1859 Mary was forty-one, and she closed the book of the "remoter past" with the death of her tenth child, Elizabeth. The next chapters of her *Memoirs* she called the "actual present," concentrating on the Civil War years and the death of her husband. Samuel Maverick had fought for Texas's entrance into the Union and felt that the union of the states was sacred. He firmly stood by his feelings that "a dissolution of the Union ought not to be harbored for a moment," and felt that the Civil War had been forced on the Southerners. What lay before them, to Maverick, was an "irrepressible conflict."

When Texas joined the Confederacy Mary and Sam's two oldest sons enlisted in the army. As George turned sixteen he enlisted in his brother Lewis's cavalry unit, and in January 1865 Willie was mustered in. After the war Mary wrote of her soldier sons, "I sent my boys to the front, and my prayers went with them, and neither they nor I can ever be ashamed of the sense of honor which led them to battle for the Lost Cause." When the fighting ceased George and Willie enrolled in college; young Sam remained in San Antonio. Lewis, who had not been well during the war, died soon after returning home.

Then the greatest blow of all struck. Although Samuel Maverick was only sixty-six in 1869, his health began to fail. He took Mary Brown to school in Virginia and seemed to benefit from the trip. Mary begged him to take a cure at one of the mineral springs, but Sam refused and continued to weaken. On September 2, 1870 he died.

Mary continued the active life of the matriarch of the Maverick clan. "Ma Maverick," as her retinue of children and grandchildren called her, remained a stalwart Episcopalian, writing in her *Memoirs* until 1881. She dedicated the reminiscences to her husband and children, noting with joy and satisfaction that, "If Mr. Maverick were to look in on us today, he would be gratified at the good will, the good health, and the good fortune which have come and remained with us during the ten years past."

When she died in 1898 the nineteenth century was drawing to a close. Mary Maverick had lived through the tumultuous years of Texas's settlement and growth. When Rena Maverick Green edited and published her grandmother's memoirs, they soon became one of the rare and poignant reminiscences of life in frontier Texas written by an Anglo-American woman. The frontispiece shows a picture of Mary surrounded by her boys, with Mary Brown sitting happily on her mother's lap. There is an enduring twinkle in the matriarch's eye, as if the daguerreotypist had just made a pleasing remark about her little group — the first generation of the famous Mavericks of Texas.

REFERENCES

Bracken, Dorothy Kendall and Maurine Whorton Redway. *Early Texas Homes.* Dallas: Southern Methodist University Press, 1956.

Brown, Alice Cook. *Early American Herb Recipes.* New York: Bonanza Books, 1966.

Brown, Dee. *The Gentle Tamers: Women of the Old West.* New York: Bantam Books, 1958.

Freytag, Walter P. (ed). *Chronicles of Fayette: The Reminiscences of Julia Lee Sinks.* La Grange, Texas: n.p., 1975.

Gaillardet, Frédéric. *Sketches of Early Texas and Louisiana.* Austin: University of Texas Press, 1966.

Green, Rena Maverick. *Memoirs of Mary A. Maverick.* San Antonio: n.p., 1921.

Green, Rena Maverick. *Samuel Maverick, Texan: 1803-1870.* San Antonio: n.p., 1952.

Weems, John Edward. *Dream of Empire: A Human History of the Republic of Texas, 1836-1846.* New York: Simon and Schuster, 1971.

Mary Adams Maverick, Matriarch of the Texas Maverick family.

"La Patrona"

Henrietta Chamberlain King

When Henrietta Maria Morse Chamberlain King died on March 31, 1925 she went to her grave escorted by nearly two hundred *vaqueros*, the men who worked the cattle on the mighty King Ranch. Dressed in their range clothes and mounted on their horses, the *vaqueros* waited solemnly until the casket of the woman they called "La Patrona" had been lowered into the ground. They rode once around the open grave, single file, hats held at their sides, then followed the lead horse back to the land and cattle that Henrietta King had helped build into the greatest ranching kingdom the United States had known.

Henrietta King left her family an estate of nearly a million acres of land, a gigantic ranching establishment even by Texas standards, and almost 95,000 head of cattle. It was a queenly heritage, unlike any that Texas had witnessed before or probably would ever know again. How different her life had been from the one she had prepared for in her native Missouri or during her school days in Mississippi. As the wife of Richard King, the Rio Grande riverboat captain who exchanged the life of a steamboat owner for that of one of the world's most famous ranchers, Henrietta experienced an adventure in empire building that few Texas women could even conceive of.

Born in Boonville, Missouri on July 21, 1832, Henrietta Chamberlain was the daughter of the Reverend Hiram Bingham Chamberlain and his wife Maria. Maria Chamberlain died when her daughter was three years old, and young Henrietta had had two other mothers by the time she was ten. Chamberlain's third marriage, however, was a lasting one, and in time produced three sons and another daughter. Sent from the family home in Somerville, Tennessee to a female institute in Holly Springs, Mississippi, when she was fourteen, Henrietta studied literature and composition, painted on velvet, and learned to play the piano — rather frivolous pursuits for a young woman destined to live out her life on a frontier ranch. Forced to spend long hours listening to lengthy discourses on the Bible, Henrietta breathed a sigh of relief when at last she could return to her family.

Soon after her return to Tennessee Hiram Chamberlain set out in search of a remote missionary field and moved his family to the Texas Rio Grande border, the southern limits of the United States. When the Chamberlains arrived at Brownsville in February 1850, the only place the pastor could find to house his family was the *Whitehall,* a steamboat moored on the river. Chamberlain set about establishing the first Presbyterian mission in South Texas, and seventeen-year-old Henrietta busied herself with teaching school, singing in the choir, and serving as a devout member of her father's flock. A self-possessed young woman with a distinct air of remoteness that remained with her throughout her life, Henrietta did not attend social gatherings at the army base nor did she dance at the Gem, the principal cafe at Brownsville, where other young couples waltzed merrily to the accompaniment of a well-tuned string orchestra.

Meeting Captain Richard King, however, was adventure enough for Henrietta. When King attempted to dock his boat and almost rammed the *Whitehall,* he let out a string of seaman's epithets. Henrietta promptly appeared on deck to deliver a stinging reprimand to the young captain. The determined young woman made a lasting impression on King, and he could not forget her luminous brown eyes. Although church-going was hardly a way of life for a steamboat captain, the handsome King soon was attending Reverend Chamberlain's services.

No two frontiersmen were more different than King and Chamberlain. The pastor had much to learn about the ways of life on the border. On several occasions he delivered uncomfortably long sermons at public hangings. He also unwisely took the side of American businessmen in a merchants' war against Brownsville's neighboring city, Matamoros, Mexico. King, on the other hand, was an old hand at frontier life. He had come ashore at Brownsville in 1847 during the Mexican War, a fullfledged boat captain. At twenty-one, he became an important figure in the business life of the border town. With his partners, Captain Mifflin Kenedy and merchant-banker Charles Stillman, he gained control of the riverboat trade and then launched into ranching with as much frontier gusto. Setting up his headquarters on Santa Gertrudis Creek north of the Brownsville border he chose a location almost depopulated, a treacherous land overrun with bandit brigades.

Henrietta and Richard's courtship followed the accepted pattern of well-chaperoned visits, and often Henrietta was seen leaning on her captain's arm as the couple explored the town. King was careful enough of the minister's daughter's sensibilities to avoid walking by the saloons where drunks often lay outside in the streets. Nevertheless, the captain's courtship of his daughter was met with a "certain cold abrasiveness" on the part of the Reverend Chamberlain, and for the first time in her life, Henrietta seriously clashed with her father.

King was as persistent in his wooing as he was in establishing his cattle ranch, and in early December 1854 the Reverend Chamberlain married the young couple. Henrietta in her peach silk wedding dress was a radiant bride, and she left for her honeymoon on King's Rancho Santa Gertrudis with high expectations. King had already built corrals with a stockade and blockhouse of mesquite logs, with a squat brass cannon set in full view. A short distance away stood the mud and stick *jacales* that housed the *vaqueros* who worked his cattle, and Henrietta's first home was a *jacal* so small she had to hang her large platters on the outside wall.

King had imported his cattle and cowboys from Mexico, and soon the *vaqueros* were calling the ranch owner "Señor Capitan" and Henrietta "La Patrona." Henrietta gave King the first permanent home he had ever known and set the tone for life at the ranch. Never a day passed that she did not read her Bible, a wedding gift from her father, who had written on the flyleaf the admonition, "Read, Believe, Obey, and Live," and the men on the ranch soon realized that the whiskey and mescal had best be kept out of sight. There was a full measure of hospitality, however, at Henrietta's table, and John Salmon "Rip" Ford wrote that Henrietta had "raised the cattle ranch from a bachelor establishment to a first-class married establishment, indicating good sense and refinement."

When King purchased his cattle in Mexico he also inadvertently acquired an entire village. With their livestock trailing across the river to Texas the Mexican villagers followed the new owner. They simply packed up their children and old people, their game chickens and dogs, their clay pots and holy objects, and came with the *vaqueros* to the King Ranch. They settled on the ranch and soon became known as *Kiñenos,* King's people.

In the mid-1850s Henrietta and Richard met Robert E. Lee, then stationed with the United States army on the border, and the young officer often rode with King over the ranchlands. King Ranch legend has it that Lee urged King to "buy land and never sell" and he pointed out a high spot at the Santa Gertrudis, telling King where to locate his ranch headquarters.

When King acquired the land controlling Santa Gertrudis Creek, he set about creating a compound. He built a commissary, a kitchen with an eating gallery, a blacksmith shop, corrals, and sleeping quarters for extra hands. For travelers and livestock buyers he built a dormitory; for himself he had a watchtower resembling a sea captain's deck. From his tower he could see his entire ranch headquarters and home with its own stone kitchen and dining room situated on the spot Lee had designated.

While King spent more and more time on horseback riding over the shimmering sea of grass far from the muddy Rio Grande, Henrietta became an integral part of ranch life. She never walked past a charming small *Kiñeno* without giving a loving pat to ward off the dreaded *mal de ojo*, or evil eye. She had absorbed many Mexican folkways, including the curative powers of garlic to alleviate wasp stings, ringworm, or the jealousy of an older child for a newborn brother or sister. King designed her HK brand and registered it in March 1859 at the Corpus Christi courthouse in the name of "Mistress Henrietta King, wife of Richard King." Soon Henrietta had her own herd of cattle mingling with those marked with King's running W, brand. By the late 1860s the *viborito* or "little snake," as the *Kiñenos* called it, was a well-known mark among Texas cow men, identifying Santa Gertrudis cattle.

During the years of growth of the King Ranch, cattle raids from Mexican bandits plagued all the ranches along the Rio Grande. Mifflin Kenedy moved his cattle further inland to join King's, and before the Civil War Henrietta moved their growing family of three children to the ranch. With the outbreak of the war "the mouth of the Rio Grande became the Confederacy's back door" and the road to the back door led directly through Richard King's ranch. As Tom Lea states, King "did not go to war, the war came to him," as hundreds of wagons loaded with Southern cotton arrived at the Santa Gertrudis. The ranch served as an official receiving station before the cotton was sent on to Brownsville and from there to England.

The war years meant many changes for the Kings. One of the happiest events was the birth of their daughter Alice at the ranch in 1862. They added "Gertrudis" to her name in honor of their home, and Alice was the only one of their five children to be born on the ranch and to live out her entire life there. In 1863 Union forces captured Brownsville, and a mounted troop set out for the ranch to capture the rebel Richard King. He escaped, but Henrietta, seven months pregnant, remained behind to see her guard murdered and her home ransacked and plundered. She quickly fled to San Patricio where her son Robert E. Lee King, named for their friend the Confederate general, was born. Then she moved her family to safety in San Antonio, while King rode off to join Captain James Richardson's company of home guards.

The cattle at the Santa Gertrudis suffered during the war years. The *Kiñenos* cared for them during the winter drought of 1863 and 1864 that ravaged many South Texas herds, but the King herds weathered the extreme cold of the historic "Big Drift" that drove cattle as far south as the Santa Gertrudis. When the war ended, King, who had been paid for his services to the Confederacy in gold, could afford to buy more land. At the same time he was able to withstand the depression of 1873 that ruined many western cowmen. Raids by Mexican bandits, however, continued, and the ranch was not secure enough for Henrietta and the children to return.

When the Kings were finally resettled on the Santa Gertrudis there were five lively youngsters plus Henrietta's three Chamberlain half-brothers who often joined in the ranch activities. Soon the girls and young Robert Lee went off to school in St. Louis, where Henrietta visited them, meeting Richard when he came to join his men at the end of the cattle drives. Overcoming Henrietta's strong Puritan scruples, Richard King showered his daughters with expensive ornaments that were remembered as all "those diamond things," to complement their elegant city clothes. He also presented Henrietta with diamond earrings, which put her conservative ideas into direct conflict with her loyalty to her husband. She wore them, but she had their brilliance dulled with a coat of enamel. With Richard King's becoming an increasingly powerful Texas cattleman, Henrietta gradually became reconciled to their growing wealth. She hardly blinked an eye when her husband sent young Richard off to college in Danville, Kentucky with his own carriage and a manservant to attend him. Years later she presented her grandson Robert Kleberg with an expensive Packard automobile on his fifteenth birthday.

Despite their wealth, tragedy struck the Kings when their young son Robert Lee died in St. Louis. While Henrietta remained there too ill to be moved, Richard returned to the ranch, resolved to sell his holdings. By the time the deal he had made fell through, however, he was ready to ride out again and resume control of his cattle and land. Henrietta returned home, and life began again for the Kings. The three older children married, and young Richard and his wife moved to an adjoining ranch to make their home near the Santa Gertrudis.

From 1881 to 1885 events occurred that changed Henrietta's life and the destiny of the King ranch. The pivotal event revolved around Richard King's losing a land case to a young attorney, Robert Justus Kleberg. Always quick to seize an opportunity, King hired the lawyer to do his legal work. Soon Kleberg was riding out to the King ranch to court Alice Gertrudis, but their marriage had to wait. Richard King suffered severe stomach pains, and when Henrietta and Alice took him to San Antonio in the early spring to consult a doctor, the diagnosis was stomach cancer in its final stages. King accepted the news with the courage he had always displayed and died in April 1885.

All of his land, property, and livestock King willed to Henrietta to be "used and disposed of precisely the same as I myself might do if I were living." Henrietta's inheritance was more or less balanced—half-a-million acres of land and half-a-million dollars in debts, and she immediately set about hiring a manager for her ranch. Her choice was a logical one: Robert Kleberg, the lawyer whom Richard King trusted and Alice loved. Within a year the young people were married in a simple ceremony at the ranch, and when they set out on their honeymoon, Henrietta accompanied them.

Henrietta's faith in Robert Kleberg was well placed. The *Kiñenos* called him "El Abogado," the lawyer, but he proved to be more than just a man to give legal advice. He had inherited a love of land from his mother Rosa, and he proved a worthy steward of the King holdings. He embarked on a program of upgrading the livestock and discovered sources of water for newly-fenced pastures. He sold some land to pay off debts on the property, but by the 1890s could return to King's policy of purchasing additional ranchland.

Even with Kleberg as manager Henrietta kept tight rein on her legacy, accepting her stewardship of the land as a Christian responsibility. In time Alice and Robert's family of three girls and two boys added gaiety to the ranch. Henrietta's stern discipline was tempered by Alice's gentleness, and brightened by Robert's vigorous good humor. Often in the evenings the entire family gathered around the piano to sing Mexican and German songs, and when grandmother Rosa Kleberg came from DeWitt County to join the family gatherings she would sing the songs she had learned as a child in Germany.

Henrietta's health gradually declined. Still she managed to walk in the garden each morning, carefully choosing the vegetables for the day's meals. Dressed in the widow's weeds she continued to wear for her husband, she strolled each evening down the old familiar path to the front gate, leaning on Alice's arm. She continued to take an active interest in the spring and fall cattle workings, setting out in her old carriage to join the roundups, protected by bonnet and gloves, and surrounded by her numerous grandchildren. No one had to explain to Henrietta King the state of her ranch, how the cattle looked, or the conditions of the pastures. She recognized the old hands and greeted new ones, making the ever-expanding family of *Kiñenos* aware of her caring presence.

As the cattle business expanded, the headquarters was enlarged so that "guests were reminded of the baronial halls of England which open to all well-behaved comers." Once a year at the annual Christmas party for the *Kiñenos* Henrietta's strict rules against dancing were relaxed, and all the ranchhands and their families sang and danced, while "La Patrona" dispensed the traditional gifts of petticoats and shirts for the adults and tarlatan stockings filled with fruit and candy for the children.

Gradually Henrietta began to spend the winters at her Victorian mansion in Corpus Christi with Alice who brought the children to school in town. She visited very little but took an active part in civic affairs, donating funds to a modern hospital for the community, the Presbyterian church, and the public schools. Sunday was a quiet day at her home, not one to be given over to frivolous enjoyments, but to be spent in quiet contemplation. Summers found the Kleberg and King clan vacationing in Colorado or Michigan to escape the Texas heat. A pair of private railroad cars transported the entourage, while Henrietta in her own private car led the group.

Under "La Patrona's" watchful surveillance Robert Kleberg expanded the Santa Gertrudis ranch holdings to almost a million acres. With Henrietta and other South Texas ranchers granting right-of-way lands, he supported the railway that ran from Corpus Christi to Brownsville, and when the first train arrived at the new settlement of Kingsville on the fourth of July 1904 Henrietta was among the group that gathered to meet it.

Kingsville, named for her beloved husband, became Henrietta's special province, her own planned community. She invested in an ice plant and milling company, a cotton gin and cotton oil mill, and the weekly newspaper. Her stern views decreed that no liquor could be sold in town, and she granted each church a town lot. Her keen interest in education led her to build the community's first public school, and she subsidized the Texas-Mexican Industrial Institute located near Kingsville for the vocational training of Mexican-American youths.

With the coming of the railroad South Texas began to boom. Cameron and Hidalgo counties were divided into three more, Jim Wells, Willacy, and Kleberg, named for Robert Justus Kleberg, Sr. King ranchlands extended into the new counties and into adjoining Nueces County as well, and Henrietta's ranchhouse became a famous gathering place for celebrities. When the splendid old homestead burned to the ground in January 1912, family members remember tiny, black-clad Henrietta fleeing her burning home with only two small bags, then turning to blow a kiss to the old house that Richard King had built for her.

Henrietta's only requirement for the new ranchhouse was that anyone could walk in with boots on, and the tile floors that were laid enhanced the new white stucco headquarters, massive in size and of hybrid design combining Mexican hacienda, Moorish palace, and the popular Mission style. Although much of the gentleness of the old wooden structure was missing, banana trees, palms, and salt cedars soon blended with the native mesquite, ebony, and willow to give the new headquarters the old feel of the South Texas cattle country.

The fortress-like design stood the Klebergs in good stead when bands of marauding Mexicans roamed the land pillaging the ranches. On one occasion the *Kiñenos* mounted guns on the roof of the house after engaging the Mexicans in a pitched battle further south. After a careful inspection of the artillery "La Patrona" calmly announced that everything was in good order and she was going to bed.

Border troubles, droughts, and debts plagued Henrietta King's last years. When Robert Kleberg became ill, Henrietta turned the management of the ranch over to her young grandson, another Robert Kleberg, who made two land sales for almost a million dollars to carry the King Ranch through the hard times in Texas.

By the 1920s Henrietta was in her eighties and the deaths of her children saddened her. Seeing so much that she loved disappearing, she deeded the Santa Gertrudis ranch headquarters and the land around it to her daughter Alice. Gradually she began to slip into the past, and died in March 1925. If the dead take a memory with them, then surely the soft beauty of the South Texas spring went with Henrietta King, who gave so much of herself to the Texas ranch she loved.

REFERENCES

Anders, Evan. "Boss Rule and Constiuent Interest: South Texas Politics During the Progressive Era." *Southwestern Historical Quarterly*, LXXXIV (January 1981).

Bell, Florence. *A History of the First Presbyterian Church.* Brownsville, Texas: n.p., c. 1943.

Brown, Dee. *The Gentle Tamers: Women of the Old West.* New York: Bantam Books, 1958.

Broyles, William Jr. "The Last Empire: The King Ranch Saga." *Texas Monthly* (October 1980): 150-193; 234-278.

Chatfield, W.H. *The Twin Cities.* Brownsville, Texas: Brownsville Historical Association, 1959.

Clarke, Mary Whatley. "Scions of the Great King Ranch." *The Cattleman, XXXVII (March 1951): 23; 66-70; 74-76.*

Domenech, The Abbé . *Missionary Adventures in Texas and Mexico.* London: Longmans, Brown, Green, Longmans and Roberts, 1858.

Doughery, E. "The Rio Grande Valley." *Magazine of History,* 35, 1867.

Fearey, Mrs. Porter. *Letter* to Crystal Sasse Ragsdale. New Braunfels, December 1980.

"Guest of Great Renown." *State Topics,* I. n.p. (December, 13, 1903): 12.

La Torre, Dolores L. *Cooking and Curing with Mexican Herbs.* Austin: Encino Press, 1977.

Lea, Tom. *The King Ranch.* (reprint). Boston: Little, Brown and Company, 1974.

Lord, Walter (ed.). *The Freemantle Diary.* New York: Capricorn Books, 1960.

Luci-Smith, Edward and Celestine Dars. *How the Rich Lived.* New York: Paddington Press Limited, 1976.

McCampbell, Coleman. *Texas Seaport.* New York: Exposition Press, 1952.

Patch, Minerva King. Papers and Collection. Corpus Christi, Texas.

Rankin, Melinda. *Texas in 1850* (reprint). Waco: Texian Press, 1966.

Report of the Permanent Committee Appointed at a Meeting of the Citizens of Brownsville, Texas, April 17, 1875. Brownsville, Texas: n.p., 1875.

Rippy, J. Fred. "Border Troubles Along the Rio Grande 1848-1860." *Southwestern Historical Quarterly,* XXIII (October 1919).

Rister, Carl Coke. *Robert E. Lee in Texas.* Norman: University of Oklahoma Press, 1946.

Robb, Thomas P., et al. *Report of the Commissioners For Inquiring Into the Depredations Committed On the Texas Frontiers.* Washington: House Inquiry Report, 39, 1872.

Sheehy, Sandy. "A Historic King Ranch Home Restored: La Puerta de Agua Dulce." *Texas Homes,* 2 (September-October, 1978): 36-40; 88.

Viele, Mrs. Brigadier General Egbert L. *Following the Drum.* Philadelphia: T. R. Peterson and Brothers, 1864.

INTERVIEWS

Minerva King Patch and E'Lane Carlisle Murray. Corpus Christi, April, May 1981.
Mrs. Parker Feary and Crystal Sasse Ragsdale (telephone). New Braunfels, December 1980.

RICHARD KING.

Captain Richard King.

Courtesy Panhandle-Plains Historical Museum, Canyon

"The Darling Of
The Plains"

 Mollie Goodnight

When Charles Goodnight first glimpsed the woman who was to become his wife, she was riding horseback accompanied by a small boy and a retinue of soldiers. The soldiers were an escort for schoolteacher Mollie, who arrived at Goodnight's mother's inn one Indian summer day in 1864 on her way with her young brother Walter to the school at Black Springs on Keechie Creek. Born on September 12, 1839 in Madison County, Tennessee, Mary Ann Dyer came to Texas with her parents, Joe Henry Dyer and Susan Lynch Miller Dyer, both descendants of prominent North Carolina and Tennessee families.

Dyer had resigned his post as attorney general of Tennessee and moved his family to Fort Belknap, Texas in 1854. The deaths of her parents left Mollie the sole provider for her five brothers. When the two eldest moved away, Mollie became a schoolteacher in order to support young Leigh, Sam, and Walter. Now in 1864 only Walter remained with her, and when the Confederate soldiers withdrew from Parker County leaving the isolated farms and ranches defenseless against marauding Indians, Mollie sought a military escort for her trip to her new school at Black Springs.

The young schoolteacher already knew who Charles Goodnight was, for his reputation as the ranger scout and Indian fighter who had discovered Cynthia Ann Parker among the

Comanches was well known in Fort Belknap. She had an excellent opportunity to discover more about this scout-turned-cattleman in the days ahead, for Mollie's lively good humor and winsomeness appealed to the often humorless Goodnight, who had had little childhood and was often driven by a "stubborness of action."

Although Goodnight had had but little opportunity for schooling, both he and Mollie shared a frontier experience and a sense of family responsibility. When he was five years old his father died, and soon afterward his mother married Hiram Daugherty. The opening of the frontier west of the Mississippi in the 1840s offered cheap land for farming, so Daugherty took his family and joined a wagon train to Texas. Ten-year-old Charles rode his horse bareback all the way to Milam County. Not long afterward Charlotte Collier Daugherty divorced her second husband, and her two Goodnight sons, Charles and Elijah, became the only means of support for their mother and three young sisters.

While Elijah took a job, Charles remained at home farming, training horses, and working at whatever odd jobs he could find. When his mother married preacher Adam Sheek in 1853, Charles Goodnight was on his own and the cattle business was his aim in life. Caring for a herd for a percentage of the calf crop was a slow way to become a cattleman, but Goodnight had a talent for handling cattle, and his honesty and unfailing judgment of character made him a respected cattleman. The only time he even took a few hours away from his work was when Mollie moved to Weatherford to teach, and he came to town to walk to school with her.

Mollie was a single woman in a frontier society and suitors for her hand were plentiful. The only way that Charles Goodnight could afford to marry her was to become an independent cattleman, and the way to independence lay in a joint venture with his friend Oliver Loving. With cattle on the Texas ranges abounding in "luxurious uselessness," Goodnight and Loving saw the advantages of trailing cattle west and north to New Mexico, Colorado, and Wyoming.

They moved their herd across the desert from the Concho to Horsehead Crossing on the Pecos River, then up to Fort Sumner, New Mexico. The trail was perilous and the herd showed losses from Indian attacks and lack of adequate water. The venture was a financial success, however, and the legendary Goodnight-Loving Trail immediately became the route for moving Texas herds north to Denver and Cheyenne. The two men moved other herds up the trail, braving Indians, weather, and dry water holes. While Loving was neither thoughtful of his personal safety nor ecstatic about working with cattle, Goodnight was a careful scout and "found his keenest joy in physical contact with cattle."

In mid-1867 the two men made their last drive together, for Loving was wounded by Indians and died at Fort Sumner. Goodnight sold their remaining cattle and fulfilled a promise to his partner to return his body to Texas so that his bones would not lie in alien soil. Then he gathered another herd, working to close out the Goodnight-Loving interests. At the end of two years when the profits were divided between the Loving family and himself, Charles Goodnight had half of the $72,000 profit to invest in his own cattle venture.

Goodnight had attained a reputation as a legendary trail driver, and now he was to create his own saga. He and Mollie had visited each other hurriedly between trail drives, while she continued to teach school and rear her brothers. Goodnight and Mollie became engaged in 1869 "after a long acquaintance." A year later they were married in Hickman, Kentucky in the parlor of her uncle's home among numerous Dyer and Hickman kin.

After the wedding the Goodnights set out for his ranch in Pueblo, Colorado accompanied by Mollie's three brothers. Charles saw that the boys were "ranch broke," but only Leigh became a successful rancher. As Mrs. Mary Ann Goodnight, Mollie was an important part of the new West her husband and other cattlemen like him were creating, and the loneliness and the dangers of the frontier did not perturb her. But when they arrived in Pueblo they found two outlaws hanging from telephone poles, victims of frontier justice, and this did bother her. Mollie insisted that they return to Texas, away from the Yankees and ruffians of Colorado, but Charles quieted her and insisted she wait a few days. He made a special effort to see that she met women of the town whom she found to be "quite as human as she."

Gradually Goodnight spent less time gathering and trailing cattle and more time on the ranch where Mollie was making a home. He increased his business holdings in Colorado and put Mollie's three brothers to work. While Leigh worked the herds for a one-fourth interest, Sam grubbed willow roots for an irrigation project and Walter counted cattle.

Goodnight became more and more a business force in southern Colorado, organizing a bank and investing in city property. He expanded his interests into mining, and laid out an irrigation project on the Arkansas River. So prosperous were his investments that when Mollie felt a need for church services in Pueblo, Goodnight, at his own expense and with the help of his business associates, built the first Southern Methodist church in the area.

Then drought ruined Goodnight's farming and ranching business, and the financial crash of 1873 wiped out his sources of credit. Bankrupt at thirty-seven, the adventurous Goodnight turned to the Texas High Plains for a new beginning. Led by a Mexican guide he found his way to the fabulous Palo Duro Canyon, rich with luxuriant grama grass, unbroken buffalo turf, and precious water supplies. Goodnight staked his claim over a hundred miles from towns in New Mexico, Kansas, and Colorado, and moved his hands and cattle to the new ranch. While Goodnight was seeking financing an indignant Mollie wrote her husband that if he would not "leave the Panhandle and come out to civilization," she would come to him.

The Irish financier John George Adair agreed to back Goodnight, and the two men and their wives started out with supply wagons to Palo Duro. Cornelia Adair, a durable sportswoman, rode a huge white horse, while Mollie journeyed in a specially equipped wagon or "ambulance." The home ranch that they came to on the JA was the first ever established on the Panhandle plains, and there Goodnight built corrals, a smokehouse, and a half-cave, half-cabin dugout for his men.

His partnership with Adair was the only way that Goodnight could find to finance the cattle and ranch he dreamed of, but the five-year agreement that was made between them was a strain on both his time and energies. In addition, Jack Adair with his aristocratic ways insisted on treating the men on the ranch as servants. Even though Adair made only rare visits to the ranch he was never popular with the hands, and some fifty years later Goodnight regretted that he had not pulled the arrogant Adair off his horse and "beaten him up." The rancher's courtly manner and masculine air was not lost on his lady boss, however, and Cornelia Adair and Goodnight got along well. That the Goodnights survived the Adairs' periodic visits to the ranch remains a credit to their good humor and forceful perseverance.

Goodnight had drifted with his cattle to a wilderness almost unknown to civilized man, but the area had been familiar for centuries to migrating buffalo herds, the Comanches who hunted them, and Mexican shepherds who drove their flocks into its protecting shelter. At the JA Mollie began her life as the first white woman on the Llano Estacado, the staked plains of Texas. Soon the cow men referred to her as the "darling of the plains," for Mollie knew and understood men and boys. She would listen and respond to their hurts and disappointments without revealing a confidence, and she had a home remedy for every ill. Among her litany of cures were "coal-oil for lice, prickly pear for wounds, salt and buffalo tallow for piles, mud for inflammation and fevers, and bufflo meat broth for a general tonic."

Her presence was constantly felt in the cow camps, carrying huge cobblers out to camp and sending cakes to the lonely men at the distant line camps. When the men rode the pastures Mollie often went along riding sidesaddle. Her husband soon devised a second horn for her left knee to make the long rides safer and more comfortable, and his design was so innovative that the Goodnight saddle was soon used both in the United States and Europe.

Sundays were special to Mollie and she held a Sunday school for everyone at the ranch. If a new recruit was unusually attentive at his first Sunday gathering Mollie did not even suspect that the oldtimers had let him know just what kind of behavior Mrs. Goodnight expected of him. She was "Aunt Mollie" to the men at the JA, and on one occasion all hands pooled their money and ordered a silver tea service from New York for her, surely a unique idea on the High Plains. Her good works and good humor did not go unnoticed by her husband, who presented her with a grandfather's clock as a tribute. An engraved plaque carries his message:

> In Honor of Mrs. Mary Dyer Goodnight, Pioneer of the Texas Panhandle. For many months, in 1876-1877, she saw few men and no women, her nearest neighbor being seventy-five miles distant, and the nearest settlement two hundred miles. She met isolation and hardship with a cheerful smile, and danger with undaunted courage. With unfailing optimism, she took life's varied gifts, and made her home a house of joy.

The homage of her husband and the respect of the men were music to Mollie's ears, for there were few luxuries or even necessities to give her joy. One writer recalled that the general merchandise stores might well have displayed a "For Men Only" sign since there was nothing in stock that a woman might buy. No frontier mercantile store sold women's hats, so women made their own bonnets, washing and ironing them when they needed it. Washing clothes in itself was an ordeal, for walls and floors of dirt were omnipresent on the High Plains, and the dirt-laden wind was a dreaded and never-ceasing presence. Boiling clothes in lye soap failed to remove the dingy hue caused by the silty waters of nearby ponds and springs, and it was not until wells were drilled and windmills pumped water from deeper stratas that a bright wash hung from the clothesline.

The desolate life did not defeat Mollie, for she pursued a routine that she found of limitless interest. One of her "domestic blessings" was a gift of three chickens that one of the hands brought her. "No one can ever know how much pleasure and company they were to me," she remembered. "They were someone I could talk to. They would run to me when I called them and followed me everywhere I went. They knew me and tried to talk to me in their language. If there had been no outside dangers the loneliness would not have been so bad."

As Mollie's home was deep in a canyon with tall walls extending a hundred miles to the east, she was seldom a victim of the "overwrought nerves" caused by the ceaseless force of the winds. Ever a student, she began a systematic study of the natural history of the Palo Duro, learning the names of the wild flowers in season and relishing insect noises and bird calls. She came to know the buffalo, the dry land turtle, and the running curlews; she beckoned the prairie dogs and scurried from bear cubs when their mother in a nearby tree pointed her sensitive nose in the air.

When the Goodnights moved to the plains the heavy boom of the buffalo rifle was only an occasional sound. Then it became a continual and ominous crack in the stillness of the prairie, and the pitiful wail of the motherless buffalo calves stirred Mollie's heart. She asked her husband and brother to bring in buffalo calves for her to raise, and the calves were put in with range cows and thrived. Soon the Goodnight buffalo herd was famous throughout the world.

Goodnight set up a separate herd of cattle for his wife and registered her PATM brand in Colorado and the Flying T in Texas. In partnership with Walter she sold her first herd and the brand with them, then invested with Sam in one thousand fine-blooded cattle. Unknowingly Sam drove the cattle across a range infected with the deadly Texas fever tick, and only a dozen or so survived.

When Mollie returned to Pueblo she purchased books and paintings for her ranch home. The Goodnights commissioned artist J. C. Cowles, a pupil of Albert Bierstadt's, to paint the old home ranch and the canyon, and a photographer to record life on the Palo Duro. Unfortunately, a fire destroyed the pictures.

By the end of the 1870s English and Scottish investors had discovered the Palo Duro, and small farmers were flooding in to buy West Texas lands. Windmills pumping from wells replaced natural watering holes, and barbed wire soon limited the open range. By the end of the financial depression in the mid-1880s railroads brought in hundreds of land-hungry squatters, and the day of the free and limitless cattle range was over.

John Adair's death in May 1885 ended the Goodnights' great adventure at the Palo Duro. Finding it difficult to manage the ranch and deal with Cornelia Adair's financial advisers, who knew nothing of the problems of a West Texas ranch, Goodnight divided the JA land and cattle and began again.

With the close of the nineteenth century the Goodnights established a ranch in northeast Armstrong County near Clarendon. As the ranch grew, Goodnight Station on the Fort Worth and Denver Railroad became Goodnight, Texas. Soon Goodnight built a Methodist church for Mollie and her neighbors to attend. A many-gabled modern ranch house followed, well suited to Mollie's taste, but Goodnight added a den with a fireplace for himself and an upstairs sleeping porch, where he could look out over the plains by day and at night gaze up at the West Texas stars.

In 1898 Mollie's long interest in education resulted in the couple's founding Goodnight College, located across the hill from their ranch. Ranch and farm boys and girls came to take junior-college courses, often paying their tuition with beef and hides, or by working the college gardens and dairy herds. "Aunt Mollie" mothered and entertained the students, but "Colonel Goodnight," always ready to help the school financially, was often rude to the students when they wanted to engage him in conversation. When West Texas State Teachers College opened in Canyon in 1910, students began attending the larger school, and today the only trace of the old Goodnight College building is a pile of brush-covered stone off U.S. 289.

In twentieth-century Texas the ways of the West were dying out, and the Goodnight ranch, with its herds of buffalo, crossbred cattalo, and fine shorthorn cattle, became a tourist attraction. The house became a museum. Often people appeared unannounced, and, as there was no hotel in the vicinity, people often stayed and ate at the ranch. While Mollie at times acted as guide for the visitors, "Colonel Goodnight" was robbed of his privacy.

By the 1920s Mollie had reached her eighties and was in failing health. In early April 1926 she died, leaving Charles Goodnight without his faithful companion. He did not long survive her. It had been half a century since Oliver Loving's death had caused him to change plans and seek his destiny as an independent cattleman. Adair had died, and now his "darling of the plains" had left him. Although he was cared for by his young second wife, Corine, until his death in 1929, his bonny Mollie with whom he pioneered always held a special place in his heart.

The Goodnights had numerous West Texas neighbors who revered them as the patriarchs of the plains. One old friend extolled them as special people who were enshrined "in the hearts of old-timers as well as later settlers." To the people of the High Plains, Charles and Mollie Goodnight stood among the "honored galaxy of heroes who contended with and finally overcame every obstacle and danger of a country given over to savagery . . . ."

REFERENCES

Adair, Cornelia, *My Diary, August 30th to November 5th, 1874* (reprint). Austin: University of Texas Press, 1965.

Brown, Dee. *The Gentle Tamers: Women of the Old West.* New York: Bantam Books, 1958.

Carmack, George. "Blazing trails." San Antonio *Express* (July 19, 1979).

Fischer, John. *From the High Plains.* New York: Harper and Row, 1978.

Haley, J. Evetts. *Charles Goodnight, Cowman & Plainsman.* Norman: University of Oklahoma Press, 1949.

Hamner, Laura V. "How Charles Goodnight Took 'Roundance'," *The Cattleman,* IX (August, 1922).

Hamner, Laura V. *The No-Gun Man of Texas, 1835-1929.* Amarillo, Texas: n. p., 1935.

Hunter, J. Marvin (comp. and ed.). *The Trail Drivers of Texas.* San Antonio: n.p., 1924.

Kerr, W. G., *Scottish Capital on the American Credit Frontier.* Austin: Texas State Historical Association, 1976.

Lewis, Willie Newberry. *Between Sun and Sod.* Clarendon, Texas: Clarendon Press, 1939.

Paxson, Frederic L. *History of the American Frontier, 1763-1893.* Boston: Houghton Mifflin Company, 1924.

Potter, Jack. "Jack Potter's Map of Cattle Trails, 1866-1895." Barker Texas History Center, The University of Texas at Austin.

Prose and Poetry of the Live-Stock Industry of the United States, Volume I. Denver: National Live Stock Historical Association, 1905.

Scarborough, Dorothy. *The Wind* (reprint). Austin: University of Texas Press, 1979.

Warner, Phoebe Kerrick. "Story of the Plains' First White Woman." *The Southwest Plainsman* (January 9, 1926).

Warner, Phoebe Kerrick. "The Wife of a Pioneer Ranchman." *The Cattleman,* VII. (March, 1921).

Charles Goodnight

The Reverend Hezekiah Williams with his wife Lizzie Johnson Williams.

Courtesy Nell Cox Shelton

A Texas Cattle Queen

Lizzie Johnson Williams

Elizabeth Johnson Williams led a legendary life, and when she died the tales concerning this pioneer cattlewoman and businesswoman only increased. The notice of her death on October 9, 1924 merited only a few lines in the Austin newspaper, but for the next several years she was the subject of local gossip,and Austinites regaled strangers with stories of this eccentric financial wizard who lived like a miser in her old age. One childhood acquaintance recalled that the legendary Lizzie had been stingy even as a young girl, saving her hair ribbons while borrowing those of her sisters. When she left no will townspeople commented, "She didn't feel she needed one. She planned to take it all with her."

Stories were numerous along Congress Avenue of Lizzie's living a bare-bones existence in a building she owned at Tenth and Congress, and oldtimers told of how she would go to the Maverick Cafe and order a bowl of vegetable soup with crackers or bread at the summertime cost of ten cents a bowl. When vegetables were no longer plentiful and the price of a bowl of soup rose, Lizzie shrewdly contracted with the cafe owner to have her soup at the year-round cost of only ten cents.

Another tale widely circulated concerned the illustrious Lizzie's raucous greeting to dignified Major George W. Littlefield, investor, cattleman, and founder of the American National Bank in Austin. When he and Lizzie met on the street, the courtly major doffed his hat to his customer, who devilishly shouted to him above the sound of horses' hooves on Congress Avenue: "Hello, you old cattle thief!" When she died, she owed his bank $5.00.

Claims on her estate were as numerous as the legends of her fabulous life, and at her death relatives combed the Brueggerhoff building, where the "Hetty Green of Texas" lived out her final years. Her real estate holdings amounted to some $200,000, but her nieces and nephews uncovered some three thousand dollars in cash tucked away in old bookcases and hidden among Lizzie's random accumulations. She secreted bonds and notes in small crevices much as a child puts away a cherished doll, and the search went on for the real treasure — Lizzie's fabled diamonds.

One relative recalls Lizzie's stealing the show at the wedding of her Shelton nephew. The marriage took place in 1916, and the eccentric Lizzie eclipsed the entire wedding party by appearing at the church in a carriage drawn by two white horses and swept into the church in a turn-of-the-century dress proudly displaying rings, tiara, and a breast pin of magnificent diamonds. No one had seen the diamonds since, but they were finally uncovered carefully wrapped in a scorched towel and tucked away in an unlocked, unmarked box.

Crammed into the rooms she occupied was the history of this fabled businesswoman's life. Yards of silks, brocades, ribbons, and laces testified to her love of ornate clothing. Quilts, quilt tops, counterpanes, and forty-five pounds of feathers for feather beds, pillows, and bolsters testified to her days as a thrifty frontier homemaker; and the riding skirts and heavy petticoats were reminiscent of her days spent working cattle. There was even a black lace shawl and a pistol, remnants perhaps of the time she spent in Cuba marketing cattle.

One trunk contained her silk, beribboned wedding dress; her brimmed wedding hat with a plume; shoes; and a frilly, feminine parasol nestled between nine yards of iridescent silk for an elegant dress never made. Of the most sentimental value to Lizzie perhaps were a handful of feathers from her pet parrot, and a bunch of dried flowers from the Reverend Hezekiah Williams's funeral wreath — a testament to her husband who had lived thirty-five years with a woman who began her career as a writer and teacher, drove cattle up the trail, and then parlayed her real estate and ranch holdings into a fortune.

Lizzie Johnson, who lived and died a lonely, private person, was born in Jefferson City, Missouri around 1843, the second of the six children of Thomas Jefferson Johnson and his wife, Catherine Hyde Johnson. Her father, a schoolteacher, brought his family to Texas, settling first at Huntsville to be near quality private schools and well-established Protestant churches. Johnson was a devout Presbyterian, and education and religion were uppermost in his consideration of a choice for a living site.

Johnson, however, wanted to run his own school and soon located at Webber's Prairie, the present Webberville, downriver from Austin. The surroundings did not please Johnson, for the school was located adjacent to the Manor Cemetery, just east of the town's notorious Hell's Half Acre and racetrack, and he soon moved to Lockhart. The open country appealed to him more, and he next located the Johnson Institute in Hays County at the edge of the wilderness, a day's ride and some seventeen miles southwest of Austin. In 1852 he built his first log-cabin school on a three-hundred-acre tract of land at the foot of Friday Mountain between the branches of Bear Creek.

One story has it that Johnson was offered the site of the present University of Texas if he would establish his school in the capital city. He refused, however, insisting that he preferred the unsettled, open spaces far from the temptations of saloons he found in town. At Johnson Institute he set about teaching higher mathematics and Latin, and although he was a hard taskmaster, he was acknowledged to be a fine teacher. Catherine Hyde Johnson, known to the students as "Aunt Katie," served as dorm mother to all boarders, supervised the housekeeping and cooking, and spent her free moments giving piano lessons to the girls. She also served as neighborhood doctor, often riding out sidesaddle to help care for one of the community's sick.

Although the school was not attached to any church, Johnson would often give Sunday Bible talks with people from the northwest part of Hays County attending. Influenced by her father's religious views, Lizzie read her Bible daily and looked on liquor as an evil influence. All of the Johnson children attended the institute, and Lizzie and her brother John had additional schooling in Washington County, Lizzie at Chappell Hill Female Institute and John at Soule University.

When the Civil War began John joined the Confederate army, while Catherine Johnson and her three daughters spent their time spinning and weaving to make clothes for the soldiers. The end of the war brought many changes, for Thomas Johnson died and his son Ben took over the management of the school. Lizzie's sisters Annie and Emma married and moved away, while Lizzie continued to teach at the institute. She taught the basic subjects plus bookkeeping and (some say) French. She gained the reputation of being a harsh, unrelenting teacher, and in one instance brought the wrath of the community down on her for her severe punishment of a German boy.

Lizzie moved from the school in 1863, teaching at Lockhart from 1865 to 1868. She also taught a year at Pleasant Hill, just south of Austin, in the two-story stone Masonic Hall, which is still standing, then three years at Parson's Seminary in Manor. She returned to the institute for one year in 1871 and then taught at the Oak Grove Academy. When her brother closed the institute in 1873 Lizzie was teaching in Austin. She had her own roll book that she took with her from school to school, marking down absences and attendances and writing down her thoughts on scraps of paper tucked among the pages. One piece with arithmetic sums on the back contains the cryptic lines: "Today is another day when spirit steals, To write just what one thinks." The lines show Lizzie's vivid imagination, which she would use to good advantage in the stories she wrote for *Frank Leslie's Illustrated Weekly*.

At Lockhart, the gathering place for cattle driven up from

the brush country of South Texas, she began to keep books for the cattlemen, picking up a trick or two, such as the practice of selling cattle by "book count," resulting in a profit for the seller. Years later she said that she preferred the company of cowmen to that of bankers, and her language, or what is remembered of it, often had the flavor of the range learned from men who never got beyond the "fly-leaf of a primer."

During her years as a teacher in Austin she continued to keep books for her cattlemen customers and began writing the anonymous fictionalized stories which Leslie's weekly magazine published. Such stories as "The Sister's Secret," "The Haunted House Among the Mountains," and "Lady Inez or The Passion Flower, an American Romance" had a wide readership among the American public, and Lizzie's income from fiction helped underwrite her first cattle investment. She parlayed $2,500 worth of stock in a Chicago cattle company in three years into a one-hundred percent profit, then sold her stock for $20,000. With this as seed money she began buying both land and cattle, and in 1871 in Travis County recorded her CY brand she bought along with a herd of cattle.

Her life took a pleasant change when she met and married the tall, charming preacher, Hezekiah G. Williams, a widower with several children. The couple married on June 8, 1879, when Lizzie was thirty-six. She must have had some serious misgivings about "Hez's" drinking habits and his lack of business sense. Her brother laughingly commented that while the Reverend Williams was preaching his Sunday sermons, his sons were out stealing the congregation's cattle. Lizzie had enough business acumen for both of them and soon came to watch over all her husband's possessions. When they married Reverend Williams signed a waiver to any rights to her property or to any property she might acquire during their lifetime together.

Lizzie kept strict account of their cattle, seeing that her stock was always kept separate from Hez's. She would almost always sell her cattle for more profit; Hez tended to gamble with his livestock, losing money on his investment. They bought a

ranch at Driftwood, and the ranch foreman was often given conflicting instructions. Lizzie told him to mark Hez's calves with
her brand, while Reverend Williams gave similar instructions
regarding Lizzie's calves. Nevertheless, when her husband could
not meet the bank payments on his cattle loans, Lizzie always
bailed him out, but being Lizzie she insisted that he pay back
his debt to her.

Hezekiah Williams had dreams of being a colonizer, and
when the Hays County courthouse in San Marcos burned to the
ground in 1908 he laid out a proposed new county seat on their
land near Driftwood. Although his Hays City was near the
geographic center of the county and Hezekiah laid off lots,
named the main streets Johnson and Williams, and built a two-
story hotel, livery stable, and church, few lots were sold and the
town he dreamed of never developed.

The couple spent a good deal of time at the ranch, but Lizzie continued her teaching, bookkeeping, and fiction writing,
working out of their home on Second Street in Austin. Lizzie
had no children and seldom showed interest in any social or
cultural life. Her entire time was consumed with her investments, and she gave up teaching to devote her time to business.
Her associates were most often the cattlemen with whom she
discussed mortgages and interest rates, calves, and range conditions. She earned their respect, and one oldtime cattleman
remembered Lizzie well, commenting: "Oh, she was smart.
Knew cattle; knew when to buy and when to sell. She always
bought good stock."

Sometime between 1879 and 1889 the adventurous Lizzie
accompanied her cattle up the Chisholm Trail, a unique experience for a woman in the days of cattle drives. Few women are
known to have gone up the trail from Texas, as cattle driving
demanded the extreme in human endurance, and it was judged
by cowmen and frontier women alike as "no place for a lady."
Lizzie and Margaret Borland of Victoria were probably the only
two Texas ranchwomen who owned the herds they followed up
the trail. Lizzie built up her own herds, while Margaret Borland
acquired her herds at her husband's death. Both accompanied

their herds in buggies during the heyday of the Texas drives. Lizzie's family surmised that she probably never had a better time in her life, basking in the attentions paid her by the cowhands, for a "calico on the trail was as scarce as sunflowers on a Christmas tree." They lavished her with gifts such as wild fruit, prairie chicken, and antelope's tongue, and Lizzie often recounted times when the hands put a rope around her and Hezekiah's bedroll to keep off rattlesnakes.

The journey was a leisurely one for a herd could stretch out for two miles or more, often covering no more than ten miles a day. Travel was often hazardous for the trail was marked by river crossings flooded from spring rains. Amanda Burks, a ranch-woman from Banquete who went up the trail in the early 1870s, recalled the fierce electrical storms that dotted the Texas nights when "lightning seemed to settle on the ground and creep along like something alive." Lizzie traveled well protected from dust and cold, swathed in petticoats, a full calico skirt, bonnet, and shawl. Armed with her tally book, she was up before the cattle each morning, counting to see if any of her precious herd was missing. She also kept a timebook, meticulously recording each hand's hours, not unlike the record she kept of her students's attendance during her schoolteaching days. When the herd reached the end of the trail, Lizzie was there, counting up her tallies and estimating her profits.

The Texas cattle business was flourishing, and Hezekiah and Lizzie spent more and more time in St. Louis, stopping at the best hotels and hobnobbing with other cattlemen and their wives. Here Lizzie could indulge her passion for clothes, purchasing at last the opulent velvets, brocades, braiding, and laces that the pictures in Frank Leslie's magazine showed her were in fashion. She bought high-buttoned shoes for daytime, slippers with spool heels for evening. For the cold St. Louis winters muffs were both warm and fashionable, and Lizzie's hats changed with the seasons, her flowered, ribboned, and plumed creations held in place by jeweled hatpins. Two of Lizzie's exquisite dresses were carefully preserved: one a bustled black sateen trimmed with black lace and jet beads; the other of gold sateen deeply ruffled at the hem and trimmed with lace. The small size of these dresses challenges the myth that Lizzie was tall and stately. Actually she was just below what is now considered average height for a woman.

On one trip to New York Lizzie giddily spent $10,000 on jewelry alone, and she wore what she bought. Choosing a pair of two-carat diamond earrings, she supplemented them with a tiara containing a center diamond of three carats surrounded by nine half-carat stones and a sunburst pin of eighty-four diamonds in a gold setting "looped back and entwined to loop again." A diamond and emerald dinner ring in an antique-gold mounting completed her purchases, but on other occasions she bought still more rings, bracelets, and necklaces, along with a serviceable "American" gold watch she wore in a pocket at her waist.

Back in Austin the practical businesswoman took precedence over the fashionable lady, although Lizzie always dressed well enough to attend church or a dinner party. Her practical everyday clothes were as no-nonsensical as her sharp business practices. Quick and observant, she confided in no one and mistrusted the bankers and lawyers she did business with. She had little to do with her relatives; one time when her brother Will wanted to purchase a certain house, he found that his sister owned it.

Investments and real estate became her life. She invested wisely, not only in the building at Tenth and Congress in downtown Austin, but in city lots on East Sixth and West Twenty-sixth streets. Her land holdings grew from acreage in Hays and Travis counties to pineywoods holdings in Trinity County and ranchlands in Culberson and Jeff Davis counties.

Not all the Williamses's time was spent in Austin, for they once journeyed to Cuba on business, spending several years out of the United States. One interesting story concerning their years there revolves around Hezekiah's being kidnapped and a large ransom being demanded for his return. Without a qualm Lizzie paid $50,000 for her beloved husband's safety, but some speculate that Hezekiah may have engineered his own kidnapping in order to have some money of his own. They arrived back in Texas even more splendid than when they had left, for Lizzie brought with her a flamboyant talking parrot. Met at the boat by a banker who showered them with flowers and reserved rooms for them in one of Galveston's more fashionable hotels, Lizzie promptly spurned him and took her business elsewhere.

When Hez's health began to fail, Lizzie took him to a number of watering places, including Hot Springs, Arkansas. When he became annoyingly ill from the effects of a lifetime of alcohol, however, she left him to his children despite the fact that she was never on friendly terms with them. Seeking sunshine and a change of climate the couple went to El Paso, and Hezekiah died there in 1914. Lizzie sorrowfully brought his body back to Austin and paid $600 for his casket, no small amount in those days. She dutifully paid his funeral expenses, and, always one to compute everything in terms of cash expended, scrawled across the bill, "I loved this old buzzard this much."

With Hezekiah gone and her relatives estranged, Lizzie began to neglect her dress, often appearing at the post office so shabby in her neglected widow's weeds that unknowing citizens offered her money for her upkeep. Then sporadically she would appear in all her finery, heavily jeweled for a special occasion. Nell Cox Shelton recalls Lizzie's attending a movie at Austin's Queen Theatre in the 1920s, dressed in an elegant black dress with a bustle, the prevailing style of some forty years before.

She moved from her home to the Brueggerhoff building, piling the accumulation of a lifetime into her tiny apartment and storing much of it in the basement. Although her supply room was piled high with firewood, she parceled it out piece by piece to her tenants and refused to burn more than one stick at a time. When churches, public and private schools, and The University of Texas appealed to her for donations, she never said "No," but kept them hopeful of her possible largesse. Her relatives felt she never cared for her family as she repeatedly refused to communicate with them.

Their bewildering kinswoman, however, continued to handle her money and see to her business well into her seventies. Her credit remained good with banks throughout Texas, and she continued to borrow money to finance her business investments. Her method of paying off her notes, however, was somewhat unorthodox. Once when she owed several thousand dollars she entered the bank, asked for her note, then drew out a large, red bandana handkerchief and proceeded to make her payment in the greenbacks she had carefully packed there.

Finally too old and ill to take care of herself, the once fabled cattle queen consented to live with her niece, Willie Greer Shelton, and her husband John. She enjoyed the comfort, the good food, and the Shelton boys, but she realized that she was not at home. At night she roamed the strange, dark house, repeating to herself, "This is the wrong street, the wrong street!" Perhaps she imagined herself wandering the streets on her way to the two-story house where she had been happy with Hez, or on her way back to the ranch, or even as a young girl going home to the institute where she began her teaching career.

When she died her "strong will and good spirit" remained a memory for many people she had known. The cowmen whom she respected and admired and the bankers with whom she bargained and bested remembered her most vividly of all. She was a singular woman in the frontier world of finance, and she reigned as queen of cattle ranching, a title Lizzie Johnson Williams earned through her own energy and wit in a time when the cattleman was king.

REFERENCES

Adams, Ramon F. *Western Words.* Norman: University of Oklahoma Press, 1945.

Brayer, Garnet M. and Herbert O. *American Cattle Trails, 1540-1900.* Bayside, New York: American Pioneer Trails Association, 1952.

Burks, Amanda. "A Woman Trail Driver." in J. Marvin Hunter: *Trail Drivers of Texas.* San Antonio: n.p., 1925.

Dobie, Dudley. *A Brief History of Hays County and San Marcos, Texas.* San Marcos: n.p., 1948.

Flanagan, Sue. *Trailing the Longhorns.* Austin: The Madrona Press, 1974.

Frank Leslie's Illustrated Weekly. New York: n.p., various issues (January 12, February 9, 1867; November 2, November 9, 1867; March 26, May 7, 1870).

Gard, Wayne. *The Chisholm Trail.* Norman: University of Oklahoma Press, 1954.

History of The Johnson Institute. (typescript). Austin-Travis County Collection, Austin Public Library, Austin, Texas.

Houston, S. D. "When A Girl Masqueraded As a Cowboy. . . ." in J. Marvin Hunter: *Trail Drivers of Texas.* San Antonio: n.p., 1925.

Lucie-Smith, Edward and Celestine Dars. *How The Rich Lived.* New York: Paddington Press, Ltd., 1976.

Marr, John C. *The History of Matagorda County, Texas.* Unpublished master's thesis. Austin: The University of Texas at Austin, 1928.

Potter, Jack. *Map Showing Cattle Trails from 1866-1895.* (manuscript). A. C. Loveless, 1935. Barker History Center, The University of Texas at Austin.

Rose, Victor M. *Settlement of Victoria, Texas.* (reprint). San Antonio: n.p., 1961.

Shelton, Emily Jones. "Lizzie E. Johnson: A Cattle Queen of Texas." *Southwestern Historical Quarterly,* L. (January 1947): 351-366.

Shelton, Mrs. John E. (Willie Idella Greer). *Statement Concerning Elizabeth E. Johnson Williams.* (typescript). Barker Texas History Center, The University of Texas at Austin.

Sniffen, John D. "Leather and Lace and a Midas Touch." *Free and Easy.* Austin: n.p., November 15-December 15, 1975.

Taylor, T. U. "An Airplane Trip over the Chisholm Trail." *Frontier Times.* 40. (August 1939).

Taylor, T. U. *The Chisholm Trail and Other Routes.* Bandera: Frontier Times, 1936.

Taylor, T. U. "Johnson Institute." *Frontier Times.* 18 (February 1941).

Williams, Elizabeth Johnson. *Probate Papers, #15915.* Travis County, County Clerk's Office.

Williams, Elizabeth Johnson. *Roll Book, 1863-1874.* Elizabeth Johnson Williams Files. Austin-Travis County Collection, Austin Public Library, Austin, Texas.

INTERVIEWS

Paul C. Ragsdale and Crystal Sasse Ragsdale. Austin, July 20, 1981.
Emmett Shelton and Crystal Sasse Ragsdale (telephone). Austin, July 6; July 13; July 18, 1981.
Nell Cox Shelton and Crystal Sasse Ragsdale. Austin, July 19, 1981.

The Johnson Institute, Hays County.

Sculptress of Statesmen

Elisabet Ney

When The University of Texas at Austin began planning for its one-hundred-year anniversary to be held in 1983, the name of Elisabet Ney was suggested as one of those who had been most interested in the founding of a state university. So ardent had been her desire for a fine arts department that this remarkable artist offered to teach sculpture classes at the new university free of charge. The first board of regents, however, did not choose to add her to the all-male faculty.

Over the years many have speculated as to why Ney failed to receive an appointment. Perhaps it was her outspoken advocacy of education for women. Or the fact that she had lived openly with Dr. Edmund Montgomery, bearing him two children, while failing to acknowledge that they were married. More than likely it was mainly a matter of her overwhelming personality.

Stories and legends abound concerning this remarkable nineteenth-century woman — many of them conflicting versions of the same incident, for Elisabet Ney delighted in stirring up controversy, telling dissimilar stories of episodes in her life depending on the circumstances at the moment.

The facts, themselves, present an interesting story, for Elisabet Ney lived an adventurous, artistic life that began in

Münster, Westphalia, on January 26, 1833. She was born to devout Catholic parents, Elisabet Wernze and her sculptor husband, Johann Adam Ney. In addition to her German heritage, there were Polish and Alsatian ancestors in her background, and Elisabet claimed to be the grandniece of Napoleon's famed Marshal Ney.

From her earliest years, Elisabet was an independent, self-confident, and imaginative person. She had no interest in her mother's role in the family and shunned all duties connected with the kitchen and housekeeping. Instead, she spent long hours in her father's sculpture studio, intrigued by the fundamentals of the sculptor's craft. As she matured she developed the strength and endurance needed to lift, pull, build, and stand for hours before a skeleton framework slathered with modeling clay.

When she was ten, she designed her own dresses, far different from the conventional modes of nineteenth-century European school girls. One costume resembled the romantic robes that Adam Ney carved on his saints and angels. At seventeen, she announced that she had learned all she could in her father's studio and that she had no intention of marrying and becoming an ordinary *hausfrau*. She planned to leave for Berlin to attend the Academy of Art to be a sculptress. She even confided to a friend her excitement and plans for meeting distinguished artists and important people in that most cosmopolitan of German cities.

Belligerent in the face of her scandalized parents' opposition, Elisabet threatened to starve herself to death. Finally her parents gave in, agreeing that she could leave home when she was nineteen. They stipulated, however, that she could certainly not go to Berlin, that center of Protestantism and whirlpool of freethinkers. Instead, she would have to be content to attend school in Munich, the capital of Catholic Bavaria.

Elisabet waited the necessary two years, studying her father's craft, following her own pattern of discipline. Her work included religious figures in clay and plaster — a madonna, a Christ risen, the martyrdom of St. Sebastian, and an apostle group. In 1852 she left for Munich, hoping to become the first fulltime woman student at the Academy of Fine Arts. While she waited for admittance, she worked at modeling with clay, drawing, studying composition, and attempting preliminary anatomical study.

Then she met the young Scotsman, Edmund Montgomery, a student at Heidelberg, just beginning studies for a medical career. Tall, handsome, intelligent, Edmund was a nonconformist with an independent income from his natural father, the Scottish jurist, Duncan McNeill. Soon after his birth Edmund's mother had taken him to live in Frankfurt, and his life and thinking were shaped by the events leading to the revolution of 1848. He turned from church authority, refusing to be confirmed, disdaining organized religion. His appreciation of the philosopher Schopenhauer had its roots in his early days of rebellion in Germany.

Soon the two independent young people were constant companions, and Elisabet gained admittance to the academy, assuring the director that she would not be a disturbing influence in the all-male classes. Wisely, she chose to concentrate on portrait sculpture, and her two years of training in Munich were profitable ones. Afterwards she decided that she must study in Berlin with Germany's greatest living sculptor, the aging Christian Daniel Rauch.

Her parents refused to finance her studies but "she loved the impossible." Edmund agreed to give her the money, and together the young couple established themselves in the Prussian city. Soon Elisabet became Rauch's best-loved pupil, working in a studio adjoining his. He secured her a scholarship to the prestigious Berlin Academy of Art, and in time Elisabet was unchallenged as the most competent and gifted woman portrait sculptor in Germany.

She adopted a personal style that became her trademark. She wore her red hair in a practical cut of clustered curls, and with her unerring sense of the dramatic, wore flowing robes reminiscent of Greek dress. Poised, slender, and queenly, her charm was firmly coupled with single-minded and ruthless ambition. Her artistic style was emotional, steeped in nineteenth-century Romanticism, heavily influenced by Rauch. She acquired a knack of visiting informally with her sitters, studying them as she worked, and incorporating into each portrait their personal qualities. Folklorist Jacob Grimm and violinist Joseph Joachim were among the notables who sat for her, and in 1858 she created a portrait of the internationally acclaimed scientist, Alexander von Humboldt.

The time she spent with Schopenhauer as she worked on his portrait endeared her to him, and until his death he continued to plead with her to return to Frankfurt. Then she visited Hanover to do a portrait of King George V. While there the court painter, Friedrich Kaulbach, painted her likeness, which shows the sculptress at twenty-six to have a remarkably attractive face, a determined mouth and chin, and intelligent eyes. She wears a flowing dress with full sleeves, and her pose is one of an intensity of feeling. A portfolio of her sketches leans against the pedestal, where the sculptured bust of George V is shown in profile.

Elisabet responded by creating a bust of Kaulbach, and rumors arose that there was more between the two artists than a professional relationship. When Queen Victoria visited Hanover she invited Elisabet to England to do her likeness in marble. It was 1863 and Edmund was in England, so Elisabet could explain in full her relationship with Kaulbach. Then she returned to Berlin and set about opening a studio.

Edmund, stricken with tuberculosis, had traveled to Madeira to recuperate. He wrote to Elisabet to join him and she rushed to his side. Edmund insisted that they be married, Elisabet acquiesed, and on November 17, 1863 the two were married in the British Consulate. Then Elisabet had second thoughts, accused Edmund of having duped her into marriage, and moved out of their house and into a villa Edmund had planned for both of them. "Formosa" became her studio, and poor Edmund was banished from the building.

Never in the couple's long life together would Elisabet admit to their marriage. She referred to Edmund as her "Best

Friend," and for the next forty-four years, Montgomery referred to his wife as "Miss Ney." Despite her public marital eccentricities, their married life was similar in domestic relationship to most other marriages of the period. At Madeira Elisabet resumed her work, creating a memorial statue of two little boys following a butterfly which she called *Sursum*, and she began work on a head of her "Best Friend."

If she was pleased with her work situation, Edmund was not. His medical practice had gradually declined, and he was chagrined that the British visitors on the island did not choose to grant the couple acceptance into their society. They left the colony after 1865, and the following two years found them at Menton on the Riviera, in the Tyrolean Alps, and in Rome. While they were in Madeira another member joned their entourage. Edmund's mother, Isabella Montgomery, enraged at Elisabet's unconventional behavior and lack of care of Edmund, sent Crescentia Simath, her personal maid, to care for her son. "Cencie" was gifted with a strong practical sense and served both as companion and housekeeper for the couple from the time they left Madeira.

An intriguing set of circumstances is rumored about the Ney-Montgomery activities during the mid-1860s. Both Elisabet and Edmund reportedly became deeply involved in spying for Prussian Prime Minister Otto von Bismarck in his efforts to unify the German states into a central government separate from Austria. It is possible that Elisabet was among the followers of the Italian revolutionary Garibaldi, reporting on his activities to Bismarck. She had easy access to his island headquarters, as she was working on a portrait bust of the hero. There was even a suggestion that the couple's house in the Alps had been rented so that secret messages could be sent between Prussia and Italy.

The year 1867 found Edmund and Elisabet again in Munich, perhaps at Bismarck's insistence. Elisabet had received a commission several years before from King Ludwig II of Bavaria to create a number of figures for the Munich Polytechnikum, and she was now anxious to complete a full-length portrait figure of him. Ludwig built a residence-studio for the artist on spacious grounds in a Munich suburb. There was a room for Edmund when he visited her. Elisabet held a salon for her fellow artists and distinguished men in public life.

As Elisabet worked on the king's statue, she also completed a figure of the chained giant *Prometheus*. Then with the figure of Ludwig cast in plaster and ready to be completed in marble, Elisabet and Edmund left Munich abruptly. With the Franco-Prussian war pending, the Montgomerys were no longer a part of Bismarck's plans, and speculation has it that the couple had to flee for their lives.

Elisabet hurriedly abandoned her studio, leaving much of her work. Bismarck tried to have the studio opened, but a court order overruled the prime minister, and Elisabet's work remained untouched and safe for over two decades, awaiting some decision from the artist herself.

With Dr. Montgomery and Cencie, Elisabet joined a group of aristocratic Germans planning to establish a Utopian colony in the United States. Seemingly unaware of the dangers to their health and the hopelessness of the area, the group chose swampy, back-country land in Thomasville, Georgia at a time when the entire South lay in tragic waste from the Civil War. In the first of an unending string of ill-fated events, the Germans became ill with malaria. In addition, their impoverished Southern neighbors were hostile to their genteel, often ludicrous, farming attempts, and even more hostile to their open sympathy for the newly-freed slaves. Ironically, the blacks also scorned the Germans' well-meaning attempts at their education, and soon the entire colony failed.

Escaping from the dismal life in the colony, the Montgomerys went to the East for Edmund to visit with fellow scientists and philosophers and then traveled to Minnesota and as far as Guatemala seeking a place to live. Edmund's financial situation had improved, and the couple could invest in both a home and studio. They headed west, passing up Louisiana where Germans had lived for a century in favor of Texas, the land that had been extolled in travel books written for migrating Germans for over forty years.

The Montgomerys, however, did not choose to live among their countrymen, but instead bought a plantation in Waller County. Elisabet fell in love with Liendo with its ancient oak trees hung with trailing Spanish moss. Although she was warned that the farm would never be a practical business investment, Elisabet was determined to have it and Edmund bought it, paying $10,000 as a down payment, with two additional payments of $4,000 and $3,500 to be paid later. Elisabet had found her place in the New World. On seeing Liendo for the first time, she is said to have proclaimed her commitment to the trees, the land, and to the startled blacks, majestically proclaiming to Edmund and Cencie, "Here will I live and here I will die."

With no more experience of American country living and cotton farming than the Utopian fiasco in Georgia, the Montgomerys set about trying to make the plantation a paying farm during the bitter, poverty-ridden economy of the Reconstruction period. Never a robust man, Edmund left the running of the farm to Elisabet and retired to his studies. He spent the rest of his life at Liendo, engaged in research and writing articles for scientific journals. In later years he became an interested, public-spirited citizen, holding office in Waller County, encouraging the establishment of a public library, and aiding in the founding of Prairie View State Normal School, now Prairie View A&M University.

His life, however, was not always easy, as he often had to abandon his studies to resolve crises caused by his wife's arrogance and haughtiness to the neighbors and townspeople. Elisabet not only held herself apart from any friendly contact with her neighbors, but often sent her long-suffering "Best Friend" to intervene in her disputes with the blacks who worked for them.

These were tragic years for Elisabet, who was deprived of her artistic outlets and thrown into a life of hard-scrabble existence on a Texas farm. Both her neighbors and the blacks of the plantation laughed at her strange clothes and at her riding horseback astride. She, in turn, scorned the Texans for their backward ways. It was difficult indeed for a woman who had conversed with Queen Victoria and Bismarck and discussed philosophy with Schopenhauer to learn to speak of farm animals and crop prices with rural Texans.

Even more difficult was the task of countering the gossip and imaginative tales the local gentry and blacks circulated about their enigmatic and exotic neighbors. When the Montgomerys' small son Arthur, whom they had named for Schopenhauer, died of diphtheria, the child's body was cremated in one of the fireplaces to keep the contagion from spreading. There was gossip about the cremation, and rumors persisted that Elisabet had made a death mask of the child and then created the little body to go with it.

A posse of men rode out to the plantation to investigate the cremation, and Dr. Montgomery, in his dry, Scot's accent, patiently explained the dangers inherent in simply burying the child. The posse accepted his explanation and left, but stories continued to circulate. Gossip and rumors were not the only troubles the Montgomerys dealt with. Liendo Plantation, mortgaged to the hilt, dragged its owners deeper and deeper into debt. None of their agricultural pursuits, not cotton, truck farming for the Houston market, nor an expensive foray into dairy and beef cattle, paid off.

Elisabet's artistic life suffered heavily. The only sculptured work she produced for almost a decade was a head of her son Lorne, which she enigmatically called "Head of a Young Violinist." Still she had met important and influential people in Texas, among them the jurist and governor Oran Milo Roberts. Roberts knew of Elisabet's training, and when he was planning the new capitol building in Austin he invited her to meet with his committee. She was asked to create statues of heroic Texans, and Elisabet was elated at the first promise of work in nine years.

She returned to Liendo, plunged into work on a self-portrait, one of Edmund, and one of the recently martyred United States president, James Garfield. Even as she was formulating designs for her statues for the capitol, plans were changed in Austin. Instead of the original, white Texas limestone, pink granite was found to be more durable. Classic figures were not considered suitable for the new stone, and Ney's work was no longer part of the finished project.

Elisabet returned to her voluntary exile, steeped in failure. Added to her sense of frustration with farming and the loss of the capitol commission was the continuing bitter relationship with her son Lorne. She had maintained complete and fatal control of the boy's rearing. She had assiduously kept him away from local young people, educated him at Liendo with foreign tutors, and dressed him in flowing Greek robes. As soon as he was old enough to assert his independence, the boy struck out on his own. Both his marriages were unacceptable to Elisabet; she would acknowledge neither his wives nor his children. Although Lorne remained at Liendo much of his life, he and his mother were never reconciled.

Thirteen years after her initial disappointment over losing the capitol commission, Ney received an offer to create the statues of Sam Houston and Stephen F. Austin for the Texas exhibit at the Chicago World's Fair planned for 1893. She would get no payment for her work, but would be supplied with working materials and a studio in the capitol basement in Austin.

She completed the plaster figure of Houston clad in the buckskin suit of a frontiersman, but there was no time to have the figure executed in marble, nor time to even complete the Austin statue in plaster. At the Texas exhibit was the statue of the dead Texas hero and the very much alive artist Elisabet Ney. The artistic power of the Houston statue and the artist's sudden emergence from an almost forgotten past plunged her into the American art world and made her an instant celebrity.

Patrons from Austin flocked to her and Elisabet determined on a studio in the capital city. Edmund secured the necessary financing, and Ney built a mock German, fortress-style building with Greek embellishments in Austin's newly-developed Hyde Park area. Now, instead of looking down rows of cotton plants, she could look down a tree-lined street to the state capitol. She called the building "Formosa" after her original studio in Madeira, and she now determined to spend the rest of her life among educated people who respected art and admired Elisabet Ney. Nevertheless, she visited Liendo with regularity.

She worked feverishly, completing commissions of Texas political leaders and prominent Austin women. Soon she had enough figures to have them completed in marble, including the figures of Houston and Austin — one pair for the Hall of Fame in Washington and the other to adorn the entrance to the rotunda of the state capitol.

At sixty-two, she made a nostalgic journey to Munich, then to Italy to see her statue *Prometheus* cut in marble and established at Linderhof Castle, joining her statue of King Ludwig. She briefly rejoined Munich's art world and spent a year in her old studio at Schwabing, working on a few new portraits and collecting all of her work to be shipped back to Texas. She left Europe to return to the home which she said "constituted the nucleus containing all in all that makes life dear to me." In Texas, her life once more revolved around "Formosa," where she often entertained under the trees, serving humble fare of tea, dry toast, and the Texas clabber she enjoyed.

In 1901 the Texas legislature finally appropriated funds to have the marbles completed of the Houston and Austin statues, and she was commissioned to honor the memory of General Albert Sidney Johnston. Her strikingly reverent work shows the recumbent figure of the fallen Confederate hero draped in a Confederate flag and lying on a battlefield bier.

Her love of adulation sustained her, and Elisabet, the artist, was uppermost in the character she presented to her admirers and acquaintances. Impractical in all financial matters, she was also quick to take offense at any slights against her talent or person. Despite her eccentricities, her circle of friends and patrons grew. Governor Elisha Pease's family was for a time numbered among her most loyal supporters, and she spent many days at the Pease mansion. She created the portrait of young Carrie Pease in both plaster and marble. Her portly figure was familiar to Austinites, as she was often seen riding about the capitol grounds clad in purple trousers with a foot-long ostrich feather waving from her turban. Or she might have been observed being helped from an overturned gig when her lively horse Pascha bolted and threw her to the ground.

In 1903 the statues of Houston and Austin were finally placed in the Texas capitol and in Washington. That same year Ney completed the statue of General Johnston, which the artist was eager to see exhibited at the St. Louis World's Fair. Elisabet had completed a statue of Lady Macbeth which she took with her to Italy to have copied in marble. Ney identified with the larger-than-life-size portrait of Lady Macbeth, perhaps unknowingly selecting the fictional portrayal of a real personality lost in time with only the myth remaining. Dr. Montgomery had finally finished his definitive work, *Philosophical Problems in the Light of Vital Organization,* printed in Boston in 1907, and he wrote of his work and of Ney's Lady Macbeth that they considered their "best bets to posterity."

In May 1907 Elisabet became seriously ill, and she died on June 29. Numbers of people gathered to pay homage to this strange woman who had brought her artistic talents and her eccentricities to Texas. Finally Elisabeth Ney made her last trip from Formosa to Liendo. She was buried near the old mansion with only Edmund, Cencie, and her son Lorne in attendance. Two blacks had dug her grave in the grove of oak trees that she and Edmund had planted some thirty years before.

Dr. Montgomery suffered a stroke soon after her death, and Cencie nursed him faithfully. During his last years he managed to complete his final work, *The Revelation of Present Experience.* When he died in 1911 he was buried next to Elisabet, who had never been out of touch with her "Best Friend" since that fateful day in Munich years before. After their deaths, Cencie burned innumerable letters, papers, and documents, so that much material dealing with the couple's relationship was lost.

The new owners of Liendo did not disturb Edmund Montgomery's study for many years, until they finally presented his books and papers to Southern Methodist University. In 1911 friends and admirers of Ney founded the Texas Fine Arts

Association and purchased Formosa. Dr. Montgomery had donated a number of Ney's sculpture pieces to The University of Texas, but the remainder of her work, tools, clothes, and house furnishings remained at Formosa, later renamed the Elisabet Ney Museum. The structure, long in need of repair, was closed in 1980 to undergo extensive renovation.

When the museum reopens, Texans will have the opportunity to explore the work of this fascinating nineteenth-century artist who made Texas her home. But perhaps the greatest monument to her American period are the statues of Houston and Austin in the capitol rotunda. Between these two heroic figures thousands of tourists pass each year; many pause to admire the work of this remarkable and eccentric woman who, in mid-career, brought her artistic talents from Germany to enoble the Texas frontier.

REFERENCES

Andreas, Christopher. " . . . and the lady who didn't exist." *Christian Science Monitor* (January 8, 1981).

Champa, Kermit S. with Kate H. Champa. *German Painting of the 19th Century.* New Haven: Yale University Press, 1970.

Delong, David G. *Historic American Buildings: Texas.* Volume I. New York: Garland Publishing, Inc., 1980.

Dielmann, Henry B. "Elisabet Ney, Sculptor." *Southwestern Historical Quarterly.* LXV. (October, 1961).

Elisabeth Ney's Sculpture Process. Austin: Austin Parks and Recreation Department, 1980.

Fortune, Jan and Jean Burton. *Elisabet Ney.* New York: Alfred Knopf, 1943.

Garwood, Ellen Clayton. *The Wild Heart.* (manuscript). Humanities Research Center, The University of Texas of Austin, 1971.

Hoffman, David. "The Elisabet Ney Studio." *Perspective* IX. (December 1980).

Keeton, Morris T. *Edmund Montgomery.* Dallas: Southern Methodist University Press, 1950.

Lindeman, Gottfried. *History of German Art.* (translated by Tessa Sayle). New York: Praeger Publishers, 1971.

Loggins, Vernon. *Two Romantics.* New York: The Odyssey Press, 1946.

Program Suggestions: The Elisabet Ney Advisory Council 1980-1981. San Antonio: The Institute of Texan Cultures (December 17, 1980).

Ramsdell, Charles William. *Reconstruction in Texas.* (reprint). Austin: The University of Texas Press, 1970.

Reiter, Joan Swallow. *The Women (The Old West).* Alexandria, Virginia: Time-Life Books, 1978.

Sagaera, Eda. *Tradition and Revolution.* New York: Basic Books, Inc., 1971.

Williamson, Roxanne Kuter. *Austin, Texas, An American Architectural History.* San Antonio: Trinity University Press, 1973.

INTERVIEWS

James D. Fisher and Crystal Sasse Ragsdale, Austin, December 1980; January 1981.

Kathleen Gee and Crystal Sasse Ragsdale, Austin, December 1980; January 1981.

The Lady
Of Bayou Bend

Ima Hogg

When Ima Hogg died in England at the age of ninety-three Houston *Post* writer Lynn Ashby wrote that the greatest gift she had left behind was an outlook on life that was "inquisitive, optimistic, peripatetic," noting that she had once written him that she had no answers to the question of life, but "only a burning desire to see something encouraging happen." Ima Hogg, whom Nellie Connally once called "the first lady of Texas," spent a lifetime seeing that encouraging things happened in the fields of music, art, historical restoration, and mental health. Her abiding passion was music, and she served as one of the original founders of the Houston symphony, spearheading the orchestra's annual drive for funds. When her brother Will named her as an administrator of his estate, "Miss Ima" used the funds, adding her own donation, to found the Hogg Foundation for Mental Health, dedicated to encouraging the mental health of the children of Texas.

"Miss Ima" was the model that others followed in the field of historical restoration. Her family home, the Varner-Hogg plantation near West Columbia, was her original restoration project, and in 1958 she donated the home and its collection of Texas antiques to Texas as a state park. Her own Southern colonial home, Bayou Bend, with its lifetime accumulation of authentic American antiques and paintings was donated to the city of Houston to serve as an annex to the Houston Museum of Fine Arts. Although she moved to a high-rise apartment after leaving Bayou Bend, touring guests were often surprised by Miss Ima's unexpected presence. At times she was glimpsed strolling about with a large bag of jelly beans, filling dish after dish so that visitors might have the feeling that they were visiting a private home.

In 1963 she purchased the historic Winedale Inn in Fayette County, planning to move it to the grounds at Bayou Bend. After researching the early German immigrant culture that the inn represented she decided to restore it in place, moving other period structures to the spot, and making it a center for the study of the cultural history of early Texas. In 1967, with flags waving and oompah bands playing, the inn was dedicated. At the presentation Nellie Connally, wife of Texas Governor John Connally, awarded Miss Ima the Texas Preservation Award in recognition of the restoration and preservation of Governor Hogg's birthplace, the Varner-Hogg plantation in Brazoria County, Bayou Bend, and the Winedale Inn. Miss Ima then presented the inn to The University of Texas, along with a handsome endowment to maintain it.

The life of service and dedication that Ima Hogg led was modeled after that of her father, James Stephen Hogg, the state of Texas's first native-born governor, and a man devoted to reform at the turn of the century. Although Houston became her adopted home, she was born in Mineola on July 10, 1882, where her father had risen from newspaper publisher to district attorney. James Stephen Hogg was joyous at the birth of his daughter, and he wrote his brother: "Our cup of joy is now complete! We have a daughter of as fine proportions and of as angelic mien as ever gracious nature favored a man with, and her name is Ima!"

Never dreaming that he was subjecting his daughter to a lifetime of cruel jokes concerning her name, he named her in honor of the heroine of the poem, "The Fate of Marvin," written by his brother, Thomas Elisha Hogg, who had recently died.

Ima's grandfather realized the folly of such a first name coupled with "Hogg," and rode into town to protest. Ima, however, had already been christened. In later life she recalled that her brother Will often returned from school with a bloody nose earned in schoolyard fights defending his sister's name.

It became a Texas joke to refer to Hogg's two daughters "Ima" and "Ura," and often even a "Wera," but Ima Hogg considered allusions to the mythical sisters as no more than a political joke that began circulating when her father campaigned for governor. Houstonians took pride in her name and often welcomed newcomers with the fact that they were members of the community when they no longer considered Miss Ima's name unusual. No doubt Ima could console herself with the beauty of her uncle's lines: "A Southern girl, whose winsome grace and kindly, gentle mien, betrayed a heart more beauteous than her face. Ah! she was fair! the Southern skies were typed in Ima's heavenly eyes."

Ima grew up in a household of men, for her mother, Sallie Stinson Hogg, died of tuberculosis when her daughter was thirteen, and Ima became the "sunshine of my household," according to her father. He wrote his sister that "My ambition is to raise my children after her [his wife's] model. If I succeed the world will be much better for it." He took his sons and daughter with him on many political trips as he campaigned for attorney general and then for governor. Visiting hospitals and penal institutions across the state he instilled in his children the need to serve others less fortunate.

Ima and her brother Will were allowed to attend their father's inauguration as governor of Texas in 1891, and in later years Ima described the grandeur of Hogg's second inaugural ball in 1893. It was a glorious occasion of gaslights, "gorgeously attired" women, and guests dancing the quadrille and the Virginia reel, with a pleasant mix of down-home square dancing. While her father was governor Ima traveled to Mexico, later recalling a ball she attended there honoring the American guests and hosted by Porfirio Diaz.

While her family lived in the governor's mansion Ima and

her brothers came into contact with many distinguished persons in the fields of the arts and politics. Throughout her life she maintained her interest in public affairs, remained a staunch Democrat, and at one time wondered aloud how "Texans of above-average intelligence could be Republicans." The Sharpstown scandal of 1971 upset her, particularly the scathing denunciation of her father by writer Harvey Katz in his book, *The Shadow of the Alamo,* that dealt with the Texas political scandal. Ima Hogg told Houston *Post* writer Lynn Ashby that when her father moved out of the governor's mansion he had so few funds that he had to borrow money to move his family's possessions.

She also told Ashby of how her father taught the family to be cautious about money. Once when she had lost her quarter allowance, she borrowed money from a servant. When her father found out about the loan he paid the money back, and subtracted a nickel from her allowance for five weeks until her debt to him was paid. Life in an Austin rented home was a good one for all the Hogg children and their menagerie of pets, which included a talking parrot. Here Ima's friends were always welcome, and on New Year's day the governor himself mixed eggs, cream, and whiskey for a festive eggnog.

Ima blossomed in the atmosphere of the governor's mansion and at Carrington Preparatory School, where she concentrated on her beloved music. Then she enrolled at The University of Texas to study English, German, and psychology. With four other young women she founded the first social sorority on the university campus, but after two years she left to study piano at the National Conservatory in New York, later continuing her studies in Germany. A photograph of Ima taken when she was a young woman shows a rather pensive face crowned by a frothy, flower-bedecked hat of the period.

Governor Hogg kept up a constant correspondence with his children at school, writing often to Ima to encourage her to write to her brothers. Will also wrote her, cautioning her to be sure to write her father each day. No doubt missing the activities of the young people Governor Hogg began to search for a permanent home for his family. His interest in land development led him to purchase acreage near West Columbia and here he found the Varner Plantation, an ideal home for them all. A permanent home to which all members of the family could return was much on his mind, and he once stated:

> Home! The center of civilization! Home! The pivot of constitutional government. Home! The ark of safety to happiness, virtue, and Christianity. Home! The haven of rest in old age, where the higher elements of better manhood can be taught rising generations by the splendid example of settled citizenship. Every man should have a home.

Soon the property became even more interesting, as the fledgling Texas oil industry began expanding near the Varner Plantation. Hogg wrote his daughter: "The oil prospects are good. It may yet turn out to be a gusher of oil." He also cautioned his children not to sell the land for some fifteen years after his death. In 1919 oil was discovered at the West Columbia field, and Hogg's children profited from his advice.

Despite her being away at school Ima and her father remained close, and Hogg wrote to his daughter how important it was that she serve as an example to her younger brothers, cautioning her that:

> With your acquaintances and large circle of friends in Texas, won by your own exemplary character and excellent behavior, you have nothing to dread in the future, provided that you do not change radically in your disposition and habits. With you or away from you I have every reason to be grateful to God for such a girl . . . .

Ima consistently maintained a close relationship with her brothers, providing them with Bayou Bend as a haven to come to, the home her father exalted.

In 1898 when Governor Hogg was invited to attend the ceremonial raising of the American flag over the new territory of Hawaii, Ima accompanied him. On the return trip Ima displayed one of her insights or "hunches," as she called them. When the group was boarding the ship to sail for California, with the baggage already on board, Ima began crying, warning her father that something dreadful was going to happen. Governor Hogg ordered the bags taken off, and the ship never reached the California shore.

In 1904 Hogg moved his law practice to Houston, staying in a suite at the Rice Hotel whenever the journey to the Varner Plantation proved impractical. When Ima returned home from studies abroad, her father was ill, and the two traveled to Colorado, hoping that the climate would improve the governor's health. The climate, however, only compounded his illness, and Ima brought her father back to Texas. She continued to care for him until his death on March 3, 1906. Then she moved from the plantation to Houston in order to teach music and piano to a group of talented students.

As early as 1902 Ima's brother Will had written his sister: "Prepare to become a comfortably rich woman. Your land at Columbia has healthy prospects of proving gusher territory . . . ." With the income from their father's estate and the profits from their oil ventures, the family founded Hogg Brothers, which included Ima, to serve as the instrument through which the family donated funds to various civic and state projects. Ever mindful of their father's advice that the greater meaning of life is service to one's fellows, each member of the family contributed to a special project. While Will founded the Texas Ex-Students Association through which University of Texas alumni could aid the school, Miss Ima began collecting funds from Houston friends to help start a symphony orchestra. She and the other donors organized the local musicians, paid them out of their pockets, and arranged for the first concert at Houston's Majestic Theater. She was often seen going from merchant to merchant soliciting advertisements for the symphony program, and she launched each season with a fund-raising party at her home.

From these humble beginnings in 1913 the Houston symphony rose to become one of the finest in the nation, and much of its success was directly related to Miss Ima's leadership. She served as president of the board for many seasons, and in 1946 she added $100,000 to the budget so that the symphony could obtain the services of Conductor Efrem Kurtz. When Kurtz's successor, Ferenc Fricsay, wired that he could not fulfill his contract for the spring season, Houston's "Empress of the Symphony," as *Time* magazine called her, hired Sir Thomas Beecham to fill the empty podium. The *grande dame* of the Houston musical scene received her own tribute in 1972, when Artur Rubinstein appeared with the symphony to celebrate Miss Ima's ninetieth birthday on December 15. She once said, "I've dreamed of enriching the lives of everybody through music," and the Houston symphony stands as a tribute to that desire.

On another occasion Ima Hogg commented, "I have done the things I have done not because I wanted to, but because I had a compulsion to do so." In 1943, against her better judgment, she allowed the members of the Houston Citizen's Educational Committee to convince her to file as a candidate for the schoolboard. She at first tried to persuade her brother Mike to run in her place, but when he refused she ran and won. As a member of the board she worked to promote art classes for black children, speaking out for more liberal policies and members of the board, and for visiting nurses in the schools. Despite the abuse she gained from more conservative members of the community, she served out her term and then decided not to run again. In 1954 she wrote a letter to the Houston *Post* at their request, citing the qualifications needed to be an effective board member. "The character and dignity of the members," she stated, "intimately affect the morale and conduct of those who seek to serve or govern," adding the attributes of an intellectually and emotionally mature personality, integrity, and understanding of the functions of the board, and a sound philosophy of education. Serving on the schoolboard was her one elective office in the field of public service.

Throughout her life nothing pleased Miss Ima more than a lavish party where she could dress up and adorn herself with jewels. Even in her nineties she appeared at balls and at the symphony gorgeously gowned in lace and chiffon, wearing on more spectacular occasions an ermine jacket. Until her later years she tinted her hair a reddish-gold and even purchased a wig to supplement her own curls. Her love of clothing, however, was surpassed by her love of antique furniture. For years her brother Will had collected the oil paintings of Frederic Remington, and with him Ima began assiduously collecting European antiques and American glass. She once recalled that she had been thrilled to sleep in Sam Houston's bed in the governor's mansion, and her fascination with antiques led her in 1920 to begin combing basements and antique shops for fine pieces of early Americana.

When her own collection and that of her brother became so extensive that they could not be adequately housed, Miss Ima commissioned Houston architect John Staub to build Bayou Bend as a home for them and their brother Mike. Then Miss Ima spent ten years arranging early American furnishings and paintings. Rare Duncan Phyfe and Chippendale furniture was complemented by paintings by American artists John Singleton Copley, Charles Willson Peale, and Edward Hicks. Miss Ima enjoyed her home, but stated that she meant to preserve the past to be enjoyed in the future, announcing on December 30, 1956 that the palatial mansion standing at the bend of Houston's Buffalo Bayou was her gift to the Houston Museum of Fine Arts to be used as a decorative arts museum. Fifteen months later the annexation was completed and tours of visitors began. Explaining that the furniture alone was worth millions, Lee Malone, director of the museum, commented that Miss Ima's gift comprised one of the three top collections in the country, rivaling that of the Metropolitan Museum's American wing and the Dupont's Winterthur Museum in Delaware.

In 1971 the American Association for State and Local History presented Ima Hogg with its Award of Merit for her contributions to art, museology, and the Houston symphony. Many Houstonians realized the high price of these awards, for Miss Ima had to resort to court action when her River Oaks neighbors protested that the noise from Bayou Bend's numerous meetings and parties disturbed the tranquility of the neighborhood. She won her case, just as she stopped an action to introduce wrestling events in the Houston Music Hall where her beloved symphony performed.

The head of a state agency once commented that "Miss Ima puts her money where her ideas are," and the restoration of the Winedale Inn proved that her energies also went into her adopted projects. She spent months researching early Texas culture, searching out pieces to complement the buildings she restored. Once when the owner of a particularly fine Texas trundle bed refused to sell the piece to Miss Ima she jubilantly announced that she had persuaded him to lease it to her. She helped to restore the German organ in the nearby community of Round Top, and then treated the citizens to a concert, playing the organ herself.

The restoration of Winedale Inn and the collection of Texas furniture occupied her time in her eighties. She traveled to other outdoor museums, consulted with restoration experts, and supervised the entire project, often ordering that her wheelchair be hauled up flights of stairs. She perused Texas almanacs to select just the right plantings, personally laying out one flowerbed in the shape of a Texas star. Her father had once commented that he wished to see Texas "a land of trees," and on Miss Ima's ninetieth birthday friends donated a sixty-acre tract of land adjacent to Winedale for an arboretum, dedicated to preserving some two hundred rare Texas trees and plants.

No greater memorial to Ima Hogg exists than her contribution to the Hogg Foundation for Mental Health at The University of Texas. She once commented, "Most of my compulsions are rooted and grounded in The University of Texas," and in 1938 she added her own contribution to the bequest of Will Hogg to fund the foundation. Constantly in touch with the activities and directors of the Hogg Foundation, Miss Ima often commented on the programs, which included sending lecturers to rural areas, working with service families, educating and training mental health professionals, publishing books and materials for the public, providing services to individual communities across the state, and contributing to research in the field of mental health.

Ima Hogg's interest in children's mental health began before child psychology was popular, and she founded the Houston Child Guidance Center, later dedicating a portion of her estate to Children's Mental Health Services of Houston and Hope Center for Youth, Inc. She was pleased in 1950 when the National Institute of Mental Health and other federal agencies contributed additional funds to the Hogg Foundation to work toward better mental health among students on campus, students from disadvantaged minorities, and the aged across the state. The University of Texas awarded her efforts on its behalf in 1962, naming her its first distinguished alumna. In addition, in 1968 she was the first recipient of the university's Santa Rita award. She was also one of the few women to have served as president of the prestigious Texas Philosophical Society.

Honors were plentiful in her later years. She was awarded an honorary doctorate of humanities by Southwestern University in Georgetown, and the Texas Heritage Foundation named her Woman of the Year. She was presented with the brotherhood award by the National Conference of Christians and Jews, and the Thomas Jefferson award of the National Society of Interior Designers. Despite her increasing age, she retained her zest for living, playing the piano for friends and relatives at her annual Christmas parties, dispensing witty comments and sage advice for all, and relishing the music of such new-age rock groups as the Beatles. She also continued to savor her famous Fishhouse punch, often dispensing it from picnic thermoses she kept handy, and she enjoyed hot dogs and chili at a birthday celebration a few evenings before her final trip to England.

Increasing age never interfered with her travels, and she journeyed to Germany to attend music festivals and made one last trip to England in 1975 to visit museums and attend concerts. Cautioned by friends about traveling abroad at her advanced age, she quipped, "When you're ninety-three, it doesn't matter where you die." A fall from a London taxi caused her to be hospitalized, and she died in London on August 19. She had printed on her Christmas cards several years before the philosophy of life that she had borrowed from her musical friend, Artur Rubinstein. Part of the quotation read: "I have adopted the technique of living from miracle to miracle." For the people of Texas, Ima Hogg made miracles happen.

REFERENCES

Ashby, Lynn. "Greatest gift." Houston *Post* (August 21, 1975): 11.

Barlow, Jim. "Ima Hogg: One of a Kind Texan." Dallas *Times-Herald* (January 10, 1971): 22.

Barlow, Jim. "Miss Ima: True Texan." San Antonio *Express-News* (January 10, 1971): 1.

Blanton, Ben. "Ima Hogg Giving Winedale Inn to Texas." Houston *Post* (April 2, 1967): 4.

Cotner, Robert C. *James Stephen Hogg*. Austin: The University of Texas Press, 1959.

"Empress of the Symphony." *Time* (February 17, 1955): 34.

"Friends Give Arboretum To Honor Miss Ima Hogg." San Angelo *Standard-Times* (August 20, 1972): 8.

Hart, Katherine. "Noted women 'lovely ladies'." Austin *American-Statesman* (September 27, 1972): 8.

Holmes, Ann. "Artur Rubinstein TV special revives memories." Houston *Chronicle* (January 26, 1977) 2-8.

Holmes, Ann. "Late Plans for Bayou Bend Museum; Miss Ima Hogg's Gift Evaluated." Houston *Chronicle* (March 30, 1958): 10.

"Ima Hogg Given Honorary Doctorate." Houston *Chronicle* (May 7, 1971): 11.

Iscoe, Louise Kosches. *Ima Hogg: First Lady of Texas*. Austin: Hogg Foundation for Mental Health, 1976.

James, D'Arcy. "The Hogg Family." *Texas Parks and Wildlife* (August 1974): 3-10.

Kennedy, Tom. "Bulk of Miss Ima's estate to foundation." Houston *Post* (August 23, 1975): 1.

"Miss Hogg Lists Standards for School Board Member." Houston *Post* (October 17, 1954): 2.

"Miss Hogg Remembers the 1893 Inaugural Differently." Houston
    Post (January 24, 1969): 7.
"Miss Ima Hogg dies at 93," Houston *Post* (August 20, 1975): 1.
"Miss Ima praised for works." Houston *Post* (August 21, 1975): 1.
Phelan, Charlotte. "Miss Ima Hogg — rare as her name." Houston
    Post (August 22, 1975): 8B.
Taylor, Lonn. "Miss Ima Hogg." *Texas Observer* (September 5,
    1975): 10-11.
"UT to mourn Miss Ima Hogg." Houston *Post* (August 22, 1975): 11.
Warren, David. *Bayou Bend*. Boston: New York Graphic Society,
    1975.

INTERVIEWS

Dr. Robert C. Cotner and Ann Fears Crawford. Austin, October
    1976.

Courtesy Austin-Travis County Collection, Austin Public Library

Vivian Brenizer and Ima Hogg circa 1900

Courtesy Library of the Daughters of the Republic of Texas
at the Alamo, San Antonio

Preserver of The
Texas Heritage

Adina De Zavala

Preservation, conservation, and historic sites may be the watchwords of many Texas groups in the 1980s; but to early twentieth-century Texans, their state's heritage, its landmarks, and its historic buildings were not as important as the expanding business development that Texas was experiencing. Particularly ignored were the rich Spanish-Mexican-Texan structures and treasures that had added so much to the history of the state during the days when Texas served as a part of Spain and Mexico.

One tiny, indefatigable, and indestructible woman, Adina De Zavala, herself a product of a strong Mexican-Texan background, spent a lifetime fighting to keep alive her state's heritage and to preserve its historic sites.

De Zavala's heritage fitted her admirably for her life's work. She was the granddaughter of Lorenzo de Zavala, that brilliant political writer and liberal leader who was an effective force in Mexico's struggle for independence from Spain. Falling from favor for opposing President Santa Anna's abrogation of the Constitution of 1824, de Zavala fled to Texas and joined the Texas battle for independence. One of the most cosmopolitan and literate men on the frontier, De Zavala used his extensive political experience as vice president of the republic of Texas.

Adina, born November 18, 1861 in her grandfather's house at Zavala Point on Buffalo Bayou in the shadow of the San Jacinto battleground, was the eldest of the six children of Lorenzo de Zavala's son Augustine and his Irish-born wife Julia Tyrell de Zavala. Precocious from childhood, Adina absorbed the stories of Texas's fight for independence from her grandmother, Emily West de Zavala. She heard of how her grandfather barely escaped the wrath of Santa Anna, and how her grandmother camped in the countryside with her three children, giving up her home for a hospital for Texan wounded and a jail for Mexican prisoners.

Adina came from a long line of courageous fighters. Her father joined the Confederate forces soon after his daughter was born, serving out the war years with the naval forces protecting the Texas coast. On his release he was so afflicted with rheumatism that he became a semi-invalid. During the Reconstruction years the entire de Zavala family felt keenly the restraints of Union occupation on their lives.

Still education was an important factor for the children, and private tutors were employed to teach them. Adina began reading at age four, and her education was continued at Galveston when her father loaded the family home onto a barge and relocated it in the coastal city. When she finished her schooling at Ursuline Academy, Adina enrolled at Sam Houston Normal Institute in Hunstville, now Sam Houston University. By 1879 she had obtained her teaching certificate and set out for Chillicothe, Missouri, to study music. Then she taught school in Terrell, Texas, for two years, before she rejoined her family, now living in San Antonio. Augustine de Zavala, in search of a higher and drier climate to ease his rheumatism, bought a ranch on the Fredericksburg road six miles north of San Antonio.

"Miss Adina," as her students called her, resumed her teaching career, her classroom reverberating with the words and deeds of famous Texans. Soon after her father's death Adina moved with her mother and two unmarried sisters to a new home on Fourth and Taylor streets in San Antonio, near the present Municipal Auditorium. Here she received letters from her brother Augustine, serving as a soldier in the Spanish-American War. And here she began to fight the battles for historic preservation that became the ruling passion of her life.

Robert Ables has written of Adina De Zavala that "her agile mind quickly perceived that the scythe of modern technology was exacting an ever-widening toll on the few remaining Spanish-Mexican-Anglo historic sites in Texas." Her first efforts began in 1889, when she and a group of civic-minded men and women founded the Texas Historical and Landmarks Association, devoted to "recording the unique history and legends of San Antonio and vicinity, and of preserving and marking historic places in the city." San Antonio proved a rich historic center, and for the first time there was a concerted effort to recognize the vast historic worth of this famous city.

Eight times a year the group met, and at each meeting De Zavala recited the group's aims: "To keep alive in the hearts of the citizens of Texas the memory of the great deeds of our heroes; the memory of the fathers and pioneers of Texas; and to inculcate a love of true liberty and righteousness." The main thrust, however, of the group's efforts became the securing of the commercial property that adjoined the Alamo, then owned by the state of Texas. The area they sought to purchase had been in the eighteenth and nineteenth centuries an open yard, ringed by high stone walls and the convent structure itself. Today these lowered walls with their recessed arches run along Alamo Plaza north toward the old central post office and then along East Houston Street.

Records and drawings reveal that these ruined walls had been rebuilt numerous times. General Cós had reinforced the walls at the time of the siege and storming of Bexar; then William Barret Travis had strengthened them in preparing for Santa Anna's attacks. The open yard had been the scene of the bloodiest fighting of Santa Anna's siege, before the defenders of the Alamo fled into the church to make their last desperate stand.

When Honoré Grenét purchased the property in 1877 he

built on the old foundations what he considered to be a historic adaptation of the original structure. The two-story, wooden building, looming high over the Alamo church, had gallery arcades and wooden towers. On the battlement top Grenét had painted the words, "The Alamo Building." Several years later the Hugo-Schmeltzer interests bought the property, and in 1889 it was condemned. Considered both inartistic and an eyesore, the property was deemed worthy of development, and Miss Adina secured a verbal option on the purchase.

In addition to the preservation of the Alamo property, the Landmarks Association also worked to retain the original Spanish names for streets in the downtown San Antonio area, and they succeeded in having public schools in the Alamo City named for Texas heroes and in requiring the display of Texas flags in schoolrooms. The association had also worked to have March 6 set aside as "Texas Heroes Days." De Zavala located the burial place of Ben Milam, who had been shot by the Mexicans as he led the Texians into San Antonio during the siege of Bexar, and a gray granite memorial marked Milam Square in his honor.

In 1892 women in Galveston and Houston established the Daughters of the Republic of Texas, and the De Zavala chapter of the statewide organization was convened in March 1893 with Miss Adina serving as the local president. Members of the original Landmarks Association who could not qualify as descendants of early Texans formed an auxiliary to the chapter.

Early in 1903 the famed sculptor Pompeo Coppini, who had portrayed many Texas heroes, alerted Miss Adina to the startling fact that plans were underway to sell the Alamo property to a hotel company. Coppini had submitted drawings for a statue of David Crockett, only to find that the sculpture was part of the proposed hotel plan. Out-of-state developers intended to purchase the property when De Zavala's option ran out.

Together Miss Adina and Coppini sought out the owners of the Menger Hotel, hoping that they might block another hotel's being built immediately adjacent to their property. Although the hotel owners were out of the city, the pair found that Clara Driscoll, a wealthy young South Texas woman with a crusading spirit to match De Zavala's, was staying at the hotel. The meeting of the two dedicated women accomplished in a few months what might not have been done for years, for Clara Driscoll had a predilection for challenging causes and a reputation for getting exactly what she wanted.

Calling on Charles Hugo to inquire about purchasing the Hugo-Schmeltzer property, the women found that the commercial value of the land had soared and that the asking price for the three acres was $75,000. They had little time to think over the offer. Driscoll toured the poorly preserved Alamo, now overwhelmed by business establishments, and offered Hugo $500 of her own money to obtain an option on the property.

Miss Adina spearheaded the efforts of the De Zavala chapter to raise $20,000 for their share of the initial down payment. Despite frenzied letter writing, personal pleas for donations, and press releases devoted to their cause, they succeeded in raising little more than $7,000 toward their share of the financial obligation.

Both De Zavala and Driscoll made numerous trips to Austin to visit with the state's lawmakers to convince them that the state should assume the financial obligation for the property. Governor S. W. T. Lanham, however, announced that he could find no "Alamo fund in the state revenue account to which the $5,000 could be charged," and the legislature adjourned without reaching an agreement on the issue. Again Clara Driscoll came to the rescue, purchasing the Alamo property herself.

It was not until 1905 that a bill to fund the Alamo purchase was passed, but both De Zavala and Driscoll held off accepting state funds until the legislature agreed that the property would be administered by the Daughters of the Republic of Texas without reservation. Negotiations continued until January 25, 1905, when the Senate passed the bill unanimously and the governor signed it the next day.

De Zavala and Coppini had long hoped for a building that would house a Texas Hall of Fame and a Museum of Historic Art, Relics, and Literature. At first Driscoll had followed De Zavala's ideas on historic restoration, commenting in the Fort Worth *Record* that a "replica of the old monastery [should] be built on the old foundations." Then in a surprising about face, Driscoll was quoted a week later as being in favor of landscaping the property, giving emphasis to the existing Alamo structure.

What began as "refined infighting" among the Daughters of the Republic of Texas soon developed into irreconcilable differences between the two groups. The convention of 1905 saw the battlelines sharply drawn between the "De Zavalans" and the "Driscollites," and soon fighting erupted in what became known as "The Second Battle of the Alamo." The ammunition included legal actions, a mass of correspondence, both secret and open, and a barrage of newspaper articles.

Court injunctions were filed on behalf of both factions; each petitioned the governor and met with members of the legislature, and each continued to claim that it was the legally anointed chapter of the Daughters of the Republic of Texas. Both groups vied for control of the Alamo property, but Clara Driscoll was in New York while Adina De Zavala remained on home ground. When the "Driscollites" sent a locksmith to change the locks on the Alamo doors, Miss Adina arrived on the scene and put him to flight. The five-foot "Angel of the Alamo" had just begun to fight.

Private discord turned into public embarrassment in April 1906, when the "Driscollites" formed a rival group, the Alamo Mission Chapter, in opposition to the De Zavala chapter. The new group, based in San Antonio, posed a threat to Miss Adina's power base. At the same time outside interests entered the fight over the Alamo. An out-of-state business group obtained an option on property just east of the Alamo for a proposed auditorium and theatre. In August De Zavala received a letter from a hotel chain stating that they had purchased the north half of the property adjoining the Alamo.

The hotel group offered to clear up Alamo Plaza of its

"common nuisance," the Hugo-Schmeltzer building, and to aid in the cost of landscaping the grounds as a park. When Miss Adina replied, describing her plan for a Hall of Fame and an art gallery on the property, a company spokesman ridiculed her plan as impractical, stating that no businessman would allow his business sense to be swayed by "misguided patriotism."

Added to the continuing disappointment concerning the Alamo project was a personal humiliation connected with Miss Adina's teaching duties. Her fight for the Alamo had interfered with her teaching, and a couple brought to the schoolboard's attention their dissatisfaction over the treatment of their daughter in De Zavala's class. Miss Adina had long been in conflict with the board, twice petitioning them for a raise in salary that would make the payment compatible with her education. She had also taken a number of leaves of absence to work on the Alamo project; and to settle matters, on January 2, 1907 she resigned from from teaching.

Although her finances were limited, she was now free to pursue with single-minded dedication her defense of the Alamo property and her devotion to Texas history. And her dedication was intense; she never allowed anyone or any cause to change the course she had decided to follow. Unlike Clara Driscoll she never married, and she never moved from San Antonio. The strong-minded pursuit of her goals, however, often led her into sharp and acrimonious conflicts with friends and supporters, members of various groups, and local and state politicians.

Controversy and discord swirled around the Alamo property, with local businessmen continuing to pressure for development of the property or a park to enhance their adjoining properties. Then, early in February 1907 the "De Zavalans" were galvanized into action with news that the convent courtyard might be leased for a vaudeville and variety show to be held next to the Alamo, and that the Hugo-Schmeltzer building would be available for leasing when the current renters moved out.

Immediately the "Angel of the Alamo" published a protest against the proposed desecration of the hallowed grounds of the Alamo. When the lease on the building expired on February

10 she personally took the place of the two spies she had sent to the property two days before. Basing her stand on the premise that "possession is nine-tenths of the law," the indefatigable Miss Adina took up a vigil inside the building, holding the fort against all comers, and swearing that she might starve to death, but she would never surrender.

When Sheriff Dan Tobin brought an injunction that stated she must leave the building, De Zavala refused to accept it or to listen to its being read. The sheriff ordered her out of the building. She declined. Two deputies were left on guard with instructions that no one else was to enter the building, but that De Zavala was free to leave at any time. Moreover, the "Angel of the Alamo" was not allowed any food or beverages. When coffee and doughnuts were brought to her, she was not permitted to have them. Permission was granted for her to drink a glass of water. When the glass proved too large to be handed through the peephole, De Zavala stooped by the door and the water was poured into her mouth.

The warfare continued, threatening to become as controversial as the original defense of the Alamo. Miss Adina's stand proved quite effective, however, and on February 11 an agreement was reached. The title to the Alamo property would pass to the state, and the grounds and buildings would be placed under its jurisdiction. When the superintendent of Public Buildings and Grounds came to inspect the property, a jubilant De Zavala gave him a grand tour. The De Zavala chapter of the Daughters of the Republic of Texas honored her with a reception, and Miss Adina, dressed in gray silk and carrying a bouquet of pink sweet peas, received the hundreds of callers who came to express their admiration for her defense of the old landmark.

Still the property remained undeveloped until the spring of 1912. Governor Oscar B. Colquitt then had the Hugo-Schmeltzer building torn down, and plans were made for the reconstruction of the old convent building and replacement of walls on the original foundations. The east wall that fronted on the convent yard was reconstructed with a series of arched doorways.

With the Alamo project finally completed Miss Adina had time to devote to her other historic projects. She made several trips to East Texas in an effort to locate the site of the first Spanish mission in Texas, San Francisco de los Tejas. She located the place with the use of sketch maps, following the historic Camino Real from San Antonio. Near Crockett, Texas a marker was placed on the suggested site of the mission.

Then she turned her energies to saving the historic Spanish Governor's Palace on San Antonio's Military Plaza. The eighteenth-century structure was the sole remaining Texas example of an aristocratic Spanish residence, and when De Zavala secured an option on the building it housed a junk shop and had been allowed to deteriorate. Miss Adina tried in vain to interest the state legislature in purchasing the property, and when these efforts failed, the city of San Antonio acquired it in 1929. The San Antonio Conservation Society restored the structure the following year.

Continuing her crusade for the preservation of San Antonio's historic structures, De Zavala led the fight to save buildings slated for destruction in the downtown section. One of these was the eighteenth-century home of Francisco Ruiz, one of the original signers of the Texas Declaration of Independence. She was among those most interested when the Witte Memorial Museum Board bought the building and moved the structure from its site near Military Plaza to the museum grounds. The elegant John Twohig house on South St. Mary's Street soon joined the Ruiz house on the museum grounds. Miss Adina's efforts to save the home and store of Jose Antonio Navarro were realized when the structure's restoration was completed after her death.

In addition to her preservation efforts De Zavala found time to serve as history editor of a newsletter, the *Interstate Index,* in 1919. This publication helped sponsor the work of the Texas History and Landmarks Association and the San Antonio Conservation Society. She authored *The Texas Year Book* and *History and Legends of the Alamo and Other Missions in and around San Antonio,* and also edited *A Collation of Kingsborough's Antiquities of Mexico,* plus writing numerous pamphlets devoted to the history of Texas.

On March 1, 1955, the eve of Texas Independence Day, the "Angel of the Alamo" died in San Antonio. She was ninety-three years old. On the way to the family burial plot in St. Mary's Cemetery, her casket draped with the Texas flag passed by the Alamo, in what might be described as a mutual salute between old friends.

REFERENCES

Ables, L. Robert. "The Second Battle for the Alamo." *Southwestern Historical Quarterly.* LXX. (January 1967).

Baker, D. W. C. *A Texas Scrapbook.* (reprint) Austin: The Steck Company, 1935.

Barnes, Charles Merritt. *Combats and Conquests of Immortal Heroes.* San Antonio: Guessaz & Ferlet Company, 1910.

Coppini, Pompeo. *Dawn to Sunset.* San Antonio: The Naylor Company, 1949.

Corner, William *San Antonio de Bexar.* (reprint). San Antonio: Graphic Arts, 1974.

De Zavala, Adina. *History of The Alamo and Other Missions in San Antonio.* San Antonio: n.p., 1917.

De Zavala, Adina. *Story of the Siege and Fall of The Alamo, A Resume.* San Antonio: n.p., 1911.

De Zavala, Adina. *The Alamo.* San Antonio: The Naylor Company, 1956.

De Zavala, Adina. *The Margil Vine.* San Antonio: n.p., 1916.

De Zavala, Lorenzo, Jr. *Letter* to H. A. McArdle, September 17, 1890. Adina De Zavala Papers, Barker Texas History Center, The University of Texas at Austin.

"Events Leading to Independence of Texas Told." San Antonio *Express* (March 2, 1919).

"Faces Starvation To Hold Alamo." San Antonio *Express* (February 11, 1908).

Fifty Years of Achievement: History of The Daughters of The Republic of Texas. Dallas: Banks Upshaw and Company, 1942.

Holley, Mary Austin. *Texas* (reprint). Austin: The Steck Company, 1935.

Houston, Andrew Jackson. *Texas Independence*. Houston: Anson Jones Press, 1938.

Howard, Pearl. "Southern Personalities: Adina De Zavala." *Holland's* magazine. Volume LIV. (1935).

"Illness Takes Life of Miss De Zavala." San Antonio *Express* (March 3, 1955).

Johnson, Lois. "Miss De Zavala Continues Shrine Fight." San Antonio *Light* (February 1948).

Looscan, Adele B. "The Work of the Daughters of the Republic of Texas in Behalf of the Alamo." *Southwestern Historical Quarterly*. VIII (July 1904).

Megarity, Margaret (Mrs. Barclay). *Letter* to Robert Ables, July 15, 1955. Daughters of the Republic of Texas Files, The Alamo Library, San Antonio, Texas.

"Miss Adina De Zavala." *Interstate Index*. Volume 13. (December 1919).

"On the Trail of Texas History." San Antonio *Express* (November 25, 1928).

Parcero, Maria de la Luz. *Lorenzo De Zavala*. Mexico, D. F.: Instituto Nacional De Antropología E Historia, 1969.

Ramsdell, Charles. *San Antonio*. Austin: University of Texas Press, 1959.

The Work of Adina De Zavala. (typescript). Adina De Zavala Files. Barker History Center, The University of Texas at Austin.

Woolford, Bess Carroll and Ellen Schulz Quillin. *The Story of the Witte Memorial Museum, 1922-1960*. San Antonio: San Antonio Museum Association, 1966.

Courtesy Austin-Travis County Collection, Austin Public Library

"Savior Of
The Alamo"

Clara Driscoll

On January 14, 1901 a young Texas woman wrote to the San Antonio *Express* that the historic shrine called the Alamo was endangered. Clara Driscoll had lived in San Antonio long enough to notice the gradual decline of the Alamo, then the property of the state of Texas. Returning from an extensive tour of Europe, Clara saw with a visitor's fresh vision the decaying and unkempt condition of the building and the grounds.

She immediately proposed that the Daughters of the Republic of Texas acquire the Alamo chapel and then embark on a project of buying the adjoining property. Her letter to the *Express* proposed that, "All the unsightly obstructions should be torn away from the Alamo chapel" and "if the matter were taken up by some patriotic Texans a sufficient amount could be raised" to get the project done.

Little did the ardent young preservationist realize that she was beginning a statewide project that would require her time and energy — not to mention her money. Her call for historic preservation at the beginning of the twentieth century was decades before its time, for the citizens of San Antonio who might have contributed generously were little interested and seemed to prefer a hotel to a historic monument. But Clara Driscoll prophesied what was indeed to become historic fact in a very few years, when she wrote that the Alamo, "weather-beaten by time, is what will endure in the memory of all who have seen or heard of the old city of San Antonio.''

Clara took matters into her own hands, and as head of the Daughters of the Republic of Texas ''Committee on Alamo and Mission Improvements,'' she wrote to Charles Hugo who held title to the property. With political canniness, she addressed her letter to him on her father's letterhead. There were few businessmen in Texas who did not know of the millionaire rancher Robert Driscoll, Sr., and few Texans who did not know that the Driscoll name had long been entwined with the history of Texas.

Clara Driscoll could boast of two grandfathers who had fought with Sam Houston at the battle of San Jacinto. Some thirty years later the two sons of her Irish grandfather, Daniel O'Driscoll, joined the Confederacy and fought against the Union forces. When they finally returned home, both Jeremiah and Robert had only their tattered uniforms and their exhausted saddle horses. They pooled their hopes and energies and soon were working cattle, taking their pay in land. As their ranch holdings grew they began to run their own cattle, and Robert dropped the ''O'' from his name altogether.

In 1870 Robert Driscoll married Julia Fox, the daughter of another prominent rancher, and their son Robert, Jr., was born the next year. It was ten years later, on April 2, 1881, that Clara was born at St. Mary's of Aransas on Copano Bay in what is now Refugio County. Before Clara was ten years old, however, a series of disastrous storms wiped out the business and port facilities that had made St. Mary's important. The brothers divided their ranch and cattle holdings, and Robert moved near Corpus Christi and established his headquarters at the Palo Alto Ranch. From there his holdings soon extended into Nueces, Duval, Jim Wells, and San Patricio counties.

Since the Driscoll ranches bordered on the King Ranch, a friendship soon developed between Driscoll and the King Ranch manager, Robert J. Kleberg. The two men and several other large landholders, including Mifflin Kenedy, pledged land for a railroad to link Corpus Christi to Brownsville and other towns in South Texas.

With the coming of the railroad in 1903 Driscoll established two townsites on the railroad line. Robstown was named for his son Robert, Jr. and Driscoll was named for his family. He had already named a railroad stop in Bee County Clara in honor of his daughter when she was only five years old. Driscoll also donated land to aid in the building of the San Antonio and Aransas Pass Railroad along the Gulf Coast to Rockport.

Like many parents in Texas at this time Robert and Julia Driscoll looked to the East for schools for their children. Robert, Jr. obtained his law degree at Princeton, and Julia chose Miss Peebles and Thompson's School in New York for Clara. Then in the early 1890s the Driscolls sent Clara to the Chateau Dieudonne, a French convent on the outskirts of Paris.

As most of her young life was spent in schools far from the Driscoll ranches, Clara developed a somewhat romantic image of ranch life in Texas. These nostalgic images later became an integral part of the fanciful stories she wrote about South Texas. Another imaginative image was fostered when Julia took her daughter on a round-the-world tour for her eighteenth-birthday present. On the last leg of the journey, however, Julia fell ill and died suddenly in London and Clara made the heartbreaking journey back to Texas alone.

What Clara brought with her to Texas was a cosmopolitan flair in clothes that, fortunately, her father's money could support, a strong sense of style which lasted throughout her life, and inherent good looks, including "indescribable brown eyes, which were almost reddish brown, amber eyes, liquid and lovely," as writer Mary Lasswell described them. Furthermore, Clara had inherited her father's firm Irish chin, and his ability to make a decision and never to apologize for it. This ability would stand her in good stead all her life, but particularly in the fight to preserve the Alamo.

The Daughters of the Republic of Texas had been negotiating with the owners of the property for some years before Clara spearheaded the fight to preserve the shrine. As early as 1892 Adina De Zavala, president and founder of San Antonio's Lorenzo de Zavala Chapter of the Daughters of the Republic, had secured an option on the property from the Hugo-Schmeltzer Company. When De Zavala and Driscoll called on Schmeltzer, they found the price for the three-acre adjoining property was $75,000. The Alamo property, in the very heart of the San Antonio business district, was prime commercial property, and the owners had set their price at fair market value.

After consulting with her father's attorneys Clara gave her own check in the amount of $500 for a thirty-day option. Then it was up to the Daughters to raise the remaining $5,500 in the next few weeks. A statewide appeal entitled "A Plea for the Alamo" went out. The Daughters asked for fifty cents from each donor and explained their intention of improving the Alamo's surroundings "in keeping with the dignity and glory of the old ruin." Nowhere was there mention of the final cost of the project.

Clara and a fellow club member traveled to Austin to request the state legislature to grant a general appropriation to help save the Alamo. While both houses of the legislature granted the request to pay the option money, Governor S. W. T. Lanham vetoed the appropriation. The legislature adjourned, and the "Save the Alamo" idea was right back in the hands of the women who had started it.

The results from the letter were disheartening—little more than a thousand dollars came in, and once again Clara gave her personal check, this time for $3,478.25. The sum of $20,000 plus interest was still to be paid the following February. Once again the Daughters launched a vigorous campaign for funds. In an effort to include every segment of the population a letter was distributed among the schoolchildren across the state. For a donation of one dollar, the Daughters promised to send each of them a photograph of the shrine and the story, "The Fall of the Alamo."

Feelings ran high about the "Save the Alamo" project. Many speculated about who should pay for the property, the state or the city of San Antonio. Others wondered if a clear title to the property could be obtained. While controversy continued Robert Driscoll watched with interest. He noted the lack of public response to the pleas for funds, and questioned his daughter as to who in Texas would be willing to guarantee the price of the property with so little hope of being repaid by the state.

Clara's answer was as positive as her father had expected. She admitted that there was only one person in the state who would guarantee the money — herself. Then Robert Driscoll promised her that there would be enough money in her account for the first payment and all others. As the Daughters of the Republic of Texas could only manage to raise the sum of $7,000, the future of the Alamo property rested squarely in the hands of Clara Driscoll. She gave the property owners her personal check for the remaining sum and signed five promissory notes. Clara Driscoll had done what no other Texan could do — she had saved the Alamo.

When Clara traveled to Austin in January 1905 to present a report on the Alamo project to the legislature, she generously gave credit to the Daughters for having raised almost $10,000, and again the legislature voted in favor of providing funds for the purchase of the property. Disagreements, however, arose over who should control the Alamo — the state or the Daughters of the Republic of Texas. Driscoll and De Zavala held out for control by the Daughters. When the state proved to have no available funds for financing the remaining debt of $65,000, once again the Driscoll money came to the rescue. Finally on August 30, 1905 the state accepted clear title and deed to the property.

The controversy over the Alamo did not cease with the purchase of the historic shrine. Soon San Antonio social and historical circles were swept into a power struggle, as the Daughters became involved in a statewide battle within their organization between the "Driscollites," members who preferred the leadership of Clara Driscoll, and the "De Zavalans," followers of Adina de Zavala. Clara, however, was no longer totally involved with the so-called second "battle of the Alamo" and began to turn her talents and energies to writing.

During the two years of the Alamo project Clara had written hundreds of pages of Texas historical material. In addition, throughout her years in Europe she had written travel pieces, and seemed to have a gift for words and phrases. That gift proved to be a prodigious one. In the next two years, she wrote two books and a musical comedy. Driscoll's novel, *The Girl of La Gloria,* was published in 1905, and a collection of short stories about Texas, *In the Shadow of the Alamo,* was published in 1906, the same year as her musical "Mexicana" was produced in New York.

What tipped the scales in favor of Clara's writing career was undoubtedly the presence in her life of a dynamic young journalist-turned-legislator from Uvalde County named Henry Hulme Sevier. When Clara came to Austin to argue for support of the Alamo project, Hal Sevier supported the project and introduced the first bill allowing the state to assume Clara's investment in the Alamo property. From that time on, the young couple's friendship flourished, and soon Sevier was Clara's escort and suitor.

As their relationship flourished, Clara's writing career also flourished. Her first book, *The Girl of La Gloria,* was based on her memory of South Texas life. Using a ranch background combined with a romantic Mexican element, she told the love story of a Mexican-American girl and an Anglo-American boy from the North. That the model for the novel's heroine was herself and the Northerner was Sevier was obvious. Driscoll followed her novel with a collection of highly romantic short stories based on historical events surrounding the Alamo. *In the Shadow of the Alamo,* published in 1906, is still good reading of the romantic sort of stories that pictured Texas as an idealized western frontier.

Not content with her success as an author, Clara was soon involved in writing a play. Hal Sevier had taken a position as financial editor for the New York *Sun,* and soon Clara also moved to New York. With two books to her credit she was ready to watch as her play, "Mexicana," went into production. Clara had used Mexico as a locale for a rather thin story of an Anglo hero and a Mexican heroine, weaving their love story into a fabric of chorus scenes and songs. After the show's opening one theatre critic questioned what had happened to Clara's knowlegeable writing about Mexico after her collaborator Robert W. Smith had rewritten her material and composer Raymond Hubbel had revamped her lyrics into the current New York vernacular.

If Robert Driscoll had no time to see that Clara's interests were protected, brother Bob did. But even his fine Princeton legal training must have been strained at drawing up contracts for the show's financing. On one side was Clara, excited at being the playwright and the "angel" of a Broadway musical; on the other, the experienced producers, Sam S. and Lee Schubert. Apparently expenditures rivaling the Alamo project were needed to finance the opulent production. Scenery and costumes were imported from Europe, and chorus girls were paid three times the going Broadway rate. The show ran from the end of January 1906 through mid-April to mixed reviews. By the time "Mexicana" closed, Clara had sensibly decided that Broadway was not for her. Besides, she was in love, and she had accepted Hal Sevier's marriage proposal.

The young couple was married in a private ceremony at St. Patrick's Cathedral on the last day of July 1906. Both Clara's father and brother attended the wedding. Then it was off to Europe for a three-month honeymoon, including champagne in Paris, the theatre in London, and sightseeing in northern Italy. All of this went on with Clara making notes on their travels, with occasional comments on her new husband's snobbishness.

When the Seviers returned to New York they began building an opulent home at Oyster Bay, Long Island. Remembering the homes she had seen in northern Italy, Clara's brick and tile Mediterranean villa had little kinship with the Texas ranchhouse where she had lived as a child, and which remained the headquarters of the Driscoll interests.

The New York years were incredibly short and unbelievably

full. For a time Clara continued to write, but the couple's social life dominated her activities. She was soon involved in the New York City Texas Club, which kept alive nostalgia for the Lone Star State. Then Robert Driscoll died, and the Seviers decided to return to Texas to make their home in Austin. The capital city was near Corpus Christi, where Robert Driscoll, Jr. had assumed control of the Driscoll family interests.

Hal Sevier established the daily Austin *American* on May 31, 1914, and Clara was soon involved in building the second of their two homes. The site they chose was a spectacular one, a lagoon on the Colorado River that Stephen F. Austin had purchased in 1832 and which had been left in its natural state since that time. The mansion Clara designed was in the Italianate style with balconies and large open terraces, and it was christened Laguna Gloria. A small copy of the rose window of Mission San José was placed near the front door, and the gardens Clara planted herself, never forgetting the large live oaks and native Texas plants, were soon the talk of Austin.

The Seviers, however, had little time to enjoy their showplace on the Colorado. The United States entered World War I in 1918, and Hal Sevier joined a group of American journalists who traveled to Chile and Argentina to counteract German propaganda. Later he became chairman of the Committee for Public Information for the United States, and attended the peace conference in Paris as special assistant to Colonel E. M. House, adviser and confidant to President Wilson.

When the Driscolls returned home in 1920 they reopened Laguna Gloria and resumed their lives as leaders of Austin society. Hal was one of the founders and the first president of the Austin Public Library Association. Clara founded the Pan-American Round Table, and worked as a member of the Austin Open Forum and the Austin Garden Club. Through the years she continued to support the Daughters of the Republic of Texas. In 1922 she was elected the first Democratic National Committeewoman from Texas, beginning a close personal and financial association with both the state and national organizations.

Robert Driscoll, Jr. died suddenly in 1929, and it was Clara's time to "ride herd," as her rancher father might have said, on the management of one of the largest estates in Texas— banking, ranches, land, gas and oil wells, a hotel chain, and numerous other investments. The Seviers moved to Corpus Christi, and Clara dutifully set up her desk in the Driscoll-owned Corpus Christi Bank and Trust Company. Hal Sevier had a desk that faced Clara's, but he was given little control of the Driscoll financial holdings. Clara found her interests and friends among business leaders and politicians. She rapidly began to understand the uses of political power and held her place among Democratic party leaders. Her salty language showed an intimate knowledge of the realities of backroom politics.

As "angel" for the Democratic party, Clara worked actively as a committeewoman through four presidential elections. She contributed $25,000 to the party coffers during the Depression years, when money was extremely scarce. In 1932 she was an active supporter of President Franklin D. Roosevelt from the time of his candidacy for president, but when Texas's John Nance Garner began gathering strong support for a presidential bid in 1939, Clara contributed both time and money on his behalf.

Roosevelt continued to hold back his announcement as to whether he would seek a third term, and Garner was listed in the national polls as the party choice. However, in a final successful coup, Roosevelt gained the nomination. Although she had spent perhaps a third of a million dollars on Garner's campaign, "Miss Clara," loyal Democrat that she was, immediately funneled money into Roosevelt's campaign.

Roosevelt appointed Hal Sevier U.S. ambassador to Chile in 1932. The press gave credit to his and Clara's friendship with Vice-President John Nance Garner. The press also cited Clara's political activities, and when Clara put her financial holdings in the hands of her boards of directors, the headlines read that for the first time in sixty years the Driscoll properties would be "run by outsiders."

At first Hal Sevier, with his range of experience in Latin

America, seemed a model diplomat. However, the glow did not last. After only a few months, there was a decided change in the embassy, and in early 1934 *Fortune* magazine reported that Clara was doing the ambassador's job, although she was not able to overcome Sevier's ineptness or unwillingness to fulfill his office. Sevier resigned his ambassadorship in 1935, amid speculation and gossip. He cited medical reasons for his resignation, and when the couple returned to Corpus Christi they took up residence in separate hotels. Clara initiated divorce proceedings, which surprised Hal Sevier, and for a time there seemed to be a possibility of her withdrawing the suit. There was, however, a complete breakdown in communication between the couple, and in July 1937 Clara was granted an uncontested divorce and resumed her maiden name.

Sevier petitioned the court to have the divorce set aside, asking for his share of some five million dollars in Driscoll properties. The case never came to court; the lawyers reached an agreement satisfactory to both parties. Sevier returned to Tennessee, and within two years of the divorce, at the age of sixty-two, he died. In Austin he was remembered as an outgoing, intelligent, well-educated, civic-minded man, but his reference file at The University of Texas's Barker History Center contains little more than a selection of obituary clippings.

Clara, meanwhile, remained a financial and political force in Texas. She built a hotel in Corpus Christi, naming it in honor of Robert Driscoll, Jr., and lived in the penthouse there for the remainder of her life. However, her true home remained the headquarters of the Driscoll ranch holdings at Palo Alto. She kept it essentially as it had always been—simple and roomy. She maintained that she liked to go to the ranch to "get away from things." She retained her love of dogs, horses, and cattle; and she seemed to have rediscovered a rancher's realistic, uncluttered outlook on life once she could spend some time in the open. It was said that of all the professions and interests for which she was known, the one she preferred was that of "cattlewoman."

Still she continued to provide money for the support and

maintenance of the Alamo and for the purchase of property adjoining it. She converted to a gift a loan of $92,000 she had made to the Texas Federation of Women's Clubs for their state headquarters. At home she took up her brother's lifelong interest in fostering the industrial and commercial development of Corpus Christi and Nueces County.

Two of Clara's numerous gifts stand out among all her acts of generosity. On December 4, 1943 she transferred the deed of Laguna Gloria to the Texas Fine Arts Association, to provide Austin with an exhibition art gallery. At the presentation she said: "Half my heart went out when I gave it." Today the Laguna Gloria grounds, as well as the art gallery, are an important part of the Austin cultural scene. Her most lasting contribution, however, was the establishment in her will of the children's hospital in Corpus Christi, given in memory of her family.

Operating on funds that compose the entire Driscoll estate, the hospital, with a branch at Robstown, opened in February 1953. Begun as a hospital providing free medical care for underprivileged children, today the institution serves all children. In addition to a total health care program for children, the hospital has developed areas in intensive care for newborns and cardiac cases.

Clara Driscoll's death on July 17, 1945, after only a short illness, left a void in public service in her native state. At her death she reaped the honors she deserved. No other Texas woman has been honored by having her body lie in state in the chapel of the Alamo. For three hours thousands of Texans paid their last respects to Clara Driscoll, the "Savior of the Alamo."

REFERENCES

Ables, Robert L. "The Second Battle for the Alamo," *Southwestern Historical Quarterly,* LXX (January 1967).

"Action Express: The Alamo and Clara Driscoll," San Antonio *Express* (November 21, 1972).

Butterfield, Jack C. and Mary Laswell. *Clara Driscoll Rescued the Alamo.* Dallas: Daughters of the Republic of Texas, 1961.

"Clara Driscoll's Body To Lie in State in Alamo," Dallas *Morning News* (July 19, 1945).

"Closed 15 Years, Laguna Gloria Opens To Public Today," Austin *American-Statesman* (March 19, 1944).

"Control of Vast Driscoll Domain Leaves Hands of Family First Time . . . ," Fort Worth *Star-Telegram* (July 31, 1934).

"Daughters of Republic," Houston *Chronicle* (April 12, 1907).

"Divorce Granted to Mrs. Sevier," Austin *American* (July 31, 1937).

"Driscoll Foundation To Erect Charity Hospital for Children," Dallas *Morning News* (August 31, 1949).

"DRT Honors Mrs. Driscoll," San Antonio *Express* (May 16, 1941).

Estes, Maurine. "Clara Driscoll's Personal Effects Reflect Vivid Life," Corpus Christi *Caller-Times* (September 4, 1953).

"In Society," *State Topics* (December 27, 1903).

Jacobs, Bonnie Sue. "Old King Ranch House is restored," North San Antonio *Times* (July 8, 1976).

Kilgore, Dan E. "Corpus Christi: A Quarter Century of Development, 1900-1925," *Southwestern Historical Quarterly,* LXXV (April, 1972).

"Laguna Gloria, Now Clara Driscoll Art Gallery . . . ," Austin *American-Statesman* (August 26, 1945).

Lea, Tom. *The King Ranch,* Volume II (reprint). Boston: Little, Brown and Company, 1974.

McCampbell, Coleman. *Texas Seaport.* New York: Exposition Press, 1952.

"Mrs. Driscoll Quits Post on Committee," Dallas *Morning News* (May 24, 1944).

Sevier, Clara Driscoll. "Letter," Houston *Daily Post* (May 17, 1907).

Turner, Martha Ann. *Clara Driscoll.* Austin: Madrona Press, 1979.

Wood, Alpha Kennedy. *Texas Coastal Bend: People and Places.* Rockport, 1979.

Laguna Gloria, home of Clara Driscoll.

Courtesy The Delta Kappa Gamma Society International

Texas's Foremost
Woman Educator

Annie Webb Blanton

The 1918 race for state superintendent of public instruction in Texas was a closely contested and highly controversial one. For the first time in Texas history a woman was challenging the traditional male candidates for the office, and feelings ran high. Annie Webb Blanton, the first woman to campaign for the state superintendent's office, was an excellent speaker, a woman who had held the office of president of the Texas State Teacher's Association, and crowds across the state turned out to hear her speak and to witness the novelty of a woman campaigning in Texas's political arena.

Blanton's decision to enter the race had been a last minute one. She had been urged to run by the State Suffrage Association, who offered to support her race with vote-getting techniques and with finances. Blanton filed on the last day that candidates could declare their intention to run and then proceeded to take on her male opponents in a bitter two-month campaign characterized by name calling and smear techniques. Her male opponents charged that she had been divorced and was an atheist. They also charged that she had been barred from serving on the State Textbook Board. One candidate, W. F. Doughty, characterized Blanton as a "tool of others," claiming that she had no chance of being elected.

In her campaign across the state Annie Webb Blanton answered her opponent's charges quietly and clearly, detailing the facts of her life as an unmarried woman and an earnest Christian. She explained that she was disqualified from serving as a member of the textbook board simply because she was the author of several textbooks used in the public schools. While the suffrage association distributed leaflets proclaiming "Why You Should Not Vote for W.F.D.," Blanton told voters that if Doughty "had carried his candidacy to the Creator in prayer as earnestly as I have, he would not have been endorsed by the breweries." During those World War I days patriotic fervor ran high, and in Texas much of it was targeted against the German brewers and the German-American Alliance, both of whom supported Doughty. The suffrage association also distributed broadsides that linked Doughty with former governor James E. Ferguson, who had been impeached on charges of taking loans from the brewers. Doughty, who had been an ardent supporter of Ferguson's, refused to make a statement about the impeachment, but the suffrage association determined to defeat Doughty for his support of Ferguson, an avowed opponent of women's suffrage. Their propaganda stressed the fact that Doughty appeared on the speaker's platform with Ferguson when the governor accused University of Texas professors of being "a lot of two-bit thieves."

The suffragists claimed that Blanton would remove the state education agency from connection with every form of machine politics, and distributed handbills extolling their candidate as " . . . impartial and democratic; a woman of principle and courage; a practical business woman; a womanly woman." While the Cleburne *Enterprise* noted that on her speaking tours, the audience gave her their attention and she "did not have to combat the prejudice which is sometimes felt toward a woman offering for office," when the July primary ballots were printed, many counties refused to list Blanton as a candidate. Only after legal threats were made did the suffragists get her name entered on the November ballot; yet she managed to defeat her opponents to become the first woman to hold an elective state office in Texas.

Much of her support came from members of the Texas State Teacher's Association, where as the first woman president of the organization she had worked to revise the constitution, to bring efficiency to the organization, to establish both a permanent fund for the organization and a retirement fund, and to publish the association's bulletin. Her friends in the group enthusiastically supported her campaign, and the townspeople of Denton, where she had taught, formed a Blanton Club. The Denton *Chronicle* actively worked for her candidacy. When she took the oath of office she sent the editor of the *Chronicle* a box of candy with a card stating, "I think you are the only editor of a paper to receive a box of fudge made by a state superintendent of public instruction."

Blanton's platform was an ambitious and progressive one in which she advocated selecting appointees on merit rather than on politics; expanding the department; improving rural schools; giving equal recognition to men and women employees; raising the scholastic and professional requirements of teachers; and working for pay raises. Not only were her programs ambitious, she had to undertake implementing them during the post-World War I economy. When she ran for a second term she ran on her own record on a ballot that included a Better Schools Amendment to provide relief for rural schools. With the support of numerous groups and an increasing number of women voters who demanded "equal rights and a fighting chance for all Texas children," she won a second term and continued her work to improve education across the state. She made effective use of the press, writing a series of articles entitled "Our School Problems in Texas: What is the Outcome to Be?" and exploring such topics as salaries, appropriations, and one-teacher schools. She actively pushed for progressive legislation, many times writing the bills herself and then lobbying for their passage through the legislature. She was ahead of her time in her views concerning minority children, working to see that black schools received supportive funding and encouraging the teaching of English to Spanish-speaking children.

Her active support of women in the field of education was the high point of her state service. Her report, *A Handbook of Information as to Education in Texas (1918-22),* included a discussion of school problems and recommendations for proposed legislation, along with a chapter entitled "Recognition of Women in Education." Here Blanton concisely set out her principles regarding equal pay and equal access to jobs, including her appointment of women to the previously all-male Summer Normal Board of Examiners. "The State Superintendent has refused to recognize a Summer Normal whose faculty does not include a fair proportion of both men and women teachers . . . ." In addition, each year when the annual schoolboard elections were approaching, Blanton sent a letter to the president of women's organizations encouraging them to help place women members on their local schoolboards.

At the end of her second term Blanton chose not to run again. Although the suffrage association had agreed to finance her campaigns, they could not raise the necessary funds, and her political debts were enormous. She sold her home in Denton and then used the money plus her professional salary, with the exception of her living expenses and life insurance payments, for the next ten years in retiring the debt. In a letter to Dr. Oscar Henry Cooper, parttime professor of history and philosophy of education at The University of Texas, she explained the difficulties she had encountered as the first woman president of the Texas State Teacher's Association and the first woman state superintendent of public instruction:

> It should be remembered . . . I worked always under this handicap — of being the first woman to hold both positions; and while I had the friendly help of many good men, there was always a faction of narrow prejudices who opposed everything that I attempted, not because there was no merit in what I was seeking,

but because of the fact that the one initiating it was a woman . . . .

After Dr. Blanton retired from public office Texas elected a woman governor and two women served as secretary of state. In addition, women had used their suffrage right to elect women to local offices across the state, and women in the teaching professions were entering more and more administrative positions. Many looked to Annie Webb Blanton as the woman who had opened the doors of educational opportunities for them, and many groups gave her accolades as "Texas's foremost educator" and "a woman whom time will call great."

The woman who was later to become Texas's best known woman educator was born in Houston, Texas, on August 19, 1870, the daughter of Thomas Lindsay Blanton and his wife, Eugenia Webb Blanton. She and her twin sister Fannie grew up in a home of seven children until Fannie died as a teenager. They began their education in private schools, and Annie attended Houston High School until her mother died in July 1879, and her father took his family to live in La Grange. Annie graduated from high school and then taught at a country school at Pine Springs in Fayette County.

Throughout her lifetime Annie Webb Blanton was proud of her Southern and Texas ancestors, including Captain William Walker, who served in the American Revolution, and John Christopher Columbus Hill, the "boy hero of the Mier expedition," who marched with the prisoners of the expedition to Mexico, attracted the attention of General Santa Anna, and remained in Mexico as an engineer in government service. Blanton often told stories of her grandfather, General William G. Webb, who served in the Texas war for independence and later became one of the pioneer settlers of La Grange.

When her father died in 1888 the Blanton family moved to Austin, and Annie Webb taught in the capital city's elementary schools and at Austin High School. During each summer vacation she enrolled as a special student at The University of Texas, and then enrolled as a regular student during her junior year. She graduated Phi Beta Kappa in 1899 with a bachelor of literature degree, and in 1901 she began teaching at North Texas State Normal College, now North Texas State University, at Denton. During the seventeen years she taught at North Texas Blanton sponsored a literary club for women students, coached the debate team, and sponsored other speech activities. She began a student literary publication, the *Journal,* and was active in women's activities in the community, helping found the City Federation of Women's Clubs and the Women's Shakespeare Society. She also authored a textbook entitled *Advanced English Grammar,* which was used for years in the public schools.

During the Denton years Annie Webb Blanton first experienced the concept of a community of professional women that she was later to use as the basis for the honorary educational sorority, Delta Kappa Gamma. She built her first home and invited a group of women teachers to live there, sharing the responsibilities of homemaking and gardening. Each teacher was given a plot of land set off by a border of violets, and here each cultivated the roses that became an important part of Blanton's life. Although the teachers took their meals at a boarding house, each Sunday evening they entertained with a buffet supper, inviting new teachers and people from the community to join them.

One of Blanton's first experiences in a leadership role came through the active role she took in the Texas State Teacher's Association. She brought to Denton five educational leaders to speak to the faculty and students, and remained an active member of the association throughout her academic life. When she was a young girl her brother Thomas Lindsay Blanton had announced that he intended to be a lawyer; Annie Webb stated that she thought she would be one too. Brother Lin told her, however, she couldn't because she was a woman. During the years she served as a member of the Texas State Teacher's Association and later as its first woman president, Blanton actively advocated equal rights for women in all fields and especially in education. As president of the association in 1916, she gained the statewide recognition in the field of education that led to the suffrage association's recruiting her to run for the office of state superintendent. During her years in public office she widened her acquaintances among women educators, and many of these women served as the nucleus of the charter membership of Delta Kappa Gamma.

When Annie Webb Blanton decided not to run for a third term as state superintendent, the members of TSTA honored her with a Christmas present of five hundred dollars, which she no doubt needed to help toward paying the campaign debt. Although she retired from public office Blanton accelerated her activities in the academic sphere. She returned to The University of Texas to complete her master's degree, entitling her thesis *A Study of Educational Progress in Texas, 1918-1922.* In 1923 she became adjunct professor of educational administriation at the university, and three years later she took a leave of absence to work on her doctorate at Cornell University. In 1927 she received her Ph.D. and returned to The University of Texas as associate professor and chair of the rural education department. In 1933 she was promoted to full professor, the third woman to attain that position at the university. As professor of rural education in the Department of Educational Administration, she took an active role in advancing the cause of rural schools across the state, and she later chaired the Department of History of Education.

While she never ran for public office again, Blanton remained active in the Democratic party,, adding to her collection of small donkeys, the party symbol, throughout her lifetime. She continued to work for the advancement of educational legislation and cooperated with the League of Women Voters on a variety of issues. Blanton also served three terms as vice president of the National Education Association and was an active member of the National Council on Education.

To many women educators, however, the high point of her

life came in 1929, when she resolved that she would form a professional society that would "help remove the barriers limiting
the advancement of women educators." Certainly the formation of the sorority was the culmination of a lifetime spent working against discrimination toward women in the educational
field. One of the keywords of her professional life had been
organization, and Blanton spent months carefully structuring
the format of the organization, planning the constitution, and
even writing the lyrics to the society's song. She hoped to have
fifteen original founders, but had only twelve acceptances by
May 11, 1929, the day chosen for the initiation of the charter
members.

Blanton and Cora Martin spent hours researching the structure of Pi Lambda Theta, a professional society to which they
both belonged, and Dr. Blanton corresponded with the other
founders at length about many items of organization and structure for the society. The one aspect that Blanton was determined
to avoid embodying in the philosophy of the group was an emphasis on scholarship; she preferred that the focus be placed on
experience for women educators.

The original twelve founders reflect the broad spectrum of
women in Texas education at the time: a grade-school teacher; a
dean of women; two high school teachers of history and one of
mathematics; three elementary school principals; college
teachers of psychology, physical education, and elementary
education; and Dr. Blanton. They came from Houston, Dallas,
San Antonio, Fort Worth, Austin, and Waxahachie. On May
11, 1929, eleven of the founders met at the University Faculty
Women's Club located at 2610 Whitis Avenue for installation
ceremonies. Anna Hiss was absent as her sister had died in
Baltimore, and she was initiated later; but Mamie Bastian, Ruby
Cole, Lela Lee Williams, Mable Youree Grizzard, Ray and Sue
King, Helen Koch, Lalla M. Odom, Ruby Terrill Lomax, and
Cora M. Martin faced Annie Webb Blanton and went through
the initiation of the society that was first named Kappa Gamma
Delta, then changed to the current name Delta Kappa Gamma

when a conflict with another organization was discovered. Tall red candles signifying the aims of the society; small red candles for each initiate; ribbons of gold and crimson; and Dr. Blanton's favorite red roses adorned the table. After the singing of the society song, the group elected officers and reviewed the society's constitution.

Recognizing the opposition that a society of women educators might foster, invitations for membership in the society were sent to Dr. Blanton under the name of Miss Katherine Graham Dalton and mailed to the university post office rather than to the faculty women's club. The founders set about combating the discrimination that existed toward women in the educational field by endowing scholarships to aid outstanding women leaders in pursuing graduate study. Thousands of women educators all over the world have been awarded financial gifts from Delta Kappa Gamma to foster graduate study. Dr. Blanton was acutely aware of the fact that women educators "were handicapped by customs which denied them administrative positions and by salary schedules that alloted lower pay to women than to men of identical training and experience."

Annie Webb Blanton realized that much of the work of organizing society chapters throughout Texas and other states would be her responsibility. She spent her own money and much of her time traveling the nation, establishing chapters and installing officers. On June 10, 1933 the fourth national convention of the society was held in New Orleans, and Blanton received the first national honor award for "her faith, her vision, her perseverance, her consecrated service to the profession and to the advancement of women educators."

In 1934 Blanton began a collection of small figures representing the states' pioneer women teachers dressed in costumes of the period each represented. She was appointed "Keeper of the Dolls" in 1936 and carried them to conventions carefully packed in nine trunks.

In 1935 Blanton was somewhat less active in the society than she had been, as she was working on a research project under a grant from the Laura Spellman Rockefeller Foundation. Her research was later published as *The Child of the Texas One-Teacher School.* Finding that her duties for the society consumed much of her professional time, Blanton requested part-time status at the university in 1939, and continued sharing her work between school and society until September 1945. Ill health forced her to resign her university post at that time, and she died on October 2, 1945. As Texas's foremost woman educator of the early twentieth century, she had more than fulfilled the prophecy that one newspaper editor made about her: "She is a woman that time will call great."

REFERENCES

Blanton, Annie Webb. *A Handbook of Information as to Education in Texas (1918-1922).* Austin: State of Texas, 1923.

Blanton, Annie Webb. *Letter* to O. H. Cooper. March 6, 1920. O. H. Cooper Collection, Barker Texas History Center, The University of Texas at Austin.

Concerning the Race for State Superintendent of Public Instruction. (broadside). Annie Webb Blanton Biographical File. Barker Texas History Center, The University of Texas at Austin.

"Denton Woman One of Texas' Leading Teachers." (unidentified newspaper clipping). Annie Webb Blanton Biographical File. Barker Texas History Center, The University of Texas at Austin.

Eby, Frederick. "Dr. Blanton was a pioneer in education." Delta Kappa Gamma *Bulletin* (Spring 1957): 39-40.

Hansard, Thom. "They Said a Woman Couldn't Win." *Daily Texan* (April 2, 1954): 3.

Holden, Eunah Temple. "Our Founder, Annie Webb Blanton." Speech presented at the birthday luncheon, Delta Kappa Gamma, Portland, Oregon, 1970.

Holden, Eunah Temple, (ed.). *Our Heritage in the Delta Kappa Gamma Society,* Volumes I and II. Austin: The Delta Kappa Gamma Society, 1960, 1970.

Howes, Durward, (ed.). *American Women,* Volume II. Los Angeles: American Publications, Inc., 1937.

Parker, Clara M. *Annie Webb Blanton, Founder of the Delta Kappa Gamma Society.* Austin: Delta Kappa Gamma Society, 1949.

Pittinger, B.F. "Annie Webb Blanton." *Texas Outlook* (January 1946): 19.
Pittinger, B.F. "Dr. Blanton as a leader and organizer." Delta Kappa Gamma *Bulletin* (Spring 1957): 39-40.
"Women Once Headed Texas Schools." Austin *American-Statesman.* (February 28, 1954): 13.

INTERVIEWS

Dr. Theresa A. Fachek and Ann Fears Crawford. Austin, July 23, 1981.
Dr. Inez Jeffrey and Ann Fears Crawford. Austin, July 8, 1981.

Courtesy Barker Texas History Center, The Univesity of Texas at Austin

"Me For Ma"

Governor Miriam

Amanda Ferguson

In 1966 when Lurleen Wallace took to the stump in Alabama's gubernatorial campaign, standing beside her on every speakers' platform was her husband George. Barred from running for a second term as governor by a one-term provision in Alabama's constitution, fiesty George Wallace entered his wife's name on the ballot, allowed Lurleen to say a few introductory remarks at each campaign function, and then took over the microphone to expound his own political views and programs. Wallace was quick to assure his loyal followers that Lurleen would be governor in her own right, but that she could count on George to be beside her, ready to "draw the water, tote in the wood, wind the clock, and put out the cat."

Alabama's rural populace may have found a man posing as his wife's "number one assistant" a novelty in their political arena, but Texans would have found the scene reminiscent of their own turbulent political history, when in the 1920s, "Farmer Jim" Ferguson, the impeached governor barred from running for public office, conceived the political master stroke of running his wife, Miriam Amanda, for governor.

The effects of the administration of Texas's first "lady governor" were far reaching. When Frances Farenthold ran for the governor's office in 1972, she often heard the refrain from men throughout the rural areas of Texas: "Well, I might as well vote for a woman in the seventies, I voted for one in the twenties." Farenthold found that many people in rural Texas still remembered the slogan that was used throughout the state during the 1924 gubernatorial campaign: "Me for Ma, and I ain't got a dern thing against Pa!"

Miriam Amanda Ferguson, Texas's first "lady governor," and Jim Ferguson, who "carried the wood" and ran the state, captured the imagination of Texas voters from the time of Mrs. Ferguson's entry in the 1924 campaign. However, despite the fact that Texas claimed the first woman governor elected in her own right, "Ma" Ferguson was governor in name only. It was "Pa" who moved his desk into the governor's office to sit at Miriam's right hand; it was Jim who extended his hand to greet the politicians when they entered the governor's office; and it was Jim who sat in on the meetings of the state's boards and commissions.

"Farmer Jim" Ferguson's flamboyant politics, a canny combination of backwoods intuition and public presence, fired the imagination of Texas's rural voters in the first part of the twentieth century. Elected to the governor's office in 1914 by the tenant farmers of the state, Ferguson soon found himself in trouble with the state legislature over his veto of the appropriations for The University of Texas. Despite the fact that a legislative investigation brought out evidence that Ferguson had appropriated state funds for his own use, had deposited state funds in a bank in which he owned stock, and had accepted and never repaid a campaign loan of $156,000 from the brewery interest, "the boys at the forks of the creeks" rallied around their advocate. When he was impeached and found guilty, barred from holding public office in Texas, Ferguson's rural supporters joined with the anti-Klan element to put his wife into the governor's office.

The Ferguson era in Texas politics was a turbulent one, growing from the roots of Populism and expanding through the Progressive era into the New Deal years. During this period Texas made the first moves toward urban growth and its accompanying problems. The era was marked by one-party rule—that of the Democratic party—and torn by the prohibition issue and that of "Fergusonism," a political philosophy that one historian has described as "a freewheeling, loose-scrupled boondocks liberalism."

During the Ferguson years, spanning the years from Jim Ferguson's first campaign in 1914 to the end of Miriam's second term of office on January 25, 1935 Texas politicians began to to rank themselves as "pro-Ferguson" or "anti-Ferguson." The political lines were tightly drawn, and one longtime Ferguson-watcher commented: "With old Jim, you were either for 'im or agin' 'im. There wasn't any middle of the road."

The other issues of the Ferguson era were similarly clearcut. From the first campaign, Jim Ferguson spoke out on the issue of tenant farming, of prime importance to the rural Texas farmers who formed the Ferguson political base. The Fergusons also encountered the problems of prohibition and the demands of the fundamentalist religion; they opposed the Ku Klux Klan and were instrumental in bringing about the first anti-mask legislation; and they became embroiled in an education controversy that pitted the advocates of higher education against the "little red schoolhouse."

The overriding issue of the Ferguson era, however, was Jim Ferguson himself and his concept of the power of the state's chief executive. Ferguson first made his mark on the state's political scene as a colorful campaigner with few equals. His gallus-snapping political style endeared him to the rural populace, and his uncanny knack for creating publicity placed him on the front pages of the state's newspapers. His war with The University of Texas, his subsequent impeachment and conviction, plus the uniqueness of his running his wife for governor and winning made national headlines.

Miriam did not even have the chance to announce her own candidacy. Jim made the decision, and, clad in an undershirt, sitting on the side of a bed in a Taylor, Texas hotel room, "Farmer Jim" announced that he was running his wife for governor. Before entering Miriam's name on the ballot,

Ferguson went to court to attempt to get his disbarment from public office turned aside. When the case was turned down, "Ma," as she was soon named by reporters for her initials "M.A.," ably assisted by "Pa," took to the stump to vindicate "Farmer Jim" and to do battle against the Klan.

Ferguson's decision to run his wife for governor was a political master stroke. Women had been granted the right to vote on August 26, 1920, and Miriam Ferguson's candidacy appealed to Texas women, many of whom had been active in both the prohibition movement and the suffrage cause. Undoubtedly, many voters felt that a woman in office would clean up the state, and the Ferguson's war against the Klan brought many supporters to the Ferguson cause, including the Dallas *Morning News,* the largest newspaper in the state and avowed enemy of Jim Ferguson.

The 1924 campaign brought flamboyant political slogans to help the Ferguson cause. "Me for Ma" stickers appeared on automobile bumpers, and voters across the state were told what a bargain they were getting in electing "Ma" and her able political aide, "Pa" — "Two Governors for the Price of One." To many voters the choice was a simple one — "The sunbonnet or the hood," a woman governor or rule by the Ku Klux Klan, and Ferguson supporters fought the "hooded monster" with poems, such as:

> Hoods off!
> Along the street there comes
> Patriotic daughters and loyal sons,
> A crowd of bonnets beneath the sky,
> Hoods off!
> Miriam Ferguson is passing by.

When a woman supporter presented Miriam Ferguson with a sunbonnet in honor of her campaign song, "Put on Your Old Gray Bonnet," Houston women requested patterns for the "Ma Ferguson" sunbonnet, and campaigners quoted:

Get out your old-time bonnet
And put Miriam Ferguson on it,
        And hitch your wagon to a star.
So on election day
We each of us can say
        Hurrah! Governor Miriam, Hurrah!

"Farmer Jim" announced the platform — anti-mask legislation designed to strip the secrecy from the Klan coupled with more economical state government — and "Ma" gave him her endorsement, telling readers of the Ferguson-owned newspaper, the *Ferguson Forum.*

> I am adopting and approving the platform which Jim has already announced, and if you elect me, I promise with all my heart to carry it out and he will help me give the people of Texas the best administration that our ability tempered with love and gratitude can produce.

While Texas women flocked to the Ferguson banner and "Farmer Jim" successfully courted the woman's vote, neither "Pa" nor "Ma" can be counted among staunch supporters of women's suffrage. Jim Ferguson had spoken out against women being given the right to vote, and Miriam followed in his philosophical footsteps. After her election she explained her views on women's suffrage in a magazine article, saying that she had originally not been in favor of women voting, but that she exercised her franchise in voting for her husband in his unsuccesful bid for the United States Senate in 1922. She explained:

> I never fought for woman suffrage, . . . but they made it law, they gave us the ballot, and I see no reason why we should not exercise our right . . . .

When "Farmer Jim" railed at the Klan, they promptly struck back, claiming that Mrs. Ferguson was fit only for the business of being a wife and mother and for feeding chickens in her backyard. Jim Ferguson knew a good campaign issue when he saw one, and when reporters and photographers from national magazines descended on Texas to cover the political campaign, there was "Ma" in her sunbonnet, feeding her prize Leghorns or canning the peaches that made campaign history. According to various newspaper accounts, at the height of the campaign, an old friend from Tyler sent Mrs. Ferguson a bushel of unusually fine peaches. Although there were telegrams to answer and speeches to be given, "the housewife was not swallowed up by the political candidate." Before the day was over, the peaches had been preserved and the candidate was back on the campaign trail.

When a Ferguson club sent her a broom to be used to "sweep and clean house at Austin of all obnoxious taxeaters," Mrs. Ferguson had her photograph taken sweeping away and released the poem that had been attached to the broom:

> 'As sure as comes election day,
> A broom to you we send.
> In sunshine use the brush part,
> In storm the other end.'

Not all Texans, however, were captivated by the idea of having a homemaker in the statehouse, and one Texas newspaper editor stated that apparently "Texas is not too old to have a governess,"while the Albany (Texas) *News* was transported by the idea of the family wash hanging on the line at the capitol and the governor laying "aside her knitting to discuss grave matters of state."

Grave matters of state, however, remained the province of "Farmer Jim," while Miriam campaigned on a platform of vindication, asking the women of the state to clear her husband's name. Appeals to women, the "boys at the forks of the creek," and the anti-Klan element combined to give Miriam victories over her Klan-backed opponent, Felix D. Robertson, in a runoff primary by a margin of 98,000 votes; and over her Republican opponent, Dr. George C. Butte, in the November general election. Texas had its first woman governor, and the Fergusons had a decisive victory over the Klan. The New York *World* editorialized:

> Ten years ago we were debating whether a woman should be allowed to vote. Today a woman is to be Governor of a great State, and most people are more interested in the principles she fought for than in the fact that she is a woman . . . .

The woman, however, who entered the governor's mansion was no backwoodswoman nor frontier folk figure. Miriam Amanda Wallace Ferguson could trace her lineage to Edward I of England and the Scottish patriot, Sir William Wallace. She was the product of upper-middle-class, smalltown Texas parents, and she had acquired more educational advantages than most Texas women of her day. Her father, Joseph Lapsley Wallace, came to Texas from Kentucky with his parents during the years of the Texas republic. After serving in the Confederate army, Wallace returned to Bell County, beginning a prosperous career as cattleman and farmer, and expanding his interests into banking and land.

His marriage to Eliza Garrison Ferguson, widow of Jim Ferguson's uncle, produced six children, of whom Miriam Amanda was the third. As Joseph Wallace's fortune increased he determined to provide his children with a good education. Miriam attended the Center Lake School, which soon proved inadequate by Wallace's standards, and he employed a tutor for his children. With her two older brothers Miriam attended Salado College and then joined her sister at Baylor Female College in Belton.

By the time she entered college, Miriam had grown into a lovely young woman, with clusters of brown curls and the luminous eyes that shine from her portraits. Her love of clothes remained with her all her life, and when she met Jim Ferguson she was one of the belles of Belton society. The couple met at a family party, and according to their daughter, fell in love at first sight. Soon Jim was a constant visitor to the Wallace home, and Miriam was the obvious target of his interests.

In January 1898 Joseph Wallace died after contracting an illness while taking a shipment of cattle to Kansas City. He left his widow a sizeable fortune in cash, cattle, and land, and Eliza Wallace turned to her young relative, Jim Ferguson, for legal advice. Ferguson then pressed his suit with Miriam, filing for city attorney of Belton and convincing Miriam that a city official needed a wife. His ardent pleas were answered, and on January 31, 1899 the young couple was married in the parlor of the Wallace home. Jim was twenty-eight; Miriam, twenty-four.

Miriam settled down to the life of a Central Texas matron, contenting herself with her home and garden, while Jim expanded his interests from being city attorney to banking. By the time Ferguson filed as a candidate for the governor's office, the couple had two children, Ouida and Ruby Dorrace.

Then Jim Ferguson decided that the time was right for him to enter politics. He announced that he would run for governor in 1913, declaring that he would veto any liquor legislation and pitching his campaign to the tenant farmers. A colorful campaigner with few equals, Ferguson's flamboyant political style endeared him to the rural farmers who put him in the statehouse.

Ferguson's arguments with the state's prohibitionists, and his veto of the appropriations for The University of Texas carried over into Miriam's term as governor, and soon the Fergusons were involved in as much controversy as Jim had been in his war with The University of Texas. "Farmer Jim" was accused of dispensing patronage with a heavy hand, of irregularities in the awarding of highway contracts, and of misuse of the pardoning power. Mrs. Ferguson issued 1,161 pardons in two years, but the Fergusons' supporters consistently defended her pardon policy by stating that the penitentiaries were filled with men who had been convicted on charges of bootlegging, and that Mrs. Ferguson believed the convicted men would better serve society by returning home to support their wives and children.

The liberal use of the pardon power was not the only issue on which the Fergusons came under attack. W. R. Sinclair of San Antonio wrote to former Governor Oscar B. Colquitt that Jim Ferguson had become "attorney for pardons, for railroads, and for highway contractors," and another San Antonio man claimed that Ferguson was becoming wealthy, as well as serving as governor by marriage. "It is quicker and surer than either an oil well or a gold mine. It is much easier than banking or manufacturing, and it has the charm of novelty," he wrote.

However, "Ma" was never criticized for being "pushy" or "uppity" as a woman. The few speeches she made were written by her husband, and on her first day in office she invited the press to stop by the mansion for hot biscuits and her homemade peach preserves. Her speeches and columns in the Ferguson newspaper, the Ferguson *Forum*, reveal her to be a typical woman of the first half of the twentieth century, both Southern and Texan in outlook. Her views swung from progressive concerning women's right to enter the business world and to dress as they pleased, to looking back to the "good old days," when women played their traditional role as homemakers and where such evils as smoking and "cigareetes" were unknown.

In her newspaper columns Mrs. Ferguson counseled women to learn a profession in case the day should come when they might need it, but not to neglect their homes. She applauded the comfort of modern female garments, and advocated that women cut their hair and wear it in any style that suited them; but warned them that when they smoked it did not look right. She spoke out strongly in favor of jazz and of young people dancing, but also extolled the virtues of rural country living, a diet of turnip greens and cornbread, the delights of gardening, and "our old Black Mammies."

One typical speech was delivered to the University Club of Houston in 1925, where "Ma" spoke on the subject, "Women in Business," urging women contemplating entering the field of business and government to retain their femininity. If women followed in the footsteps of men they would do no better than men, she warned, ending with the admonition: "If a woman is mannish, let her stay away from us."

Mrs. Ferguson's fight to vindicate her husband's name, the push to pass through the Texas legislature an amnesty bill to remove all stigma from Jim Ferguson's name, and Attorney General Dan Moody's investigation of the awarding of highway contracts soon had the Fergusons on the defensive. Many Texans believed that the Fergusons had profited from the pardoning of criminals as well as the awarding of highway contracts, although no officials were indicted in the highway scandals and no money from the rewarding of contracts was ever traced to any member of the Ferguson family. Dan Moody, however, had made a name for himself through the lawsuit against the American Road Company, and in the next election he filed for governor against Miriam Ferguson.

By 1926 public opinion had swung to Moody, although Mrs. Ferguson courted the female vote avidly, stating that she had the right to the traditional second term afforded all male governors, and charging that she was being discriminated against because she had a husband. Leaders in the women's suffrage movement and in the Women's Christian Temperance League, however, spoke out against her. The suffragist leader Carrie Chapman Catt carried a grudge against Jim Ferguson's anti-suffragist views and told the Illinois League of Women Voters that the only reason Miriam Ferguson had been elected governor of Texas in the first place was because of the Klan issue and a strong Democratic tradition in Texas politics. It was clear that the fact that Miriam Ferguson had stood behind her husband and had allowed him to speak for her had alienated her from the militant suffragist group, and even such a politically docile group as the Daughters of the Republic of Texas charged that a campaign photograph of Mrs. Ferguson in front of the Texas flag was cheap.

Although Dan Moody defeated "Ma" in 1926 by some 200,000 votes, Jim Ferguson stated that his motto was "Never say 'die,' say 'damn'," and promptly entered into another fight when his enemies sought to repeal the amnesty bill passed during Miriam's administration. Ferguson won and promptly filed for governor in February 1930. The Democratic Executive Committee, however, refused to enter his name on the ballot, and the Texas Supreme Court declared the amnesty bill to be unconstitutional.

The only way to win the governor's race was to enter Miriam once more on the ballot. Texas, however, was changing by 1930. The Depression had made its mark, and the tenant farmer issue was a dead one. More and more Texans were seeking to make a living in their state's cities. The "big oil" candidate, Ross Sterling, who described himself as "Your Big Fat Boy from Buffalo Bayou," appealed to the city interests and challenged Mrs. Ferguson in the campaign. The Fergusons won the primary, but lost to an overwhelming city vote in the runoff. "Farmer Jim" promptly attacked Sterling's business interests and his official act of sending the Texas Rangers and the National Guard into the East Texas oilfields to control runaway oil production. Labeling Sterling "the present encumbrance," Jim Ferguson ran Miriam again in 1932.

Although Mrs. Ferguson returned to the governor's mansion for one final term, her administration was relatively quiet, with the biggest event a visit from Will Rogers. The folk humorist twirled his rope in the mansion gardens, and "Ma" served him a big bowl of Texas chili. With the state in a grave economic situation, Mrs. Ferguson ordered the banks to close their doors and called for strict ceilings on state spending. She also obtained federal money through NYA, CCC, WPA, and other federal relief programs to mitigate the plight of unemployed Texans during the Depression.

Runaway oil continued to plague the Ferguson administration, and Mrs. Ferguson was successful in getting the legislature to pass a two-cents per barrel tax on the state's oil production, the first step toward regulation and conservation of the state's most valuable natural resource. The Depression, however, made more headlines than the Fergusons, and Miriam, bowing to a longstanding Texas tradition, declined to run for a third term. But when Franklin D. Roosevelt, whom the Fergusons strongly supported, announced that he would seek a third term as president, "Old Jim" concluded that the time was ripe to mount a third term for Miriam, and she responded with a widely-circulated pamphlet, *If I Should Run for Governor,* calling for a third term for Roosevelt and one for herself. The 1940s, however, heralded a new day in Texas political campaigning. The Ferguson style of stump speaking had given way to radio, and the Fergusons crossed the campaign trail of the master of radio hucksterism, W. Lee "Pappy" O'Daniel. When the votes were counted in the 1940 gubernatorial race, Miriam Ferguson finished fourth, and "Pappy" O'Daniel went to the statehouse. Jim Ferguson had to content himself with being a behind-the-scenes political manipulator.

Ferguson's involvement in the 1941 election, which pitted O'Daniel against a young Congressman named Lyndon Johnson in a battle over a seat for the United States Senate, taught Johnson one of his more valuable political lessons. Ferguson backed O'Daniel, believing that "while one dry senator in Washington might do little harm to the beer and whiskey business in Texas, one dry wartime governor such as O'Daniel could knock it cold." Ferguson not only backed O'Daniel with money, he delivered the vote. Garnering the campaign support of his Ferguson machine when Lyndon Johnson led in the primary, Ferguson called out the East Texas "corrected" vote to push O'Daniel ahead. Years later, Johnson told one reporter that "Jim Ferguson stole the 1941 election from me."

Johnson, chagrined by his loss, told his campaign aides, "If I ever get in another close election, I'm not going to lose it." The young Congressman actively courted the Fergusons' support, and in 1948 Lyndon Johnson sent his brother to call on Mrs. Ferguson. With Governor Jim dead Miriam inherited the Fergusons' legendary "black book," listing all the Ferguson supporters. Mrs. Ferguson agreed to support Johnson, and the Ferguson loyalists spread the word through East Texas. When the votes were counted in the most controversial political race in Texas's history, the East Texas boxes that had gone for O'Daniel in 1941, were solidly behind Lyndon Johnson.

Senator Lyndon Johnson never forgot a political favor, and

in 1955, when more than three hundred Texas Democrats gathered at the Driskill Hotel in Austin to honor Mrs. Ferguson's 80th birthday, Senator Majority Leader Lyndon B. Johnson made the congratulatory address. He lauded the Fergusons as politicians "who stand for the folks — four-square and without apology and no compromise . . . . "

In assessing Miriam Ferguson's accomplishments, it is difficult to divorce the results of her terms in office from the philosophy of her husband. Even as late as 1953 when the Texas Senate honored her with a special Mother's Day resolution, they overlooked her accomplishments as governor and cited her as "an example of gentle womanhood, an ideal wife, and a devoted mother." Although she campaigned in eleven statewide races between the years 1924 and 1940 and continued to support Democratic candidates down to the Kennedy-Johnson ticket in 1960, when she died on June 25, 1961 *Time* magazine summed up Mrs. Ferguson as "a college-educated, devoutly religious, well-bred woman who was about as political as peach cobbler."

Although Mrs. Ferguson claimed that her major accomplishments in office were in the field of education, in 1954 when the Texas Heritage Foundation honored Texans for their contributions to education, the award went posthumously to Governor James E. Ferguson, whom the organization praised as Texas's "foremost friend of rural education."

Perhaps Mrs. Ferguson accomplished as much as any governor of Texas could have accomplished in the difficult years that spanned the 1920s and the 1930s. The fact that she is seldom evaluated on her own terms is due to the controversy surrounding "Governor Jim" and his influence on her administrations. She ran as governor of Texas to vindicate her husband, and certainly without his backing and the effectiveness of the "Ferguson machine," Texas would not have had its first woman governor.

Suffrage leaders condemned her as a "Slave Wife" and "Mere Figurehead," and put the blame for her failures on "Governor Jim." No doubt she put too much faith and trust in her husband. Although Texas history books accord her a place in the state's long list of political "personalities," she is delegated little space in the history of the feminist movement. Her activities while governor of Texas are so little recognized outside the state that one contemporary book dealing with women in politics refers to her as "Ma Watson," and undoutedly her failure to be remembered or appreciated can be ascribed to what one newspaper designated as her political epitaph—"Too Much Husband."

REFERENCES

Adler, Barbara Squire. "Then and Now." New York *Times* magazine (April 8, 1951): 75.

Banks, Jimmy. *Money, Marbles and Chalk: The Wondrous World of Texas Politics.* Austin: Texas Publishing Company, 1971.

Beale, Howard K. *Are American Teachers Free?* New York: n.p.,1936.

Bentley, Max. "An Interview with Governor-Elect Ferguson." *Holland's* magazine, (January 1925): 55.

Biennial Report of the Attorney General (September 1, 1924-August 31, 1926). Austin: State of Texas.: 199.

Brooks, Raymond. "Ma Ferguson Plans Quiet 78th Birthday," Austin *Statesman* (June 12, 1953): 1.

Crawford, Ann Fears. *John B. Connally: The Making of a Governor, 1917-1962.* Unpublished doctoral dissertation. Austin: The University of Texas, 1976.

Crawford, Ann Fears. *The Woman in Front of the Man.* Unpublished paper delivered at the American Studies of Texas meeting (Beaumont, 1978).

Ferguson, Charles W. "James E. Ferguson." *Southwest Review* (October 1924): 27.

Ferguson, Miriam. Clippings. Archives. Texas State Library, Austin, Texas.

Ferguson, Miriam. *A Partial History of Outstanding Achievements of the Ferguson Administration.* (mimeographed copy). Copy furnished to Ann Fears Crawford by Ghent Sanderford, executive secretary to Miriam Ferguson.

Fergusonism Down to Date: A Story in 60 Chapters. n.p., 1930.

Furniss, Norman F. *The Fundamentalist Controversy, 1918-1931.* New Haven: Harvard University Press, 1954.

Gallagher, Robert S. "Me for Ma—and I ain't got a dern thing against Pa." *American Heritage* (October 1966): 46.

Gantt, Fred, Jr. *The Chief Executive in Texas.* Austin: The University of Texas Press, 1964.

Goldman, Eric. *The Tragedy of Lyndon Johnson.* New York: Alfred A Knopf, 1969.

Hall of Remembrance, Texas Heritage Foundation, Inc. (n.p. n.d.) pamphlet, Barker Texas History Center, The University of Texas at Austin.

Keever, Cynthia Pendergrass. *The Election of Miriam Ferguson as Governor of Texas, 1924.* Unpublished master's thesis. Austin: The University of Texas, 1971.

Key, V. O., Jr. *Southern Politics in State and Nation.* New York: Alfred A. Knopf, 1949.

Luthin, Reinhard H. *American Demagogues.* Glouchester: Peter Smith, 1959.

" 'Ma' Ferguson of Texas." *Literary Digest* (September 18, 1924): 24.

Nalle, Oudia Ferguson. *The Fergusons of Texas (or) Two Governors for the Price of One: A Biography of James Edward and His Wife, Miriam Amanda Ferguson.* San Antonio: The Naylor Company, 1946.

Perry, George Sessions. *Texas: A World in Itself.* New York: McGraw-Hill Company, 1942.

Street, Katherine. *Philosophy of and Plans for Education Found in the Legislative Messages of the Chief Executives of Texas.* Unpublished master's thesis. Waco: Baylor University (June, 1940).

Strother, French. "The Governors Ferguson of Texas." *World's Work* (September, 1925): 489.

"The Fall of 'Ma' Ferguson." *Literary Digest* (December 12, 1925): 7.

The Fergusons Open the Campaign for Governor at Waco, April 27, 1940. Miriam A. Ferguson file, Barker History Center, The University of Texas at Austin.

Tolchin, Susan and Martin. *Clout: Womanpower and Politics.* New York: G. P. Putnam, 1973.

Vaughn, Dick. "A Red Rose and the Ku Klux Klan." Houston *Press* (October 15, 1932): 2.

INTERVIEWS

Judge Robert Lee Bobbitt, Sr. and Ann Fears Crawford. San Antonio,
    July 1967.
Jim Bowmer and Ann Fears Crawford. Temple, June 1971.
Sam Houston Johnson and Ann Fears Crawford. Austin, February
    1976.
Lawrence P. Looney and Ann Fears Crawford. Austin, June 1977.
Judge W. A. Morrison and Ann Fears Crawford. Austin, June 1971.
George Nalle, Sr. and Ann Fears Crawford. Austin, November 1966.
Edmunds Travis and Ann Fears Crawford. Austin, July 1967.
Dorrace Ferguson Watt and Ann Fears Crawford. Austin, July 1971.

FOR GOVERNOR OF TEXAS

MRS. MIRIAM A. FERGUSON
OF TEMPLE

Courtesy Austin-Travis County Collection, Austin Public Library

Texas's "Petticoat Lobbyist"

 Jane Yelvington McCallum

In January 1927 Texas Governor Dan Moody appointed as his secretary of state the second woman to hold the office in the state of Texas. His choice for the ceremonial office was a logical one — Jane Yelvington McCallum, who had contributed her time, home, money, and influence to Moody's campaign, serving as head of the Texas Women's Citizens Committee of Dan Moody for Governor. As the organizing force behind the "Dan's the Man" clubs, McCallum established an organizational chart for each club to follow and instructed the members as to methods of contacting newspaper editors and women voters, using the poll lists. Moody awarded McCallum with the secretary of state's position, and she maintained it under his successor, Ross Sterling, holding the office from 1927 to 1933.

Governor Moody recognized Jane McCallum's dedicated service in the fight for women's suffrage, a lifelong commitment that for her included educational reform, prohibition, and reform of the child labor laws. Born on December 30, 1878 in La Vernia, Texas, Jane LeGette Yelvington could trace her family heritage in America to the American Revolution. For more than a hundred years her family had been active in literary, civic, and educational affairs in Texas, and her parents, Alvaro Leonard Yelvington and Mary Fullerton LeGette Yelvington encouraged their children to speak their thoughts during family discussions and to make up their own minds about issues and problems. Jane's intellectual growth was further stimulated at Zealey's Female College in Mississippi and at The University of Texas, where she studied journalism.

When Jane met the young La Vernia schoolteacher, Arthur Newell McCallum, she discovered that they shared an interest in Texas history, and Jane told him of the time that her father sat her on a fence post and told the whole family to watch a herd of cattle moving past their home. "It will be the last herd moving up the Chisholm Trail," her father prophesied; and it was. Jane and Arthur were married in 1896, and with her husband Jane moved first to Kenedy and then to Seguin, where A. N. McCallum served in the public schools before moving in 1903 to Austin to become the capital city's superintendent of public schools.

In Austin Jane McCallum settled down to rearing the couple's five children, but soon found that her involvement in civic affairs was playing an increasing part in her life. Her work with various club groups, including the American Association of University Women, the Colonial Dames, and Theta Sigma Phi, gave her a base to become active in the woman's movement to gain suffrage, and her interest in prohibition and the reform of child labor laws gave her the impetus to work within the political arena. So great was her commitment to women's suffrage that she resigned from many of her clubs and organizations to devote her entire energies to the movement. She later recalled that she had heard University of Texas English professor Stark Young lecture on how women "to accomplish even very small things . . . must concentrate on a few and give up many pleasures."

A concern for reform of the child labor laws and for the passage of prohibition taught McCallum the organizational abilities that she needed to spearhead promoting women's suffrage. Her diaries, kept in a rather haphazard fashion from 1916 to 1920, reflect and comment on the progress of the women's movement in Texas. Interspersed with her reports of political activities are notes that reflect a mother and homemaker's concern for her children, their activities, and events surrounding The University of Texas and the Austin public schools. Having her mother to help with the housekeeping made rearing five children somewhat easier, but still McCallum was present at football games and receptions for public school teachers as often as she was at legislative sessions. Once an irate senator, annoyed at the pressure women lobbyists were making over the suffrage question, asked her why she didn't remain at home and raise a family. Undaunted, McCallum looked him in the eye and replied, "I have five children. How many would you suggest I have?"

When she served as secretary of state she was constantly attending meetings, and a typical day during 1924 found McCallum attending a meeting of the Travis County Council of Women at Laguna Gloria, Clara Driscoll's home. She made her report, attended a meeting of the executive committee, ate lunch, and then rushed off to Clark Field for a baseball game, where one of her sons was playing. Then she was off to a tea and home finally to fix dinner for her family. Afterwards she attended a precinct meeting at Baker School, where she served on the committee to select delegates to the county convention, then dashed home to join her husband in entertaining out-of-town guests. Sundays might find her strolling leisurely with her family from their comfortable home on Austin's West Thirty-Second Street to Mount Bonnell.

McCallum recorded the history of the women's suffrage movement in Texas from its earliest beginnings in 1869 through the sustained push that began in 1903, when Annette Finnigan and her sisters organized the Equal Suffrage League in Houston and brought national suffrage leader Carrie Chapman Catt to lecture to Houston women in 1905. In 1903 the Texas Woman Suffrage Association was organized, but it became inactive when Finnigan left the state. The only group left alive was the Austin society with twenty-five members; in 1912 suffrage clubs were organized in San Antonio, Galveston, Waco, Dallas, Tyler, and San Marcos.

Women's organizations sponsored speakers on the suffrage question across the state, and by 1913 the San Antonio league sponsored a bill that was introduced in the legislature but never came to a vote. Opposition to women's suffrage centered around Governor James E. Ferguson, who was violently opposed to it, but the women suffrage leaders of the state continued to write to legislators soliciting their support for an amendment to the state constitution. With Minnie Fisher Cunningham heading the state congressional committee in 1915, the suffragists pressed for a vote in the House of Representatives. Representative Charles Metcalf fought for the issue and brought it to vote in the House, but failed to gain the two-thirds majority needed for passage.

Women's suffrage, had become one of the "leading political questions of the day," and in 1916 the group changed its name to the Texas Equal Suffrage Association. President "Minnie Fish" kept notes on legislators and their commitment to the women's suffrage cause, while "Jane Y" served as head of the ratification committee and worked with the press and publicity. The women suffrage leaders organized a sophisticated political campaign composed of letters to legislators, with McCallum calling for a Second Tuesday Suffrage Day each month. Under McCallum's leadership, the Austin Women's Suffrage Association solicited women to join their ranks and to pay the fifty cents fee to help sponsor a suffrage dance on May 19, 1916 at the Knights of Columbus Hall. Featured were such dances as the "Washington Waltz" and the "Texas Next Step."

When the legislative session opened in January 1916, the leaders of the women's groups were there to lobby effectively, expecting any legislation passed to be vetoed by their foe, Governor Ferguson. Impeachment proceedings against the governor, however, gave the leaders hope for their cause, and when Ferguson planned a speech to the Farmers's Institute to explain his veto of the appropriations for the state university, suffrage leaders strung orange banners in front of the capitol reading, "Women of Texas Protest."

McCallum attended a meeting at the University Club,

where everyone was discussing "Governor Ferguson's outrageous behavior in regard to vetoing the appropriations for The University of Texas," and she noted in her diary that, "We suffragists concluded that had we the vote, we'd impeach him — *or* rather force the legislature to do so." The suffragists realized their opportunity to rid government of an adamant foe of women's suffrage, and during the following months "Minnie Fish" called numerous meetings of the group to organize protests against Ferguson. So effective were the women that D. K. Woodward, Jr., leading the opposition to Ferguson, told McCallum:

> The impeachment of former Governor Ferguson could not have been brought about without the cooperation of the women of the State . . . The women were asked to reach the remote sections, to eradicate prejudice and leave understanding in its stead . . . They did all that was asked of them and more. The most confirmed skeptic on the question of women's participation in public life must have been converted had he witnessed the unselfish, tireless, efficient work of those hundreds of devoted women....

Cunningham decided that McCallum and Elisabeth Speer were the best lobbyists, and Jane determined to take public-speaking lessons to help her in presenting the suffrage issue to legislators and to various women's groups. In addition, she persuaded Hal Sevier, publisher of the Austin *American*, to allow her to write a column for the paper entitled "Suffrage Corner," although the editor of the paper, Edmunds Travis, was opposed to the passage of a women's suffrage amendment.

McCallum spent so much time working for Ferguson's impeachment and for the passage of the women's suffrage amendment that she became quite sensitive to criticism for her failure to support causes other than these. She noted in her diary on May 11, 1917 that she was asked to join other women in protesting sending soldiers to France to fight in World War I. She would not join the effort, noting that she felt that it would be cowardly for the soldiers not to go. Mrs. Ireland Graves rebuked her for being so "light-hearted," and McCallum went to her room and cried until she was "nearly sick." Throughout the suffrage fight McCallum often became so exhausted that her husband would call a halt and take her camping, or down to New Braunfels to enjoy the peacefulness of the Comal River.

By January 1918 the suffragists had intensified their efforts to get a federal amendment passed, and Texas women poured letters and telegrams into Washington to their congressmen. So intensive was the effort that Carrie Chapman Catt referred to it as the "heavy artillery down in Texas." On January 9, 1918 Mc-Callum noted in her diary that President Woodrow Wilson had spoken in favor of the amendment, and she commented, "Feel like I could walk to Washington just to give him a pat. Can it really be true?"

Realizing the importance of the Texas vote and with a friend of women's suffrage, William Pettus Hobby, in the governor's mansion, the women intensified their efforts. Mc-Callum was often sent to rural communities to speak to women's groups, and on one occasion she arrived in a nearby town to find only one light on. The proprietor of the local store took her to the school where she was to speak, assuring her that she was expected and that the women would appear as soon as they had finished "milking, strained away the milk, had supper, and washed up." Soon the women, with husbands and children in tow, arrived to listen to "Jane Y" speak.

With primary elections scheduled for July in Texas, Cunningham and other women suffragists established a headquarters at the Driskill Hotel and petitioned the governor to submit the issue to a vote during a special called session of the legislature in February. Hobby consented to do so, if the women could present him with a petition signed by a majority of the members of the House of Representatives and the Senate. When the women complied, Hobby submitted a bill drafted by Judge Ocie Speer of Forth Worth that would give Texas women the

right to vote in all primary elections and in all nominating conventions. Somewhat short of an equal suffrage bill, the Primary
Election Bill passed both houses and was signed into law by the
governor on March 26, 1918. Present at the occasion were the
bill's sponsor, Representative C. B. Metcalf of San Angelo, Mc-
Callum, Cunningham, Elizabeth Speer, and Nell H. Doom, the
leaders of the effort. After Hobby signed the bill, he presented
the silver embossed pen used for signing to Minnie Fisher Cunningham, but the most welcome accolade for their efforts came
from Wilson, who wired the suffragists: "Please accept my
warm congratulations on the adoption of the primary suffrage
bill by the state of Texas."

With little time left to prepare women to vote, the suffrage
leaders set up schools headed by Nell H. Doom, who earned the
nickname "The Ramrod" for her ability to get women effectively educated as to their voting rights. The group circulated
samples of ballots, studies of the issues, and candidate records,
and by election day some 306,000 Texas women were registered
— "surely a convincing answer to the statement that 'Southern
women do not want to vote'," McCallum commented.

McCallum lost eighteen pounds while busily organizing
sub-chairpersons to help get women to vote in the primary election, but she recorded ecstatically in her diary that

> The men just glory in our direct way and open way of
> doing things. They say that the day of the candidate
> with a shady record is certainly past. It never occurs to
> us to refuse to tell *who* we are for and *why*, and when
> we hear certain men are for Ferguson what is there to
> do but ask them. If they refuse to tell we put them
> down for him . . . .

She expanded her column in the Austin *American* to "Woman
and Her Ways," and by June 1918 was writing "Women in
Politics," certainly a captivating title for 1918, when American
women had not yet won the right to vote in national elections.

In October 1919 the Equal Suffrage Association became

the State League of Women Voters, and women suffragists turned their efforts to electing Will Hobby governor and Annie
Webb Blanton superintendent of public instruction for the state
of Texas. When the Nineteenth Amendment was passed and
women throughout the nation gained the right to vote in all
elections, the suffragists and members of leagues of women
voters across the state resolved that a joint legislative council
"composed of representatives of six statewide organizations
would be the quickest, most effective method of transforming
their recently acquired voting privilege into legislative power."
By 1922 the Texas League of Women Voters, the Federation of
Business and Professional Women's Clubs, the Women's Christian Temperance Union, the Texas Federation of Women's
Clubs, and the Texas Congress of Mothers and Parent-Teacher
Associations had formed the Women's Joint Legislative Council
and had acquired Senate Committee Room Five as their headquarters. Spurred by their newly-enfranchised status, the
women busily sent out press releases and interviewed legislators.
They were successful in passing through the Twenty-eighth
Legislature an emergency appropriation for public schools, re-
vised and strengthened prohibition laws, a bill providing for a
survey of conditions in Texas prisons, one for surveying the condition of public education, a provision for registering births,
and federal assistance for the care of expectant mothers and
newborn babies. So effective were they at their lobbying efforts
that legislators called them derisively, "The Petticoat Lobby," a
term that McCallum reveled in.

Called on to serve as head of the lobby effort, McCallum
refused, feeling that she was needed at home. The newspaper
column, family activities, and the suffrage fight had drained her
strength. In addition, she was learning to type. In August she
and her family vactioned at Camp Placid in New Braunfels, and
Jane took this time to assess her life and her activities, finding
herself in the typical quandary of many Americans following
World War I. She wrote in her diary:

. . . I wonder if the mere act of writing down one's problems can clarify them in a certain sense . . . I wonder if the world is really upside down and jigsawing around like everybody says or if it is just an age old cry against innovations, and the eternal clash between age and youth. I try so hard to get all points of view . . . .

The legislative council's work continued through the Twenty-ninth Legislature, with members actively interviewing candidates and pledging them to support their issues. They were successful in restoring an appropriation for the Gainesville State School for Girls, adding appropriations for rural schools, and strengthening laws prohibiting child labor in the state. In addition to working with the council, McCallum remained active in civic affairs. She campaigned throughout Austin in favor of the city-manager form of government which passed in 1924.

Faced with a choice between a Ku Klux Klan-backed candidate in the 1924 election and Miriam Ferguson, many suffragist leaders backed Mrs. Ferguson, although they continued to oppose Jim Ferguson's policies. When it became obvious that Miriam Ferguson was being directed by her husband, women leaders across the state changed their support to Dan Moody, attorney general under the Fergusons. Moody solicited the help of women leaders, and McCallum helped arrange a private luncheon for Moody and the women to discuss issues and the part that they could play in his campaign and administration. McCallum, seeing the campaign as one between Moody and Jim Ferguson, wrote Moody's aunt that she had lost eighteen pounds helping to defeat Ferguson before, and "I can easily lose 25 lbs. this time."

Serving as a member of the State Democratic Executive Committee, a delegate to Democratic national conventions, and a presidential elector strengthened McCallum's political ties with Democratic leaders, and when Moody appointed her secretary of state she saw it as not merely a ceremonial political position, but one in which she could serve as an inspiration to other women to seek political office. Many Texans honored her for finding the Texas Declaration of Independence, long forgotten in a state vault, and seeing that it was displayed for the public.

McCallum remained secretary of state under Governor Ross Sterling, who defeated Miriam Ferguson in 1930, and when the Fergusons entered the race again in 1932, McCallum spoke for Sterling over the radio, broadcasting across the state. On August 16, 1932 she spoke over WBAP-Fort Worth, telling voters that "Miriam Ferguson has never represented even a very small portion of the patriotic, intelligent womanhood of the state... Mrs. Ferguson never has and never can cause them aught but shame and humiliation." When Miriam Ferguson defeated Sterling in the second primary, McCallum was out of office, but not out of politics.

Throughout the 1940s she continued to keep the spirit of the suffragists alive and mourned the fact that women were often indifferent to civic affairs. Remembering the enthusiasm of the "petticoat lobby," McCallum called on women to put their intelligence and energy to use in national and local affairs. She commented:

> Women whose children have grown up have much free time they could devote to civic affairs. But I'm afraid they are not utilizing their talents much as those talents are needed.

She also cautioned women to study the issues and to vote for the candidate most qualified for the job, noting

> Never vote for a women just because she is a woman....It is the candidate's platform which is important — not the battle of the sexes ....

In 1945, when regents of The University of Texas fired President Homer P. Rainey, McCallum was one of those in the forefront protesting the move, and she and Minnie Fisher Cunningham signed a statement inquiring about the process used in confirming regents to the board of the state university. She remained active in civic affairs up to her death, and her last service was as a grand jury commissioner, appointed in 1957 by Judge Harris W. Gardner four days after the constitutional amendment passed authorizing women to serve on grand juries.

Her journalistic activities chronicled the women's suffrage movement and also the concerns of women throughout the 1930s and the 1940s. Her articles for the Austin *American-Statesman*, entitled "Women and War" and "Eve in the New Era" covered a miscellany of topics of interest to women, including social ills such as the treatments of the mentally ill and world affairs. "Women in Politics" was published in the "Texas Supplement" of the London *Times*, and she contributed a chapter on "Women Pioneers" to the *National History of Woman Suffrage*. She pioneered biographies of important Texas women, and published articles on Elisabet Ney, and a book, *All Texians Were Not Males*. Her book, *Women Pioneers*, was published by the Johnson Company in 1929. After her husband's death in 1943 she compiled biographical material on his life for the Austin Independent School District, and she continued as an active writer until her later years.

Jane McCallum, Texas's "Petticoat Lobbyist," died on August 14, 1957, and the editor of the Austin *American-Statesman*, Charles E. Green, wrote of her life:

> . . . She was a most vital woman . . . You who did not know her, some fraction of your life is better because she once lived, once worked in this community. She made everyone who worked in her vicinity a better person — and thus her accomplishments went ever beyond her own personal enterprises. She was a grand person, a fine lady. She had courage, backbone, and sweetness.

When women in Austin and Central Texas met for the annual Democratic Woman's Day celebration in 1957, the program was

232   *WOMEN IN TEXAS*

dedicated to Jane McCallum, who had spent a lifetime fighting for a woman's right to participate actively in government.

REFERENCES

"An Austin Woman Who Does Things." Unidentified clipping in Jane McCallum biographical file. Austin-Travis County Collection. Austin Public Library. Austin, Texas.

Anthony, Linda. "Women won battle in 1918." Austin *American-Statesman* (August 26, 1981): A-4.

"Austin Civic Leader Dies. Austin *American-Statesman* (August 15, 1957): A-1.

Barnes, Lorraine. "Leader of the Petticoat Lobby." *Texas Star* (October 3, 1971): 10-11.

Barns, Florence. "Jane Y. McCallum." *Texas Writers of Today*. Dallas: Tardy Publishing Company, 1933.

Bateman, Audray. "Texas suffragists fought hard for vote." Austin *American-Statesman* (August 26, 1981): A-4.

Bishop, Curtis. "Mrs. Jane McCallum Still Fights for Old Ideals — Recognition of Women." Austin *American-Statesman* (n.d.) Clipping in Jane McCallum biographical file. Austin-Travis County Collection, Austin Public Library, Austin, Texas.

Bowles, Willie D. *The History of the Woman Suffrage Movement in Texas.* (unpublished master's thesis). Austin: The University of Texas (August 1939).

"Civic Leader Rites Friday." Austin *American-Statesman* (August 15, 1957): A-3.

"Democratic Woman's Day Programs To Be Dedicated to Jane Y. McCallum." Austin *American-Statesman* (August 15, 1957): A-8.

"Funeral Tributes Scheduled." Austin *American-Statesman* (August 16, 1957): B-3.

Green, Charles E. "The 9th Column." Austin *American-Statesman* (August 16, 1957): A-1.

McCallum, Jane Y. "How 'Petticoat Lobby' Got Its Effective Start." Austin *American-Statesman* (July 29, 1946): 15.

McCallum, Jane Y. *Letter* to Mrs. J. B. Robertson. July 11, 1942. Copy in Jane McCallum biographical file. Austin-Travis County Collection. Austin Public Library, Austin, Texas.

McCallum, Jane Y. "Mrs. McCallum as Columnist Supports Rainey." Austin *American-Statesman* (May 26, 1946): 12.

McCallum, Jane Y. "Petticoat Lobby Gets in Action for Child Health." Austin *American-Statesman* (October 6, 1946): 17.

McCallum, Jane Y. "Primaries Opened To Women Voters By State Law in '18." Austin *American-Statesman* (October 13, 1946): 7.

McCallum, Jane Y. "Prison Reform Is Achievement of Petticoat Lobby." Austin *American-Statesman* (October 13, 1946): 9.

McCallum, Jane Y. "Should Delegation Disavowing Party Get Convention Seat?" Austin *American-Statesman* (April 30, 1944): 22.

McCallum, Jane. "The Texas Field for Writers." *Alcalde* (May 1930): 327-328.

McCallum, Jane. "Women in Politics: The Fight for Prohibition." London *Times* (Texas Supplement) (March 31, 1925): 47.

McCallum, Jane Y. "Why Put Lot of Doubt on Independence Declaration?" Austin *American-Statesman* (March 2, 1939): 1.

Moreland, Sinclair. "Jane Y. McCallum." *Texas Women's Hall of Fame*. Dallas: n.p., 1917.

"Mrs. McCallum Urges Fight Against Civic Indifference." Austin *American-Statesman* (July 18, 1948): 2.

"Notable Public Service This Texan's Monument." Austin *American-Statesman* (August 16, 1957): A-3.

"Records At Austin Prove Interesting." Dallas *Morning News* (July 10, 1943): 5.

Sager, Lois. "Petticoat Lobbyist Issues Some Tips." Dallas *Morning News* (January 20, 1946): 10.

Sager, Lois. "Women Do Dem Battles Like Their Menfolks." Dallas *Morning News* (September 13, 1944): 22.

Taylor, A. Elizabeth. "The Woman Suffrage Movement in Texas." *Journal of Southern History* (May 1951): 194-215.

Thornton, William M. "Party Members Sue For Right to Inspect Democratic Record." Dallas *Morning News* (May 19, 1944): 1.

Courtesy The Texas Collection, Baylor University.

"I Have Books
I Must Write"

Dorothy Scarborough

In 1925 the West Texas town of Sweetwater was in an uproar over the publication of a book about the devastating effects of the West Texas climate on a genteel Southern girl. *The Wind,* published by Harper and Brothers in New York, was selling rapidly across Texas and the Southwest, and speculation mounted concerning the identity of the author. The publishers had chosen to seek publicity for their realistic work of fiction by publishing it anonymously, and West Texans were outraged that the author of the book was not named. Knowledgeable Texans guessed the author was Dorothy Scarborough, a native Texan, who had used folksongs, regional Texas settings, realistic dialogue, and clear-cut characters in her previous works of fiction.

Lawyer R. C. Crane, the president of the West Texas Historical Association, wrote an article that appeared in major Texas newspapers including the Dallas *Morning News* stating that the author was at fault in regard to local and natural history and showed a "deplorable ignorance" of the region. Dorothy Scarborough, again writing anonymously, defended her work, asking Crane, "Has the West Texas wind got on your nerves, Mr. Crane, and the sand blinded you to the difference between a novel and a historical treatise? . . . ," and quoted from other reviewers who had compared her book to those of Thomas Hardy. She cited reviews that called the work, "A piece of masterly realism that rings true" and stated that it "contains many elements of colossal greatness . . . . "

The second edition of *The Wind* released in 1926 carried the author's name, and Scarborough revealed that she had agreed to publishing the original manuscript without her name when the publishers suggested that it would help sales. She wrote to William H. Biggs, her editor at Harper and Brothers:

> I am delighted you like my book . . . Fact is, I like it myself! . . . I have faith in it and believe that if it is properly presented to the public it will reach a good audience. It is different from the conventional story and it is genuine . . . .

Sales of the book began to drop, and Scarborough expressed her disappointment that the publishers had not exploited the mystery surrounding the authorship of the book to more advantage. When *The Wind* was sold to MGM as a vehicle for Lillian Gish, Scarborough worked on the screenplay with her brother, George Moore Scarborough, and she and Gish became great friends. The actress and her mother later came to New York, and Scarborough wrote to Texas for an authentic barbecue recipe to serve them.

Lillian Gish had read the book and taken it to MGM suggesting that the producers make a motion picture from the story. It was filmed in the Mojave Desert, and the actors and film crew experienced the intense heat and wind that Scarborough had so realistically portrayed. In 1928 the writer also felt the effects of the West Texas climate when the Sweetwater Chamber of Commerce invited her to speak to the group. She charmed her audience, and when Judge Crane took her on a tour to point out her numerous errors concerning climate and geography, a West Texas norther blew in and ended their conversation.

Magazine articles explored the story of how the writer from

Texas began her novel of the Southern heroine Letty Mason and her destruction by the West Texas climate. When Edna Ferber and Scarborough were riding together in a taxi on the way to a writers' luncheon, Ferber mentioned that she was nervous. ''It must be the wind,'' the Texan commented and mentioned the novel she had planned about West Texas. The two authors arrived at the luncheon and Ferber introduced the Texas writer, mentioning that she planned a novel about the wind. Scarborough went home and immediately began to write the book.

In the wake of Scarborough's novel, magazine and newspaper stories also explored the writer's background, many concentrating on the uniqueness of the writer's having begun her career as a teacher and writer in Texas and then having taught at New York's Columbia University. Uniqueness had been nothing new to Emily Dorothy Scarborough from the time she was born on January 27, 1878 in the tiny community of Mount Carmel, Texas. She was the daughter of an East Texas lawyer, John B. Scarborough, and his wife, Mary Adelaide Ellison Scarborough. The couple's eldest child, Ellison Bledsoe, died when he was young, but their other three, including the youngest, Emily Dorothy, had superior educations and all had a decided literary bent.

Martha Douglass studied modern languages at Vassar and then taught at Baylor University. She married George White McDaniel, who served as pastor of the First Baptist Church in Richmond, Virginia for twenty years. Martha McDaniel wrote three novels, her husband's biography, and a volume of poetry. George Moore Scarborough led an even more illustrious literary life. Graduating from The University of Texas Law School he practiced journalism and served with the U.S. Department of Justice. Displaying an unusual amount of daring and courage, he cleaned up a gambling ring and used his remarkable experiences in the plays he then wrote for Broadway. In 1912 his first play, *The Lure,* was produced and was as sensational a success as his sister's novel, *The Wind.* After writing and adapting a number of plays for the stage, he moved to Hollywood to write for the screen, collaborating with his sister on the screenplay of her novel.

When "Dottie" was still a young girl, her parents moved the family to Sweetwater, Texas in search of a cure for Mary Adelaide Scarborough's weak lungs. Dorothy Scarborough would later recount that

> . . . *The Wind* has its real origins in the impressions I got from hearing my mother's vivid accounts of her struggles with the climate of the West. She loved the people out there, but she did not care for the weather. . . .

Mary Adelaide's health improved, and the Scarboroughs moved to Waco in order to give their children the advantages of the educational institutions there, particularly Baylor University. A typical tomboy, "Dottie" was often found perched high in a tree scribbling stories for her family's entertainment. "I always wanted to write," she recalled later, and her parents encouraged all their children in their literary pursuits. She attended Baylor University, and when her parents died she boarded with family friends until she could complete her education.

Scarborough was granted both her bachelor's and master's degrees from Baylor and received the Burleson Fellowship in 1896. She contributed her first short piece, "A Visit to Hades," to the Baylor literary magazine in March 1893 when she was only fifteen, and she continued to be an outstanding student of literature. She taught English courses while working on her master's degree and served as editor of the literary magazine. She combined teaching classes at Baylor, including beginning the first college journalism course in the state, with postgraduate work at the University of Chicago and travel abroad.

One of the innovations that she brought to Baylor was the Modern Writers Club. The students wrote to author Frank R. Stockton concerning his famous short story, *The Lady or the Tiger?* Stockton graciously wrote to Scarborough thanking her

students for settling the question that had confounded millions
of readers and telling her that "people in the North are apt to
say it was the lady, while my readers in the South are likely to
favor the tiger." Stockton also advised her not to publish, as she
was only twenty years old and he felt it was better "to study and
to practice composition, but not to print for several years to
come."

The year 1910 was a pivotal one for the young Texas
teacher, for she took a leave of absence and entered Oxford
University as a special student. At the time Oxford did not grant
degrees to women, and Scarborough experienced the
discrimination against women still present in the academic
world. In later life Scarborough became an ardent champion of
women's rights but felt that women had to do more and do better than men to get equal recognition. She explored this theme
in her serial, *The Unfair Sex*, published in 1925 in *The
Woman's Viewpoint*, a publication devoted to women's issues.
The heroine, Nancy Carroll, called "Ginger," is an
autobiographical portrait of Scarborough herself, and Ginger's
adventures parallel those of Scarborough, including studying at
Oxford and a youthful crush on an English instructor. Ginger is
a forceful, determined, young woman who comments, "If they
[the boys] couldn't treat her right, she wouldn't play."

The Oxford experience was an exhilarating one for Scarborough, expanding her intellectual horizons and bringing her
into contact with English authors such as Christopher Morley.
When she returned to Baylor she began a lifelong study of
folklore, and in 1912 published a group of poems, *Fugitive
Verses*, that celebrated black folksongs. She was a charter
member of the Texas Folklore Society and in 1916 served as
president of the group.

Although Baylor promoted her to the rank of assistant professor, Scarborough was determined to complete her doctoral
dissertation. She obtained another year's leave to complete the
residency work on her doctorate at Columbia, and in 1917 her
dissertation, *The Supernatural in Modern English Fiction*, was
published by G. P. Putnam's Sons. With the publication of her

book by a New York publisher Scarborough was invited to teach at Columbia, and she taught courses in the short story and the novel. In 1923 she was appointed assistant professor with an expanded course load, and in 1931 she was made associate professor, the second highest-ranking woman faculty member. While in New York she served as a member of the staff of "Books and the Book World" for the New York *Sun,* and her study of modern fiction brought her into contact with the ideas of Sigmund Freud which were influencing twentieth-century writing.

Scarborough planned a trilogy dealing with the evils of the tenant farmer system and the need for cooperatives to ease the financial burden of the South's cotton farmers. She took a six-month's leave of absence to explore the cotton industry in the South, and in 1923 *In the Land of Cotton* was published, followed by *Can't Get a Red Bird* and *The Stretch-berry Smile.* In 1934 Harper and Brothers published her children's book, *The Story of Cotton.* Although her novels never approached the fame of Frank Norris's trilogy on wheat, the books concerning the cotton industry portrayed the plight of the tenant farmer and the need for reforms within the industry to aid the agricultural South.

Scarborough was beginning to gain a reputation as a regional writer for her portrayal of the Texas environment, and in 1923 she returned to her native state to receive an honorary doctorate from Baylor University, and to serve as commencement speaker at The University of Texas. She was a guest of Governor Pat M. Neff at the Texas governor's mansion, and after visiting friends in Waco she returned to New York to her teaching, book reviewing for the *Bookman* and *Dial* magazines, and completing work on *The Wind* and a collection of black folksongs. She founded a writers' club at Columbia and introduced students and writers to one another at gatherings in her apartment. Her students often had the opportunity to exchange ideas and comments with such authors as Christopher Morley, Edna Ferber, and Hamlin Garland. She maintained a lifelong correspondence with many of these same students, encouraging their efforts and criticizing their work.

Even while Scarborough was planning her next writing project, she carried a heavy teaching load at Columbia, concentrating on the novel and the short story. Among her students were the future folklorist, Roark Bradford, who later wrote *This Side of Jordan,* and Carson McCullers, who took her first writing course under Scarborough and later wrote acclaimed short stories and plays set in the South.

In an interview with Mary Moore-Sifford, writing for the Dallas *Morning News* Scarborough was quoted as saying, "I wouldn't teach if I didn't like it," but she admitted that it took a good deal of time from her writing. She spent her summers traveling throughout the South collecting folksongs and tales, or writing at her eighteen-room farmhouse in the Berkshires. She also recorded a series of radio talks on folklore and writing for a New York radio station. In her interview with Moore-Sifford she spoke out strongly in favor of a regional literature, pointing out that the South possessed everything to sponsor a regional literature except publishing companies. It had writers of great talent, an unexplored literary territory, and a growing leisure class that would support literature. She was quick to condemn Northern critics who described Southern literature as too full of "mockingbirds and magnolias," for she felt that the South was changing and its literature with it. She cited William Faulkner as one of the new breed of Southern writers.

Scarborough herself never pretended to be anything but a regional writer, basing her stories in the South and West but embracing themes that were universal. She remained throughout her life a transplanted Southerner who deplored the evils of city life and remained staunchly devoted to her Baptist faith. She once commented that, "In New York you need your religion more than you ever did before."

She also needed a place of retreat from the impersonal city, and her farm in the Berkshires, replete with its early American furniture and apple orchards, became the haven where she could concentrate on her novels and folklore. Being Dorothy

Scarborough she saw in her New England farmhouse a touch of the old South and wrote to a friend:

> . . . The thing that tempted me to buy the place was the wide porches that stretch across the front of the house and the great pillars that are more like the colonial architecture of the South than New England . . . .

She thought about beginning a series of informal essays entitled *From a Northern Porch,* to serve as a companion piece to *From a Southern Porch,* the book she had published in 1919, designed to be read on a friendly Southern porch. Scarborough's essays reflect a humor lacking in her more serious work, a lively view of life in the South, and a tongue-in-cheek attitude toward smalltown life.

It was from New England that she set out on her journeys collecting and recording folklore and folksongs. Baylor University's Texas Collection contains a photograph of Scarborough on one of her visits to the mountain people. She is pictured riding sidesaddle, and the author wrote on the picture, "Notice I ride sidesaddle — mountain etiquette doesn't hold with womanfolks ridin' *[sic]* like men!" Folklore, which became an interest of hers during her Texas days, became a consuming passion during her later years. In 1925, the same year that saw the publication of *The Wind,* Harvard University Press published *On the Trail of Negro Folk Songs,* Scarborough's collection of black folklore.

Commenting on the latter book, Dorothy Scarborough once said, "Folksongs have to be wheedled and coaxed and wooed with all manner of blandishments and flatteries," and she researched black lore and folksongs until her death. Her novels are filled with authentic folklore and songs, and the plaintive cowboy ballad, "Bury Me Not on the Lone Prairie," became one of the leitmotifs for her book *The Wind.* She wrote the entry on black folklore for *The Encyclopedia Britannica* and interviewed W. C. Handy on black music. Her lifelong study of folklore is manifested in all her novels, and *The Wind* in particular is filled with haunting folk refrains, black dialect, and Mexican expressions such as " 'Sta bueno!"

Mexicans, blacks, cowboys, plantation owners, and strong frontier women all populate her novels, and her descriptions of bluebonnets, horned toads, buffalo clover, and jack rabbits reflect an authentic feel for Texas. The traditional conservative Western values are strong in Texas, and Scarborough's novels are imbued with such values, along with the myths of the frontier. As Sylvia Ann Grider points out in the original draft of her introduction to the recent reprint of *The Wind,* the Texan portrays a naturalistic, hard-scrabble determinism in the novel. The book's heroine, Letty Mason, remains Scarborough's most clearcut character, and her defeat by the wind shows the strong force that the hard life on the frontier exerts on all who come in contact with it.

With attention to detail Scarborough depicts the defeat of Letty Mason, a sheltered, cultured Southern woman, by the harsh elements and rough life of West Texas. While she illustrates sandstroms and isolation defeating a woman, she also shows the devastating effect of droughts, blizzards, and falling cattle prices on the men of the West. As Grider states, "Texas is portrayed as harsh, cruel, tyrannical, and destructive." Letty Mason embodies the high ideals and cultured life of the South, and her search for beauty and love is defeated by the harsh realities of life on the plains.

Although Letty Mason succumbs to the driving force of the West Texas wind, many of the women in Scarborough's novel stand strong against the elements and embody the frontier virtues of strength and determination. Cora, who marries Letty Mason's cousin, personifies the rough, determined woman who accepts her fate, adapts to it, and survives the elements. Cora not only thrives on her harsh existence, she serves as a bulwark between her husband and the harrowing environment. Still, it is Letty Mason, the personification of gentleness and culture, who is the heroine of the story, and she is defeated by the relentless force of the wind. As Scarborough describes the theme of her book,

The wind was the cause of it all . . . How could
a fair, sensitive woman fight the wind? How oppose a
wild shouting voice that never let her know the peace
of silence? — a resistless force that was at her all the
day, a naked, unbodied wind—like a ghost more terrible because visible—that wailed to her across waste
places in the night, calling her like a demon lover?

Scarborough's next novel, *The Unfair Sex,* was published
only in serial form, and Nancy Carroll or "Ginger" is far less a
compelling heroine than Letty Mason. The author, however,
uses the novel to advance her views on the role of women in a
man's world, and to show that discrimination against women
exists both in the country and in the city. Like many writers of
the early twentieth century Scarborough espoused the view that
the city represented evil and that goodness and virtue existed
only in smalltown America.

She explores this theme to its fullest in her novel *Impatient
Griselda,* published by Grosset and Dunlap in 1927. Based on
the legend of Lilith, the demon wife of Adam, *Impatient
Griselda* is a tragic love story that spans two generations of Central Texas people. Lilith in the novel is seduced and becomes
pregnant in New York, where she dies tragically in childbirth.
To Scarborough there were basically two types of women — the
selfish and the unselfish; and her final novel expands her idea
that it is the selfish and strong whose influence prevails.

Scarborough next edited a collection of short stories that
was published in 1935 and continued her research on black
folklore and songs. In 1930 the Council on Research in the
Humanities at Columbia awarded her a grant to continue her
collecting and editing of folklore, and she worked diligently on
her book, *A Song Catcher in Southern Mountains,* spending an
entire two years revising her manuscript. She neglected her
health during her travels through the mountain areas and
became seriously ill in the fall of 1935. She died on November
7, 1935, and the revision of her manuscript was completed by
two of her colleagues. They quoted her as saying only a short

time before her death, "Why, I have books I must write that will take me more than a lifetime!" She was planning another novel at the time of her death, and Columbia University Press published *A Song Catcher in Southern Mountains* posthumously in 1937.

At the memorial service at Columbia one minute of silence was observed in her memory, and then the writer who had written so much about Central Texas came home to Texas to be buried in the family plot in Waco. Her work in black folklore stands as her most memorable contribution, and her novel *The Wind* remains one of the most realistic portraits of the Texas frontier in the 1880s. Her tragic heroine, Letty Mason, was reintroduced to Texans when The University of Texas Press reprinted *The Wind* in 1979, and *Texas Woman* magazine serialized the novel in three installments.

Although the popularity of many of Scarborough's works has died out, she remains a "writer of place" who depicted her native Texas and the Southwest as the harsh environment that it was. She has been ranked with Mary Austin and Willa Cather as an outstanding woman writer of Southwestern fiction. She wrote with a sense of realism about women and the countryside in opposition to the often romantic view espoused by other writers. Like Mary Austin she works the rich tapestry of the Southwest in both a colorful, yet realistic, fashion. Her reputation remains secure with the realistic portrayal of her heroine, Letty Mason, and to many Texans Dorothy Scarborough will always be remembered as the woman who wrote *The Wind* and outraged a state.

REFERENCES

Beard, Joyce Juanita. *Dorothy Scarborough: Texas Regionalist.* Unpublished master's thesis. Fort Worth: Texas Christian University, 1965.

Cranfill, Mable. "Dorothy Scarborough: An Account of the Career of the Most Representative Texas Novelist and Teacher." *The Texas Monthly,* IV (September 1929): 213-227.

Cranfill, Mable. "Dorothy Scarborough — An Appreciation." Baylor *Bulletin*, XL (August 1937): 38-45.

Dixon, Arline Harris. *The Development of the Novel: Lectures of Dorothy Scarborough.* Unpublished master's thesis. Waco: Baylor University, 1943.

Ferguson, Charles W. "Miss Scarborough Trails the Elusive Folk-Song." *Books and Bookmen* (undated clipping). Dorothy Scarborough file. Barker History Center. The University of Texas at Austin, Austin, Texas.

Grider, Sylvia Ann. *Introduction to the Wind.* Original typescript. The Texas Collection, Baylor University, Waco, Texas.

Moore-Sifford, Mary. "Dorothy Scarborough Is Champion of Southern Writers." Dallas *Morning News* (February 10, 1929): 22.

Muncy, Elizabeth Roberta. *Dorothy Scarborough: A Literary Pioneer.* Unpublished master's thesis. Waco: Baylor University, 1940.

Neatherline, James William. *Dorothy Scarborough: Form and milieu in the work of a Texas writer.* Unpublished doctoral dissertation. Ann Arbor: University of Michigan, 1973.

Scarborough, Dorothy. *Impatient Griselda.* New York: Grosset and Dunlap, 1927.

Scarborough, Dorothy. *Letter* to William H. Briggs of Harper and Brothers, New York, April 28, 1925. The Texas Collection. Baylor University, Waco, Texas.

Scarborough, Dorothy. *Letter* to C. A. Hubbard of Chapel Hill, North Carolina, August 8, 1935. The Texas Collection. Baylor University, Waco, Texas.

Scarborough, Dorothy. "The Unfair Sex," (serial). *The Woman's Viewpoint* (November-June 1925): various pages.

Scarborough, Dorothy. *The Wind* (reprint). Austin: The University of Texas Press, 1979.

Shook, Virginia. "Dorothy Scarborough Has Fingers in Many Literary Pies." Dallas *Herald-Tribune* (March 17, 1935): 6.

Smith, Goldie Capers. "Dorothy Scarborough." *The Creative Arts in Texas: A Handbook of Biography.* Dallas: Cokesbury Press, 1926.

Stockton, Frank R. *Letter* to Dorothy Scarborough from Charleston, West Virginia, December 12, 1899. The Texas Collection, Baylor University, Waco, Texas.

Whitcomb, Virginia Rowland. *Dorothy Scarborough: Biography and Criticism.* Unpublished master's thesis. Waco: Baylor University, 1945.

Dorothy Scarborough

"Mrs. Secretary"

Oveta Culp Hobby

When President Dwight D. Eisenhower named Oveta Culp Hobby as the nation's first secretary of Health, Education, and Welfare in April 1953, U.S. Senator Lyndon Johnson and Senator Price Daniel joined in presenting Hobby to the senators who confirmed her appointment. "She's the type of woman you'd like to have for a daughter or a sister, a wife or a mother, or the trustee of your estate," Johnson told his fellow senators. Throughout her lifetime positions of respect and responsibility have been Oveta Hobby's, and self-assurance has marked her progress from a smalltown Central Texas girl to the publisher of one of Texas's largest daily newspapers.

Born on January 19, 1905 in Killeen, Texas, Oveta was the second of the seven children of Isaac William Culp and his wife, Emma Hoover Culp. Her mother named her Oveta, an Indian word for "forget," after a character in a romantic novel and because the named rhymed with that of the Culp's first daughter, Juanita. Oveta grew up the pampered favorite of an adoring father, surrounded by books. The family had to pull her away from reading to go for Sunday afternoon drives or to attend movies, but by the time she was in the sixth grade she had such a command of the language that when her teacher announced the prize for the best speller would be a handsome Bible, Oveta told her that she might as well write her name in the Bible there and then. True to her word, by the end of the school term, the Bible was hers.

Emma Hoover Culp was one of Texas's dedicated suffragists and an active campaigner for the young gubernatorial candidate Will Hobby, when he ran against Jim Ferguson in 1918. Oveta recalls her mother, dressed in a neat blue suit, white straw hat, and white gloves telling her daughters that the summer peaches had to be canned and that the job was their responsibility. She was off to campaign for Will Hobby.

When Ike Culp, a popular lawyer throughout the Central Texas area, was elected to the state legislature in 1919, Oveta accompanied him to Austin, still managing to graduate from high school at the top of her class. The world of politics and law fascinated her, and when Culp was elected to a second legislative term, Oveta left Mary Hardin-Baylor College and joined her father in Austin, where she audited courses at The University of Texas law school. Her legal and legislative experience proved helpful when she went to work codifying bank laws for the Texas State Banking Department, and later as a clerk for the judiciary committee of the Texas House of Representatives. She was appointed by the Speaker of the House as parliamentarian in 1925 and kept the job for six years. She served again as parliamentarian during the 1939 and 1941 legislative sessions, and later wrote a book on parliamentary procedure, *Mr. Chairman*, which was used as a textbook in public schools both in Texas and Louisiana.

Expanding her political activities, Oveta worked with local Democratic organizations in Houston and participated in the National Democratic Convention held in Houston in 1928. She commuted to the Bayou City from Austin, sharing a room with Florence Sterling, an ardent suffragist and sister of Ross Sterling, president of Humble Oil and Refining Company and later governor of Texas. When Sterling bought the Houston *Dispatch* in 1925 and the Houston *Post* in 1926, combining them as the Houston *Post-Dispatch*, he installed William Pettus Hobby, former Texas governor and longtime newspaperman, as president.

Oveta began working in the circulation department of the *Post*, and in 1929 she announced that she was a candidate for the state legislature from Harris County. Her defeat by a Klan-backed candidate, who regaled his campaign audiences with tales of her experiences as a "parliamentarian," caused her to abandon elective politics. Working for the *Post* brought her into contact with Will Hobby, who had been a friend of her father's and whose wife, Willie Cooper Hobby, had died in 1929. Soon the two were attending concerts, plays, and other social events in Houston, and on February 23, 1931 they were wed.

Oveta Hobby later commented that her father warned her prospective husband that she had little interest in clothes and would embarrass him by not dressing up. During the years of their marriage, however, Oveta cultivated a personal style of her own, which included stunning hats; took elocution lessons to soften her Texas twang; and learned to manage a large household establishment, while keeping her hand in politics and maintaining ever-increasing responsibilites at the Houston *Post*. She was active in Houston social circles, working with the Junior League and becoming a patroness of the Houston symphony, still managing to find time to serve as state president of the League of Women Voters.

Oveta married Will Hobby at a particularly low ebb in his business fortunes; he was facing bankruptcy as a result of an unfortunate venture in an insurance company. Becoming the other working half of the "Hobby Team," she wrote a syndicated column on parliamentary law, rose from research editor to book editor to assistant editor; and then was appointed executive vice president by *Post* board chairman J.E. Josey. Emphasizing women's news, she changed the format and many of the departments of the *Post* and helped her husband by serving as an executive director of his radio station KPRC; and as his interest in radio and banking increased she gradually took over the management of the Houston *Post*.

Visiting New York in 1941 for a convention of the American Newspaper Publishers Association, Oveta Hobby commented to a reporter, "It is not so difficult to combine matrimony and a career in a small city like Houston," but she went on to prove that she could add the responsibilities of motherhood. Never letting down on her political commitments, even appearing at her desk at the *Post* in a neck brace as a result of a riding accident, she gave birth on her own birthday, January 19, 1932 to William Pettus Hobby, Jr. Governor Hobby was overjoyed and commented to his wife, "I had no idea babies were so popular, or I would have had them in my platform." Five years later, and again on her birthday, Oveta gave birth to a daughter, Jessica Oveta Hobby.

When Will Hobby acquired ownership of both the *Post* and radio station KPRC, Oveta helped with reorganization of the business departments of both the "Hobby Team's" ventures. In addition, she expanded her writing interest to interpretation of current events both on the national and the international scene, commenting on such diverse subjects as Turkey's constitution and Britain's pact with Egypt. Under her direction the *Post* began covering events important to Houston's black community and featuring blacks in newspaper stories. Even with growing responsibilities at the newspaper and with rearing her children, she found time to pursue legal studies at Houston's South Texas School of Law.

The Hobbys became increasingly opposed to President Franklin Roosevelt's New Deal, and they lent support to Wendell Willkie when he ran against Roosevelt in the president's bid for a third term. When Roosevelt was reelected, however, the *Post* called for national unity behind the president and for preparedness in the face of war. On July 30, 1940 Oveta was appointed to a dollar-a-year job in Washington as head of the newly created women's interest section of the Bureau of Public Relations of the War Department. She was stationed in the munitions building, and her office turned out stories for women news commentators and kept track of items that would be of interest to women. One of her main jobs was to prove to American mothers that the army provided for the welfare of their sons; and her staff, soon convinced that Oveta Hobby could more than handle the job assigned to her, called her the "Charming Chief."

Oveta was on her way home to join her husband and

children when word reached her of the bombing of Pearl Harbor. She never made it home, but returned to Washington to help the War Department establish a Women's Army Auxiliary Corps. Before the Congressional committee considering legislation proposed by Congresswoman Edith Nourse Rogers she testified that the "army could not rely on haphazard, unorganized voluntary assistance from women." On May 12, 1942 the Women's Auxiliary Army Corps was organized, and on May 16 Secretary of War Henry Stimson appointed Oveta Culp Hobby as director of the corps with the rank of colonel.

By September 1942 Hobby was engaged in meetings with army staff officers and in representing the WAAC's before the Military Affairs Committee in Congress. Explaining that "this is a serious job for serious women," Hobby pushed for and received a listing of some 239 jobs that women were certified to fill, enabling her to expand the corps from a few thousand women to 100,000. She instituted the famed billed army hat known as the "Hobby hat," and when soldiers gawked at pink lingerie hanging on the washlines, she ordered khaki underwear for her troops.

The WAVES and the SPARS were organized as a result of successful recruiting on the part of the WACs, which dropped the "Auxiliary" from its name in 1943 when the force received full army status. Time and time again Colonel Hobby had to fight army brass for equal treatment for her "G. I. Janes," and when officials decreed that women who became "pregnant without permission" while serving in the WACs would be dishonorably discharged with loss of rights and pay, she successfully defended her women, pointing out that male soldiers who fathered illegitimate children should receive the same treatment. She won her point, and WACs who became pregnant were granted honorable discharges.

Hobby took seven-year-old Jessica to Washington with her, while teenager William remained at home in Houston with his father. By 1945 Hobby was exhausted, and she resigned her command. On December 31, 1944 she was awarded the Distinguished Service Medal, the third highest decoration that the army gives; she was the first army woman to receive the medal. In 1972, when her son was running for lieutenant governor of Texas, she told one reporter of her pride in the medal plus the Philippine Merit Medal she received. "Democracy is a wonderful thing. All of us ought to bear military service," she stated, pointing out that she felt that in the future women would be drafted.

Houston welcomed Hobby home with a testimonial dinner which included congratulatory telegrams from General Eisenhower, President Truman, and General George C. Marshall. Oveta referred to Will Hobby as "my partner, my friend, my husband," and cited his active supportiveness that had allowed her to fulfill her army duties without the extra care of household responsibilities. Soon the "Hobby Team" was reorganizing the *Post*, supporting the United Nations, and encouraging a move by the Texas legislature to support states rights. Oveta became so active in conservative Democratic politics that Houston reporters speculated that she might run for governor of Texas. She served as the first woman director of the American Society of Newspaper Editors, and on November 10, 1948 she was named president of the Southern Newspaper Publishers Association. She also was appointed to the United Nations Conference on Freedom in Information, served as a consultant for the Bipartisan Committee on the Organization of the Executive Branch, and served on the board of directors of the Citizens Committee for the Hoover Report, an attempt at governmental reorganization.

During the 1948 presidential campaign the Hobbys found little to admire in Harry S Truman, the candidate of the Democratic party; editorials on the front page of the *Post* warned that Texas's offshore oil lands, the tidelands, were in danger of being lost and that the Republicans were the answer to their safety. Oveta visited with Thomas E. Dewey in Dallas, and the Republican candidate promised that, if elected, he would approve a tidelands quitclaim bill. When Truman won the election and the Supreme Court ruled in a California tidelands case that the federal government had paramount rights in oil lands offshore a state's borders, the Hobbys deplored the usurpation of what they considered to be purely a states rights issue.

Early in 1952 Dallas oilman Sid Richardson traveled to SHAPE headquarters in Paris to convince General Dwight D. Eisenhower to run for the presidency — as the candidate of the Democratic party. Texas Republican Jack Porter, however, assured the Texas party that Eisenhower would run as a Republican, and the Hobbys conducted a poll in the *Post* that showed that a majority of their readers favored Eisenhower. As the new coeditor and publisher of the *Post*, Oveta announced her support of Eisenhower well in advance of the nominating convention, supported him and his policies favoring state ownership of the tidelands, and published a political primer which was instrumental in getting pro-Eisenhower Texans into many Republican precincts.

The Eisenhower Republicans met strong opposition from "Old Guard" Republicans who favored Senator Robert Taft; but when the Texans arrived at the Chicago convention, Porter and his contesting delegation of Eisenhower supporters were seated. Governor Allan Shivers and Texas attorney general Price Daniel organized "Texas Democrats for Eisenhower," and Oveta Hobby spent months working at the national headquarters of Citizens for Eisenhower in New York. Will Hobby continued to support Eisenhower on the editorial and front pages of the *Post*, and on November 4, 1952 Eisenhower won the presidential nomination, with Texas bolting to the Republican column.

On November 25, 1952 Eisenhower appointed Oveta Culp Hobby as administrator of the Federal Security Agency, the department of the federal government in charge of the health, education, and economic security of individual citizens. Texas governor Allan Shivers said of her appointment that it was one in which all Texans could take pride, citing Hobby's "invaluable service to the Eisenhower political campaign."

Plans were in the making to raise the agency to Cabinet status, and Eisenhower asked Hobby to attend Cabinet meetings and sent a request to Congress to raise her status.

When Health, Education, and Welfare became part of the Cabinet, "Mrs. Secretary," as Hobby preferred to be called, began a grueling six-day-a-week schedule that included both inaugurating new programs and dismantling Democratic plans advocating a health insurance plan that she felt bordered on socialized medicine. By March 22, 1954 she was drafting a new bill dealing with health insurance, to encourage private insurance companies to offer greater protection.

While her son William completed his work at Rice Institute, daughter Jessica lived in Washington with her mother and attended school. When Hobby was chosen, along with Mamie Eisenhower, as one of the best-dressed women in America, Jessica expressed her embarrasment at having such a well-dressed mother. To American women, however, a Cabinet member who wore fashionable hats to her redecorated mulberry-and-cream office, lunched at her desk on cottage-cheese and fruit salad, and had her hair done at Elizabeth Arden's was newsworthy. As the second woman Cabinet member in the nation's history, her words and actions often made headlines. The male members of the Cabinet, who noted her arrival at Cabinet meetings in a government-owned, powder-blue Cadillac limousine, often greeted her entrance with: "Here comes baby blue and you know who!"

Controversy marked the final days of Hobby's tenure as secretary of HEW. When the recently-developed polio vaccine, named for its creator Dr. Jonas Salk, was released for general use, fourteen children died from allergic reactions to the new medication. Hobby expressed her heartbreak over the deaths, removed the vaccine from use, allowed time for further testing, and then returned the medication to the market. The national uproar was much like the swine flu crisis, she recalled, but the decrease in deaths from polio among both children and adults was well worth the wait.

Will Hobby became ill, and Oveta resigned her Washington position and returned to active control of the Houston *Post*. When Secretary of the Treasury George M. Humphrey received word of her resignation, he said, "What! The best man in the Cabinet resigning?'' She returned to Houston and more honors for her success as a Cabinet member. Texas businesswomen had named her an Outstanding Texas Woman in 1951, and she received honorary doctorates from Bard College and the college she attended many years before, Mary Hardin-Baylor. In 1967 she was named the first woman to serve on the board of trustees of Rice University, and she was a member of the board of regents of Southwest Texas State Teachers College. In 1966 she was elected to the board of directors of General Foods Corporation and served on the board on the board of trustees of the Mutual Insurance Company and as a director of General Aniline and Film Corporation. *Harper's Bazaar* named her one of ''100 American Women of Accomplishment,'' and in 1968 President Lyndon Johnson named her to the Public Broadcasting Board. In October 1978 she was presented with the George Catlett Marshall Medal for Public Service, the highest award given by the Association of the U.S. Army and awarded for ''selfless and outstanding service'' to the nation. She was the nineteenth recipient of this award and the first woman.

Although she began to resign some of her corporate offices as she approached her seventies, Oveta Culp Hobby still remains chairman of the board of the Houston *Post*, running the multimedia corporation while her son serves as lieutenant governor of Texas. She lost a legal battle over deed restrictions in her neighborhood and had her large family mansion torn down. Moving to a townhouse, where she lives among her collection of magnificent antiques, silver, and paintings, she is still known for her regal posture, her fashionable clothes and hats, and her magnificent manner that earned her the tribute from one Texas writer: ''The Last of the Great Ladies.''

REFERENCES

Brinkerhoff, Mary. ''Volunteers Won't Be Replaced by Machine, Lady Editor Says.'' Dallas *Morning News* (September 11, 1965): 22.
Clark, James A. (with Weldon Hart). *The Tactful Texan: A Biography of Governor Will Hobby*. New York: Random House, 1958.

"Colonel Hobby First WAC to Get DSM." Dallas *Morning News* (January 1, 1945): 4.

Duckworth, Allen. "You Know What a Bargain Newspaper Brings?" Dallas *Morning News* (October 31, 1949): 10.

"First Woman to Serve — Mrs. Hobby Named to Rice University Board." Houston *Post* (June 18, 1967): 1.

Hobby, Oveta Culp. *Scrapbook*. Barker History Center, The University of Texas at Austin.

"Hobby receives honor of Marshall medal from Army association." Houston *Post* (October 19, 1978): 1.

"Hobby's Army." *Time* (January 17, 1944): 57-61.

Hurt, Harry. "The Last of the Great Ladies." *Texas Monthly* (October 1978): 143-150.

"Lady in Command." *Reader's Digest* (August 1953): 7-10.

" 'Major' Hobby's WAAC's." *Time* (May 25, 1942): 12.

"Mrs. Hobby." *U.S. News and World Report* (December 5, 1952): 25.

"Mrs. Hobby Heads Group." Dallas *Morning News* (November 10, 1948): 3.

"Mrs. Hobby Urges Equal Opportunity for Women." Houston *Post* (September 20, 1963): 1.

"Oveta Culp Hobby on Educational TV Panel." Houston *Post* (November 11, 1965): 2.

"Oveta Hobby: 'women will be drafted.' " Dallas *Times Herald* (April 12, 1972): 1.

"Presenting—Oveta Culp Hobby." *Pathfinder* (January 17, 1943): 3.

Serrin, Judith. "Hobby sees need for more women in Cabinet." Dallas *Times Herald* (January 31, 1977): 1.

"Texans To Honor Two Dallas Women." Dallas *Morning News* (February 4, 1951): 1.

"Texan's Wife Named Head of Woman's Army Corps." Dallas *Morning News* (May 16, 1942): 1.

"The Pioneers in HEW." *Newsweek* (February 28, 1966): 16.

"WAAC Chief Declares Women Aid War in All Ways Except Fighting." Dallas *Morning News* (February 17, 1945): 1.

"Wife of Former Governor Writes Book on Parliamentary Procedure." Austin *American-Statesman* (October 11, 1936): 1.

Williams, Norma Joe. "Behind Hat, Orchid, There Stands A Woman." San Angelo *Standard Times* (April 16, 1972): 1.

Oveta Culp Hobby with her husband, former Governor Will Hobby.

Courtesy Dallas Morning News

"The Little Lady On The Big Bench"

Sarah Tilghman Hughes

On November 22, 1963, when U.S. District Judge Sarah T. Hughes administered the oath of office to her longtime friend and political ally Lyndon B. Johnson, most Texans recognized the name of this petite woman advocate because of her distinguished career on the federal bench. Few recalled that the first woman to administer the oath of office to an American president had almost failed to be appointed to a federal judgeship, and even fewer might have remembered that the distinguished jurist had served two terms and part of a third as a successful member of the Texas House of Representatives, coming to the legislature in 1931 at the age of thirty-four, at that time the youngest woman to be elected to the House.

In 1961 she was appointed to a federal judgeship in Texas, the first female federal judge in the state. It was, however, merely the culmination of a lifetime in which Sarah Tilghman Hughes had spent fighting for equal rights for women. Born August 2, 1896 in Baltimore, Maryland, Sarah Tilghman spent her early years working in her mother's boarding house, probably the hardest work she ever did.

Her mother instilled in her the idea that she could do anything in life that she wanted to do, and when, at age sixteen, she graduated from high school second in her class, her mother declared that she should have been first.

What Sarah Tilghman wanted to do was to go to law school, and the first step was graduating Phi Beta Kappa from Baltimore's Goucher College. She minored in math and took three years of Latin, two subjects that helped develop her fine sense of logic. Two years teaching physics, chemistry, and zoology at Salem Academy and College in Winston-Salem, North Carolina, earned her the money to enter George Washington University to work on a law degree. She supplemented her income by working as a policewoman in the Washington, D.C., police department's woman's bureau. Her work there with juvenile offenders established a background that she was to use later, when as a state district judge she helped establish a separate juvenile court and a detention home for juvenile offenders in Dallas.

Graduating from law school in 1922 she gained admittance to both the District of Columbia and Texas state bars in that same year, and in 1937 the young attorney was admitted to practice before the United States Supreme Court. After graduation she married a fellow law student, George E. Hughes, a native Texan. When her law professor advised the couple, "Pick your town. You can make a living anywhere. Find a place you can make a life." To Sarah Hughes, that meant Dallas.

While her husband worked for the Veterans Administration, Sarah Hughes learned her first lesson in discrimination. Having written letters of application to major Dallas law firms, she found that in a state where women were not allowed to sit on juries or to make legal contracts, women lawyers were not in demand. One law firm did allow her to sit in their outer office, as they had no secretary, and they gave her a few legal cases to handle. She later recalled:

> When I started out there were only four women lawyers in Dallas. We certainly couldn't specialize in our practices. We had to take whatever cases we could get.

She soon became a force in the political life of the city,

speaking out against a Dallas schoolboard policy of not allowing married women to teach in the schools. She and her husband shared the household duties, and while he seldom thought that she could win a political race, he was supportive of her and proud when she entered the local political field and won her first election to public office.

Her first successful race in Dallas came in 1930, and she used her own money—a total of $300—and methodically campaigned in car barns, factories, fire houses, and police stations, "visiting everybody in town," as she recalled. She won her race, and went to Austin to take her seat in the Texas House of Representatives. Hughes served in the Forty-second and Forty-third legislative sessions and was beginning her third term in the Forty-fourth session when Governor James Allred appointed her to the Fourteenth District Court in Dallas. She became the first woman to serve as a regular district judge in Texas.

Hughes's first term in the state legislature marked the first time that there had been as many as four women House members, and she served along with Helen Moore, Lee J. Rountree, and Mrs. N. R. Strong. When her second session in the legislature opened in 1933, however, Sarah Hughes found herself the only woman member of the house. At the end of her second session in the legislature, the media voted her "Most Valuable Member of the House."

Moreover, during the two full sessions that she served Hughes gained a reputation as an effective legal opponent and a forceful debater, fighting for a West Texas land bill and the Colorado River Valley Authority measure providing for the completion of Buchanan Dam on the Colorado River. Citing Hughes as "capable, conscientious, and courageous," Allred pushed for her appointment as a state district judge, despite the fact that Senator Claude Westerfield of Dallas objected to a married woman holding a judgeship on the Texas bench.

On February 7, 1932, when the confirmation vote on Hughes's nomination came before the Senate Committee on Governor's Nominations in open session, only Senator Roy Sanderford voted against her, but Dallas attorney Harry Lawther appeared in opposition. Lawther advanced the argument that there were constitutional objections to her appointment, as she was a member of the House when the appointment was made. Her fellow House members, however, commended her in a petition, and two hundred Dallas lawyers also presented a petition in her favor. Ironically, Senator Weatherford's choice for the post, Dallas attorney C.F. Cusak, appeared in support of Hughes, citing the fact that

> No one has opposed Mrs. Hughes because of doubt of her ability . . . but only because she is a woman and I do not think that is a valid reason. I am for her because I know her qualifications and I have had my ears knocked down in court when opposing her . . . .

Gaining Senate confirmation Hughes served on the bench at a time when Texas women were not even allowed to sit on juries. Her political career, however, was not always so successful. She ran for the United States Congress in 1946, but was defeated by J. Frank Wilson in a runoff campaign. One of the issues in the campaign was a strong stand that women should be drafted into the armed services along with men. She challenged Justice Joe Greenhill for a seat on the Texas Supreme Court in 1958, but again lost the race.

When she was offered a post with the Federal Trade Commission by President Harry Truman in 1950, Hughes turned down the offer, saying, "My contacts with federal agencies have been such that I wouldn't want to be a member of any of them." She remained on the state bench, working for women's rights, including the right of Texas women to sit on juries within the state. She remained active in professional clubs, among them the Business and Professional Women's Club of Dallas, serving as president of the organization and on both the state and national boards. Later she was elected first vice president of the International Federation of Business and Professional Women's Clubs.

Sarah Hughes often expressed her love for political campaigning, even down to putting bumper stickers on cars, and in 1952 she had a chance to work in one of the shortest campaigns in political history. As national president of the B&PW clubs, she again called for the registration of women for the draft. The national organization voted to call for the draft of women when necessary, and Hughes responded: "And that time is now."

The organization backed her for vice president of the United States on the Democratic ticket, and Maine Senator Margaret Chase Smith for the same place on the Republican ballot. Although she admitted that she enjoyed her short-lived campaign, Hughes later declared that the purpose of naming her as a vice-presidential candidate was not really to gain the nomination. She had promised House Speaker Sam Rayburn of Texas that she would withdraw the nomination as soon as it was entered.

Sarah Hughes's love for political involvement was once again in the forefront when she campaigned actively for the Kennedy-Johnson ticket in 1960, serving as co-chairperson for the campaign in Dallas County. In 1962 John F. Kennedy appointed her to a federal judgeship in the Northern District of Dallas, a post she had wanted for some time. Again she met with opposition to her appointment, this time from the American Bar Assocation. The legal body objected to Hughes's appointment not because she was a woman, but because she was sixty-five years old. She responded in the peppery manner that had made her famous:

> 'The ABA apparently feels that if a person is over 65, they're senile. If I ever become senile, I hope I can recognize this and get out.'

She managed, however, to become a federal judge. When the objections to her appointment were revived at the Senate confirmation hearings, Vice-President Lyndon Johnson and U.S. Senator Ralph Yarborough appeared, and both stated that they differed with the bar association's protest. Yarborough said that the ABA had incorrectly interpreted federal retirement, adding "ABA makes a grave mistake by placing age over ability." Johnson, in speaking out for Hughes's appointment, added: "I have never known a more competent and humane public servant . . . I am confident she will make one of the great judges of our time."

And a great judge she was. Her work for women and juveniles made her a legend on the district court bench; and, on the federal bench, she tried major cases dealing with abortion, fair housing, welfare, and drug smuggling. In a landmark case she ruled that the Dallas County jail practices did not meet state legal standards. Her decision was later upheld by the United States Supreme Court.

Since the time she accepted the appointment of judge on the district court bench, she had worked for the reform of the Texas prison system, and she constantly spoke out on the need for probation of prisoners. She once stated that

> . . . punishment of the criminal is not enough; we have to rehabilitate. If we haven't done a good job of making the prisoner fit back into society when he is released, he will simply go back to jail.

The most spectacular case heard by Judge Hughes was the Securities and Exchange Commission's stock fraud suit against officials of National Bankers Life Insurance Company, a suit brought about by the 1971 Sharpstown scandals that began on the floor of the Texas House of Representatives, where many years before, young Sarah Hughes had begun her political career. SEC lawyers had approached Judge Hughes in February 1971, asking her to grant a restraining order to prevent trading of the stock of companies involved in the suit and from the wasting of corporate assets of the businesses under investigation. One of the individuals involved was former Texas Attorney General Waggoner Carr, who Hughes ruled was not involved in the complicated scheme to manipulate corporate stocks. All the participants, however, including Carr, were indicted, and on September 16 Judge Hughes, ignoring the political aspects of loans to prominent state politicians, stuck strictly to the business and corporate aspects of the case and handed down her decision. She held nine businessmen and four corporations guilty of illegal stock manipulations and enjoined them from any further stock dealings. This case caused headlines and eventually led to the indictment of other state officials, including Speaker of the House Gus Mutscher.

The swearing in of Lyndon B. Johnson as president of the United States aboard Air Force One in Dallas was the act that brought Judge Hughes her first national attention. Arriving home from the planned luncheon that was to honor President Kennedy after his motorcade parade, Hughes received a telephone call from U.S. Attorney Barefoot Sanders. Vice-President Johnson was on the other line and asked her to come out to Love Field to administer to him the oath of office as president of the United States.

The Kennedy assassination also brought Hughes a great deal of criticism. She had angered a number of people when, as a federal judge, she continued to appear at partisan Democratic functions. When Hughes referred to Dallas as the ''city of hate,'' her remarks were printed and many Dallas citizens spoke out against her. She defended her statements later, saying

> There was a climate of hate in Dallas that was not evident in any other place. I definitely think that the feeling in Dallas contributed to the fact that Oswald would do this deed here rather than in some other city. . . I believe now that the leaders of Dallas realized what the situation was here and have gone all out to change it.

In 1968 the Press Club of Dallas named her their All-Time Headliner, and she received a distinguished alumna award from George Washington University, along with an honorary doctor of laws degree from her alma mater, Goucher College. Awards and recognition have come to the woman advocate, and women's groups have honored her for her work for the Equal

Rights Amendment. She has been quick to point out that many women lack the necessary drive to push for their rights, but counsels that

> For too long women have been deprived of promotions in business and politics. Women have contributions to make and their abilities should be made use of.

Not until she reached the age of seventy-nine did Sarah Hughes ask to take senior status, opening the way for a new federal judge but retaining the right to take additional cases for hearings and trials. When she announced her decision, Judge Robert Porter commended her as a "remarkable person, a delightful lady, and an outstanding judge," adding that

> She never wanted any criticism of her performance just because she was a woman. . . so she worked harder than anyone around her to prove she was top notch — and she was.

REFERENCES

Castleberry, Vivian. "Everything You Wanted To Know About Sarah Hughes and Were Afraid To Ask," Dallas *Times-Herald* (October 24, 1971): 24.

Crawford, Ann Fears. *From Ferguson to Farenthold: Texas Women in Politics.* Unpublished paper delivered at the Texas State Historical Association (San Antonio, 1978).

Crosby, Kay. "She's Short in Stature, Long on Statutes," Dallas *Morning News* (October 24, 1971): 5.

"Dallas Woman for Veep?" Dallas *Morning News* (June 12, 1952): 1.

Deaton, Charles. *The Year They Threw the Rascals Out.* Austin: Shoal Creek Publishers, Inc., 1973.

Eyre, Ruth. "Judge Hughes stays in the swim at 78," Dallas *Times-Herald* (August 22, 1974): 18.

Feldeman, Trude B. "An Emergency Call to Judge Hughes in Dallas," Houston *Post* (November 21, 1965): 1.

"Judge Sarah T. Hughes Has Proved Men Wrong," Houston *Chronicle* (April 29, 1965): 4.

"Little Lady on a Big Bench," Houston *Post* (April 25, 1965): 1.

Mashek, John. "Body Ignores ABA on Hughes Protest," Dallas *Morning News* (March 8, 1962): 1.

Oden, Marjorie. "Judge Hughes Says Draft Women Now," Dallas *Morning News* (July 14, 1951): 1.

Pederson, Rena. "Judge Hughes Leaves Post," Dallas *Morning News* (August 5, 1975): 4.

"Sarah T. Hughes Appointed Judge of District Court," Dallas *Morning News* (February 2, 1935): 5.

Thornton, William M. "Hughes Nomination Favored By 8 to 1 Vote of Committee," Dallas *Morning News* (February 8, 1932): 16.

Weddington, Sarah, et al. *Texas Women in Politics.* Austin: Foundation for Women's Resources, 1977.

Courtesy Babe Didrikson Zaharias Memorial Museum, Beaumont

"The Texas Babe"

Mildred "Babe"

Didrikson Zaharias

On October 14, 1975 film stars Susan Clark and Alex Karras arrived in Beaumont, Texas, for a personal appearance at the premiere of the made-for-TV film "Babe," scheduled for showing over CBS on October 23. The citizens of Beaumont turned out to honor the stars and the legendary athlete who was the subject of the film. "Babe" Didrikson Zaharias had risen from the sandlots of South Beaumont to become one of the immortals of the sports world, winning Olympic medals, some eighty-two golf tournaments, and the accolades of such notable sportswriters as Paul Gallico and Grantland Rice.

The TV film was a success and has been shown over network television a number of times. Susan Clark, who trained for the role on the UCLA track, looks amazingly like photographs of Babe Didrikson, and the film follows with accuracy the events of the athlete's life. The next year the citizens of Beaumont attended the opening of the Babe Didrikson Zaharias Museum, a project begun by the athlete's husband, George Zaharias, which cost $154,000 and took eight years to complete. Her trophies and medals were moved to the museum, where tourists by the hundreds come to view the memorabilia that mark the life of one of America's sports greats.

Born Mildred Ella Didricksen in Port Arthur, Texas on June 26, 1911, she was the sixth of the seven children of a former

Norwegian ship captain Ole Didricksen, and his wife Hannah. In later years Babe changed the spelling of her name and often obscured the date of her birth, claiming it to be 1913, 1914, or 1915 on various occasions. Ole Didricksen had immigrated from Norway to Texas and worked three years before he sent for his wife and three children. Hannah Didricksen never became accustomed to the Texas heat or the ugliness of the Texas Gulf Coast, and after she gave birth to her seventh child during a hurricane she was so terrified that her husband moved the family to Beaumont, seventeen miles away.

Babe Didrikson grew up on Beaumont's south side, a tough, scrappy youngster, who played in sandlot baseball games and enjoyed boxing with her brother Louis. "I never played girls' games when I was a youngster," she later told a reporter. "Dolls just didn't interest me. I wanted to play the boys' games." Her family encouraged her, all of them participating in sports. Babe claimed in later years that the Didricksen children got their natural athletic ability from their mother, who had once been a skier and ice skater in her native Norway. Mother Hannah also passed on to her children the love of an orderly household and cleanliness. While Babe learned to slug with Louis and slide into third base with brother Arthur, she also learned to cook and sew. Throughout her life Babe Didrikson remained "crazy about clothes," according to her high-school friend, Lois Blanchette, and she won a seventy-five dollar prize at the Texas State Fair for a dress with a box-pleated skirt that she made.

Beaumont High School was not so quick to accept her into the ranks of its star athletes. Although she had gained her nickname "Babe," which she always preferred to Mildred, by hitting a long ball in her sandlot baseball games, when she was sixteen the officials at Beaumont High School ruled her out of competition on the basketball team as "too small, too frail, and liable to serious injury." Babe took the judgment in stride, working out with a coach, and soon made the team, gaining the reputation of a girl with an "eye for the basket." She spent so much time practicing basketball that her parents complained, and Babe calmly teamed up with Blanchette to win at women's tennis, then went on to play every sport that Beaumont High School offered.

The girls' basketball team, however, was where she caught the eye of Tiny Spurlock, sportswriter for the Beaumont *Enterprise and Journal.* After games in the armory on College Street Scurlock would take the girls out for dinner, and he and Babe struck up a friendship that lasted throughout her lifetime. She often wrote to Scurlock telling him of her wins and her losses, and Scurlock wrote the first stories that told people that Babe Didrikson was on the road to athletic fame.

On February 18, 1930 Colonel M.J. McCombs saw her make basketball history as high-point scorer against a Houston team and signed her to play basketball for the Employers Casualty Company in Dallas. Babe dropped out of school, went to work for the company, and reportedly sold ten insurance policies her first day. She proved a winner on the basketball court also, leading the Employers Casualty Golden Cyclones to victories and becoming an All-American basketball player three years in a row.

To provide the girls with athletic experience during the summer months Colonel McCombs inaugurated a series of track and field events, undoubtedly with an eye to the 1932 Olympics. Babe trained at all events from the broad jump to the javelin throw and spent her spare time practicing fancy diving. In the 1930 women's national A.A.U. championships, she propelled the Golden Cyclones to second place and scored national records in the javelin and baseball throw. In 1931 she repeated her successes, setting records in the baseball throw and in the eighty-meter hurdles.

In 1932 Babe gained international fame, taking the Olympic world by storm. The Associated Press had named her Woman Athlete of the Year in 1931, and all eyes were on her at the Los Angeles Olympic Games. Her brother Arthur rode the rails to watch her perform, and she proved herself a real champion, throwing the javelin 143 feet-4 inches and winning the eighty-meter hurdles in 11.7 seconds. Famed sportswriter

Grantland Rice wrote of her, "It was a treat to watch her stroll into the high jump the moment some official set up the crossbar. She had less wasted effort than any athlete I have ever seen in action." Headlines touted the exploits of "The Amazing Amazon," "Belting Babe," "The Texas Tomboy," and writer Paul Gallico named her "The Texas Babe," a name that seemed to sum up her Texas bravado and the boastful manner that caused many of her Olympic teammates to scorn her. Some years later Gallico used Babe as the model for his short-story heroine "Honey" in *Vanity Fair*. Honey Hadwell, as Gallico portrayed her, was a brash and breezy South Carolina girl with a Southern accent you could cut with a knife.

After her Olympic victories, Babe returned to Dallas to a heroine's welcome. She was bombarded with roses and confetti, while the local newspapers ran full-page "Welcome Home, Babe!" stories heralding her homecoming. Then it was home to Beaumont, where the entire town turned out to welcome the hometown girl, acclaimed "The world's greatest athlete." The sports pages across the nation were filled with story after story of her triumphs, and Didrikson helped to spread the myth of her athletic superiority. Asked by one reporter when she first became aware of her sense of coordination, Babe told a story of teasing an old farm bull, then jumping onto a fire engine to outwit him. Another legend she helped create concerned her entry into the field of golf. Challenged by sportswriters Rice, Gallico, Westbrook Pegler, and Braven Dyer to a game of golf after her Olympic triumphs, she reportedly drove the ball 265 yards down the fairway. Although she claimed this was the first time she had picked up a golf club, she had played golf as early as her Beaumont High School days, and her picture is featured in the 1929 high school annual as a member of both the golf and tennis teams.

It was a blow to Babe's career when the Amateur Athletic Union declared her ineligible to play in amateur athletics, as she had accepted a gift of a Dodge automobile and the company used a photograph with her car for advertising purposes. Protesting the AAU decision, Didrikson departed for a whirlwind tour of the RKO vaudeville circuit, performing on a treadmill and playing her harmonica. Then she barnstormed with a basketball team called Babe Didrikson's All Americans, and pitched for the House of David's all-male baseball team. As a promotional gimmick Connie Mack allowed her to pitch an inning for his Philadelphia Athletics against the Brooklyn Dodgers.

Babe added to her reputation as a brazen opportunist, and her flamboyant style and boyish figure gained her a reputation as a "muscle moll." Women were not openly accepted in the sports world, and Babe's exuberance and outgoing manner plus her frank enjoyment of often beating men at their own games led many people to look on her as a freak. The press, however, loved her, relishing her high-spirited antics, her willingness to play the harmonica and entertain, and her frank, open comments. As Babe began to become a celebrity in the world of golf, her publicity increased and reporters quickly realized that "The Texas Tomboy" was good copy for the sports pages. The singer Hildegarde once asked Babe what she could do to improve her own golf game, and Babe quipped: "Just take off your girdle and swing hard." When asked which was her favorite sport Babe quickly answered, "The one I'm playing," and once on a radio show when the irrepressible Babe was asked what she could do besides play golf, tennis, and win Olympic titles, she whipped out her harmonica and played hillbilly tunes.

Her approach to learning to play championship golf was a simple one — practice, practice, practice, and win! "I've always been a fighter," she told one reporter. "Ever since I was a kid, I've scrapped for everything. I want to win every time. If a game is worth playing, it's worth playing to win." After eight hours a day on the golf course perfecting her game for tournament play, her hands often bled so hard she had to play with them covered with tape. Her goal was the Texas Women's Amateur Championship in 1935, and although she qualified the members of the Texas Women's Golf Association ignored her. The girl from Beaumont's south side might have been lacking in social status, but she was a member in good standing at the Beaumont Country Club, and when she arrived at Houston's prestigious River Oaks Country Club, she was determined to win.

Playing in a Texas downpour, Babe won the semifinals with a dramatic putt on the last hole, and the Associated Press labeled her "America's wonder girl athlete and probably the most promising woman golf player in the United States." She went on to win the tournament in a tough match against Peggy Chandler, who had snubbed Babe and was one of the more feminine and well-dressed golfers on the women's circuit. Ever her champion, Paul Gallico chortled that "The Texas Babe seems to be working out a lifelong vendetta on sissy girls," and Grantland Rice celebrated her victory in verse:

> The Texas Babe now shifts the scene
> Where splashing drives are far
> Where spoon shots find the distant green
> To break the back of par.

The "sissy girls" struck back by complaining to the U.S. Golf Association that Babe was ineligible for amateur play as she was a professional athlete. The USGA agreed and barred her from competing in all tournaments but the Western Open.

Babe, with the help of Bertha Bowen of Fort Worth, resolved to beat the "sissy girls" at their own game. An influential member of the Fort Worth golfing scene, Bowen took "The Texas Amazon" to Neiman-Marcus for seven hundred dollars worth of new clothes, advised her on a more feminine hairdo, and applied subtle makeup; but try as she might, she could never get Babe to play golf in a girdle. Nevertheless, the rough-and-tumble tomboy disappeared, and the press took notice of the new Babe's silly hats and red fingernail polish.

The woman who had once been called a "muscle moll" was soon designing more comfortable and attractive clothes for women on the golf circuit, and in later years she designed a golf dress that was manufactured by Serbin, a shirt with buttons on the sleeves to allow for a wider swing, and a golf shoe with removable spikes. Babe had a decided flair in her dress and once appeared on the golf course wearing a pink shirt embroidered with black palm trees and matching pink socks.

She played the Western Open as a professional and signed a contract with the Wilson Sporting Goods Company to publicize their products. Her new image was much in evidence and she told reporters:

> I'm very happy. My new job thrills me and I know that women's golf has a greater future in this country than men's golf. Golf is a game of coordination, rhythm, and grace. Women have this to a much higher degree than men, as dancing shows.

Disappointed when she lost her chance in the winner's circle in the quarterfinals, Didrikson took to the exhibition circuit with professional Gene Sarazen. On their two-month tour Babe perfected the art of playing to the gallery, and challenged the president of one exclusive country club to a game of tennis, playing barefoot and beating him. She developed a standard challenge to her male partners, yelling for everyone on the links to hear, ''Come on pardner, let out! Why allow little me to pass you all the time?''

Romance came into ''The Texas Tomboy's'' life when she was teamed with wrestler George Zaharias and a minister at the Los Angeles Open in 1938. The minister won the game, but Babe challenged George with a mighty drive down the fairway. When George drove the ball three yards further, Babe said, ''I always said I could fall in love with a man strong enough to out-drive me.'' Soon ''The Belting Babe'' and ''The Groaning Greek from Cripple Creek,'' as sportswriters called Zaharias, were a steady twosome, writing each other love notes and signing them ''Romance.'' The couple married on December 23, 1938, and Zaharias began promoting Babe's career, convincing her that she should quit professional golf and apply for amateur standing once again.

Babe threw herself into homemaking, watering the rosebushes around her West Los Angeles duplex, sewing curtains, and cooking gargantuan meals, including homemade cinnamon rolls, to please her husband. She also took up tennis and bowling with a passion, still keeping her golf game up to par.

The Zahariases lived an uprooted life, often changing their homes as they moved about the golf circuit. Though George Zaharias was a restless man, often on the go, Babe craved the security of a home of her own. She also wanted a baby, but after one miscarriage never talked of having a child again. She thought that she had found a permanent home when the couple moved to Denver. There Babe became active in many community projects, and in 1943 Denver juvenile court judge Philip B. Gilliam appointed her a probation officer and recreation consultant, adding that Babe would be a hero to the children of the city. Babe accepted her job without salary with great spirit and spent hours teaching children in detention and orphan homes to play ball, swim, and play golf.

World War II and her lack of amateur status kept Babe from the golf links, but in 1943 she regained her amateur standing and challenged Clara Callender to a match at the Desert Golf Club in Palm Springs. She beat her opponent, broke the women's record, and went on to win her third Western Open championship. When she won the Texas Women's Open in 1945 the Associated Press named her the outstanding woman athlete of the year, an honor she won six times in her lifetime. From 1945 to 1947 she won seventeen straight tournaments, including the National Women's Amateur championship.

International fame came again when she won the British Women's Amateur golf title in Gullane, Scotland, defeating Jacqueline Gordon of London in the final round five games to four. Babe was unused to the wet, cold British weather, and the Scots sent her heavy clothing that she called "Bundles for Babe." She chose a baggy pair of light blue slacks, or "slocks" as the Scots called them, and they soon became her calling card on the links. The staid British public found the irrepressible Babe and her Texas-style enthusiasm a delight. She took to the fairways with a "Hi, ya everybody!," danced a highland fling barefooted and wearing a kilt on the clubhouse lawn, and performed highjinks never seen in Scotland before. The Scots took her to their hearts, insisting that she change from her sweater and skirt into her lucky "slocks" for her final victory against Gordon.

Didrikson sailed for home an acclaimed heroine, cheered by a British farewll of "Auld Lang Syne," and George met her with kisses and a tugboat of reporters. She signed a contract with agent Fred Corcoran, reveling in being named "Woman of the Year" along with Helen Hayes, Helen Traubel, and Ingrid Bergman. *Time* magazine cited her as a "crowd puller," and commented that " . . . Babe in her showmanship is as subtle as a punch on the nose." She signed a contract for $300,000 to star in movie shorts about golf, and then went home to Denver where ten thousand citizens turned out to honor her with a Western-style celebration and buffalo barbecue. The governor of Colorado attended, and when the mayor presented her with a fourteen-foot, gilt-plated key to the city, Babe responded that she thought it was "the biggest, grandest thing" that had ever happened to her.

The girl from the Beaumont sandlots was an international celebrity, and George Zaharias promoted his wife's fame into a fortune. When "Queen of Sports," a movie short starring "La Babe," opened she made a personal appearance on the Denver stage. She wrote a book called *Championship Golf,* and then turned her energies to writing a series of syndicated columns entitled "The Babe Says — ," practical golf tips aimed at women golfers. In her column Babe challenged women to concentrate more and more on hitting the ball instead of just swinging, and the strength and the drive that characterized her own playing helped change the focus of women's golf.

In 1948, with financial support from the Wilson Company, Babe and five other women golfers established the Ladies Professional Golf Association, and competition among women golfers intensified. The Zahariases bought their own golf course, renamed it the Tampa Golf and Country Club, and Babe entered the 1950s as a top money winner on the women's circuit.

Although Babe continually credited George Zaharias with promoting her career and cited him as the guiding hand behind the formation of the LPGA, the couple gradually grew apart. George gained an enormous amount of weight, and Babe once quipped that when she had married him he was a "Greek god," but he had turned into a "goddamn Greek." Zaharias, however, was at her side when doctors discovered that she had a femoral hernia. After an operation in 1952 she returned to the golf circuit, only to experience a lack of energy and intense pain. She appeared in Beaumont to win the first Babe Zaharias Open, created in her honor, and then returned to Hotel Dieu Hospital for a series of tests. Doctors discovered cancer of the lower intestine, and in 1953 they performed a colostomy to help prevent the spread of the disease.

Babe rallied to help President and Mrs. Eisenhower inaugurate the 1954 Cancer Crusade, and then took to the golf circuit once again. She was awarded the Ben Hogan Comeback of the Year Award, winning five tournaments including the U.S. Women's Open. Then she checked into the hospital again; the cancer had returned. Her family and friends in Beaumont visited her, and fans filled her room with flowers. During her entire stay in the hospital Babe kept her golf clubs close at hand, and her protegé on the golf circuit, Betty Dodd, abandoned her own professional career to be with Babe, often cheering her by playing the harmonica. Lois Blanchette recalls that Babe never accepted the fact that cancer could defeat her, but she would often turn her head away and ask, "Why me, God?"

The next two years were spent in and out of hospitals, and Babe sought peace and comfort at her Tampa home, often asking her husband or Betty Dodd to take her to a golf course just so she could bend down and touch the turf. On September 27, 1956 the woman sportswriters had named "the world's greatest athlete" died in Galveston's John Sealy Hospital.

Babe had become a legend in her lifetime, winning every woman's championship at least once. She helped build golf into one of the premier sports for women, and she held a spot in the annals of sports as one of the great natural athletes of all times.

Wherever sports figures gather to discuss the "greats" in the sports world the name of Babe Didrikson Zaharias is the woman always mentioned.

REFERENCES

"Babe Didrikson Wins Again." Los Angeles *Examiner* (August 5, 1932): 1.

"Babe Zaharias 'Woman Athlete of '46.' " The Denver *Post* (January 5, 1947) in Babe Didrikson Zaharias *Scrapbook,* Babe Didrikson Zaharias Museum, Beaumont, Texas.

Barrier, Smith. "Shifting Sands: Golf Main Street." *The Woman Golfer* (August-September 1947): 6-7.

Blane, Thomas. "Southern Personalities: Babe Didrikson World Athlete." *Holland's* magazine (October 1932): 23.

Caldwell, Betty. "This Is It Folks! Today Denver Pays Honor to Our Babe." Rocky Mountain *News* (July 3, 1947): 3.

Carberry, Jack. "The Second Guess." Denver *Post* (January 5, 1947) in *Scrapbook.*

Cunningham, Bill. "Texas Flash." *Collier's* (August 6, 1932): 26.

"Dallas Welcomes Babe Didrikson Home." Dallas *Dispatch* (August 11, 1932): 1.

Daniel, Dan. "Babe Toast of Florida." Rocky Mountain *News* (February 18, 1947) in *Scrapbook.*

DeGrummond, Lena Young and Lynn de Grummond DeLaune. *Babe Didrikson: Girl Athlete.* New York: Bobbs-Merrill Co., Inc., 1963.

Didrikson, Babe. "Thrills." *The Amateur Athlete* (September 1932) in *Scrapbook.*

"Didrikson British Champion." New York *Times* (June 18, 1947) in *Scrapbook.*

Duke, Kerry. "Babe's memorial to open." Beaumont *Enterprise-Journal* (November 27, 1976): 3-A.

Gallico, Paul. "'Honey'." *Vanity Fair* (April 1933): 46-47.

Johnson, Erskine. "The Women in the Olympics." Rocky Mountain *News* (June 26, 1932) in *Scrapbook.*

Johnson, William Oscar and Nancy P. Williamson. *"Whatta-Gal":*
The Babe Didrikson Story. Boston: Little Brown and Company,
1977.

Keck, Harvey. "Babe Zaharias Wins Acclaim of Former Stars." Pitts-
burg *Sun-Telegraph* (August 16, 1947) in *Scrapbook.*

Mazza, Bob. " 'Babe' Bows in Home Town." Hollywood *Reporter*
(October 14, 1975): 1.

Menke, Frank G. "Intimate Glimpses of the Olympic Miracle 'Babe'
Didrikson. Denver *Post* (October 23, 1932) in *Scrapbook.*

Parker, Dan. "There Never Was a Girl Like Babe." Unidentified clipping in *Scrapbook.*

Povich, Shirley. "This Morning." Washington *Post* (May 17, 1947) in
Scrapbook.

Rice, Grantland. "For Men Only." *Collier's* (September 24, 1932):
19.

Roe, Dorothy. "Five New Faces Join 'Woman of the Year'."
Associated Press release in *Scrapbook.*

Rogers, Dave. "Bubba Didrikson: A proud brother recalls the
'Babe'." Beaumont *Enterprise-Journal* (May 25, 1981): 3-B.

Smith, Cecil. " 'Babe' Ode to an Athlete Dying Young." Los
Angeles *Examiner* (March 10, 1975): 2-A.

"The World's Greatest Girl Athlete." Pittsburgh *Press* (August 23,
1938): 2.

"Whatta Woman." *Time* (March 10, 1947): 69.

Zaharias, Babe Didrikson. *This Life I've Led.* New York: A. S. Barnes
and Company, Inc., 1965.

INTERVIEWS

Lois Blanchette and Ann Fears Crawford. Beaumont. August 13,
1981.

Courtesy Babe Didrikson Zaharias Memorial Museum, Beaumont

"That Woman"

Frances "Sissy" Farenthold

"I am a candidate in order to give the people of Texas a choice — a choice other than between two contaminated candidates and a legislator from the Fifties." With these words, Frances Tarlton "Sissy" Farenthold launched her campaign for governor of the state of Texas in 1972. Texans had not heard such bold words as "Reform . . . integrity . . . equal rights for women . . . environmental responsibility . . . humanized government . . . eradicating police state tactics" in a governor's race for many years.

These words were also a far cry from the words and expressions that had sparked the political speeches of Miriam Ferguson in her gubernatorial campaigns during the 1920s and the 1930s. Women flocked to the banner of "That Woman," as Farenthold was called, and turned out the vote for a woman gubernatorial candidate. Liberals and ethnic minorities as well as women responded to the reformer many heralded as destined to carry the banner of the "New Populism" in Texas, and Farenthold gave them their rallying cry:

> Three kinds of words cover the needs of a woman who wants to make it in politics. The first is 'awareness.' Look at the facts of the status of women and women in politics. The second word is 'asser-

tiveness.' I say assertiveness because it means aggression; the word "aggression" tends to strike fear in the hearts of men. The third word is 'audacity' . . . even members of my family flinched when I thought of running for governor. But then I realized I was running against two law school dropouts . . . I'm working now for the day when the unqualified woman, Black, or Chicano, can join the unqualified white man in politics.

Reformer, insurgent, populist, product of upper-middle-class Texas society, inheritor of a long tradition of service to the state of Texas, Frances Farenthold epitomized that convergence of Texas first families that had produced both men and women of stature whose dedication to their state had made their names known to many.

Her Irish Dougherty forebears had come to colonial Texas in the 1830s. Her grandfather, Benjamin Dudley Tarlton, a Central Texas lawyer, had served in the Texas legislature from 1881 to 1886, when Governor James S. Hogg appointed him to the Texas Court of Appeals. He had run for the Texas Supreme Court and later lectured at The University of Texas Law School, where the law library now bears his name. Her grandmother, Kate D. Bluntzer, was one of the first public schoolteachers in Corpus Christi, and her aunt, Lida Dougherty, served San Patricio County as the first woman school superintendent in Texas.

Farenthold's father, Dudley Tarlton, was a well-known Corpus Christi attorney who served as a campaign manager for Railroad Commissioner Ernest O. Thompson in 1938 when he lost the gubernatorial race in an upset victory to W. Lee O'Daniel. Born in South Texas on October 2, 1926, the daughter of Tarlton and Catherine R. Bluntzer Tarlton, Frances Tarlton attended Hockaday School in Dallas and then returned briefly to Corpus Christi, where she became known as the "barefoot debutante," for her habit of removing her shoes in reception lines. Then she attended Vassar College, graduating as a member of Phi Beta Kappa with a degree in political science.

Despite the strong family tradition of public service and political involvement in both state and national politics, to many Texans "Sissy" Farenthold may have had more than three strikes against her as a candidate for governor of Texas. She had gone East to attend college; she had become a "lady lawyer" by attending The University of Texas Law School, graduating with honors; and instead of marrying a South Texas rancher, she had married a Belgian nobleman and longtime Texas resident, George Farenthold. In addition, while serving a second term as the only woman in the Texas House of Representatives, she had led a group of insurgents who were called the "Dirty Thirty" in opposition to the Speaker of the House of Representatives and his lieutenants in what became known as the Sharpstown scandal.

The road that led Frances Farenthold to a race for the statehouse began with a traditional woman's concern, public welfare, and moved during her first term in the legislature to what she termed "people problems." She had little political experience, except as a campaigner for her cousin Dudley Doughtery, when he ran for the state legislature, and for John F. Kennedy in his 1960 presidential campaign. The death of a child, however, led her to apply for a job as director of the Nueces County Legal Aid Association, where she learned at first hand the inequities of the welfare system in Texas. Service on the Corpus Christi Human Relations Commission reinforced her beliefs that many Texans lived in appalling conditions and that state agencies failed to respond to their needs.

In February 1968, when attorney Jake Jarmon, a colleague from her law school days, suggested she file for a seat in the Texas legislature, she barely made the filing deadline to become the first woman candidate to run in District 45, the rich farming, cattle, and oil-producing counties along the lower Gulf Coast. Poorly financed and lacking support from her own Democratic party organization, her campaign was conducted under the keywords, "ethics, efficiency, education, and ecology." Compounding all the organizational problems of a political campaign was the fact that the candidate was a naturally shy person. On one occasion her husband deposited her at a shopping center, handed her campaign cards and a dime, and told her to call him when she had handed out all the cards.

However, 1968 was a presidential election year, with Hubert Humphrey leading the Democratic ticket, and Democrats came out to vote. When Dr. Hector Garcia, a knowledgeable politician and close advisor, assured her that she was going to win, Farenthold didn't believe him. She beat the Republican incumbent, however, after successfully challenging three other Democrats in the primary and a Chicano in the runoff election. Her first session in the legislature was a learning experience and reform became her byword. She later recalled:

> I was in the legislature about two weeks before I decided that reform had to be my major concern. I went there knowing blacks weren't represented, knowing Mexican-Americans weren't represented. I found that Texans weren't even represented.

Her legislative successes were balanced by significant defeats. She spoke out against an anti-riot bill, House Bill 431, championed by Attorney General Crawford Martin. Considering the bill a threat to civil rights and an overreaction to civil disorder, she succeeded only in getting it amended, but she was successful in passing an antiquities bill, which gave the state of Texas its share of treasures and artifacts found in Texas waters and along the coast. She supported a bill that allowed district courts to pay up to twenty dollars a day to jurors with economic hardships, but failed in her attempt to secure passage of legislation to establish a Governor's Committee on Children and Youth or a state Human Relations Commission. Welfare reform went begging, despite repeated attempts on her part, and when she proposed placing three students on The University of Texas Board of Regents, Frank Erwin, a member of the board, stated that students had no valid interest nor place in the deliberations of the regents.

"Advocate of lost causes" was the way many of her colleagues viewed her, but she campaigned for a second term, despite a broken leg acquired during a skiing holiday with her children. "Integrity, Courage, and Competence in the '70s" was her campaign slogan, and the Corpus Christi *Caller-Times* called her victory a "runaway," despite both Democratic and Republican opposition. Her second term brought the Sharpstown bank scandal, which propelled House Speaker Gus Mutscher and members of the House leadership into the courts and Farenthold and the "Dirty Thirty" to the front pages of state and national newspapers.

House Committee Resolution 87, introduced on the floor of the House by Farenthold, called for an investigation of Sharpstown, but when called for a supporting motion, Mutscher overruled her. The Speaker and his allies struck back at her by redistricting Farenthold's political home base, but "Sissy" used the Sharpstown scandal to good advantage during her 1972 gubernatorial campaign.

Shunning races for attorney general, a seat on the Texas Railroad Commission, or state senator, Farenthold withheld her announcement as a candidate for governor, waiting on veteran U.S. Senator Ralph Yarborough's announcement on a possible race for the statehouse. "Had Yarborough run for governor, I thought it would be feasible to run for attorney general. But what I was worried about was if he did not run for governor, there would be very little visibility [for me] in the attorney general's race," she commented later.

Roy Evans, then president of the state AFL-CIO, discouraged her from running for either governor or attorney general and failed to get her labor's endorsement. When Yarborough announced again for the Senate, Farenthold announced for governor. The 1972 race pitted her against incumbent Governor Preston Smith from West Texas and the "golden boy" of Texas politics, Lieutenant Governor Ben Barnes of Brownwood, both implicated in the Sharpstown scandal, and Uvalde rancher Dolph Briscoe, a former state legislator and an unsuccessful gubernatorial candidate in 1968.

Underfinanced and understaffed, the Farenthold campaign focused on the thirty counties in the state with the largest population, and Farenthold's candidacy immediately became more a crusade than a campaign. The candidate insisted on women being placed in key campaign positions, and her women supporters, wearing T-shirts labeled "Sissy's Kiddy Corps," campaigned in suburbs, supermarket parking lots, and smalltown squares. The only large donations of money to her campaign came from family members, and "Sissy" boasted that over sixty percent of her other contributions were women.

With only a three percent name identification factor, running against a slick, well-financed media blitz on the part of Dolph Briscoe, "That Woman" announced her candidacy in twenty-four cities across the state in four days. Her call for a corporate profits tax to replace the state's regressive sales tax struck terror in the hearts of Texas businessmen; and her call for curbing the state's elite police corps, the Texas Rangers, elicited more angry letters than any other issue in her campaign.

When Farenthold managed to win a place in the runoff against Briscoe, the conservative political establishment closed ranks behind one of their own. The Uvalde rancher usurped "Sissy's" campaign issue by stating in newspapers across the state that, "Dolph Briscoe has no radical or extreme proposals for Texas government; only a commitment to put government back into the hands of the people." When the votes were counted, Briscoe had won with fifty-five percent of the vote, but Farenthold had made a formidable showing, obtaining forty-five percent. The candidate, however, commented philosophically: "We are midstream in a journey, We have a distance to go. We are working for public government so long overdue. We are not going to give up that fight."

Despite her loss in a hard-fought governor's race, Farenthold managed to knock out of the race the two candidates who had been tainted by the Sharpstown scandal; and Ben Barnes, the anointed successor to Lyndon Johnson and John Connally, retired from politics. Many speculated what the meaning of the Farenthold candidacy had meant in Texas. Her forthright campaign had encouraged women to serve as active campaigners and to hold positions of authority within the campaign organization. Moreover, Farenthold had proven that women as gubernatorial candidates would no longer be an oddity in Texas.

Although temporarily out of state elective office, Farenthold was active on the national political scene. Campaigning for George McGovern for president at the Democratic national convention in Miami, she became a possible candidate for vice president on the Democratic ticket. Three students from Baylor University circulated a petition on her behalf, and, when Congresswoman Shirley Chisholm of New York decided not to seek a place on the ticket, the National Women's Political Caucus took up the Farenthold banner. Feminist leader Gloria Steinem nominated Farenthold, with David Lopez, Fannie Lou Hamer, and Allard Lowenstein seconding her nomination. Although "Sissy" gained four hundred votes, most of them from women delegates, she lost a place on the ticket to Thomas Eagleton, United States Senator from Missouri. Nevertheless, she campaigned throughout the state and nation for the Democrats, serving as national co-chairperson of Citizens for McGovern.

Leaving the political field, Farenthold began teaching at Texas Southern University School of Law, speaking on political issues, and serving as chairperson of the National Women's Political Caucus. She remained a vital entity in Texas political circles, moving her home base to Houston and co-chairing efforts to gain support throughout Texas for Senator Edward Kennedy's health bill. Liberal politicians began looking toward the gubernatorial race for Farenthold in 1974. They prophesied that the "New Populism" had gained credibility and clout because of Farenthold's entry in the 1972 race for governor and encouraged her to enter the campaign.

On February 4, 1974 she announced that she would again challenge Briscoe for the governor's chair, commenting: "I view this as a rematch. One down and that was Barnes, and one to go and that's Briscoe." Her announcement speech served as a clarion call to women throughout the state:

. . . Women need to not only run for office and get into policy making positions in the parties but they also need to contribute money to women candidates. I had more contributions from women than men . . . I went to a girl's preparatory school and a woman's college and never studied a thing about women's suffrage. I studied law but never studied one case about sex discrimination. The barriers are slowly being broken in Texas. At least now no one is strangling over a woman running for office . . . .

Farenthold made public her 1973 federal income tax statements and challenged Briscoe to do the same. "He should be willing to reveal all his financial dealings or should . . . retire to his banks and ranches as a private citizen," she stated. She attacked Briscoe's appointments to political office and his lack of leadership during a Texas energy crisis. Her claims that Briscoe had made himself inaccessible to legislators and to Texas citizens were sparked by the fact that beginning in 1975, the governor of Texas would serve four-year terms instead of two-year ones. "I love this state, just like you do," she told the Texas Women's Political Caucus. "We can't afford to let this state sleep for four more years."

Farenthold's campaign, however, lacked the fire and conviction of her 1972 race. While Briscoe toured the state in his private plane, "Sissy" was reduced to using public transportation, often arriving late at rallies to find her crowds already dispersed. Her campaign was also greatly hampered by lack of money. Attacking Briscoe's record and failure to act on such issues as Texas's critical public school finance program, she found that the reform spirit inspired by the 1974 Sharpstown scandal had grown listless. Many of her former supporters failed to rally to her stand, and voters around the state were apathetic to a reformer's appeals. When the votes were counted Farenthold had captured only twenty-eight percent of the vote, giving Dolph Briscoe the second term traditionally afforded Texas governors.

After her second defeat, many Texans expected Frances Farenthold to retire from active political life, but she continued her speaking engagements on behalf of the National Women's Political Caucus. A conference on women's rights in 1975 took her to Wells College in Aurora, New York, and in 1976 she returned there to become the thirteenth president of the prestigious women's college.

One of her first moves as president of Wells was to take down the office portraits of her twelve male predecessors and send them to the library. "There wasn't a role model among them," she declared. She immediately launched into an energy-saving program, trimmed the budget, and extended a recruit-ment campaign across the nation to increase Wells's enrollment. She also publicized the college, accepting speaking engage-ments in various sections of the country. Education, to Faren-thold, became a driving force equal to that of politics, and the college newspaper gave her full credit for being, "tough, truthful, and caring."

During her term as president, she spoke out in favor of women's colleges, stating that the atmosphere "gave women the opportunity to experience self-assurance." Recalling her own college experience, she said, "I personally know I wouldn't have survived The University of Texas Law School without the confidence I gained at Vassar." Serving as president of the col-lege was a rewarding experience for Farenthold, but she still felt that she was not an academic person. In addition, she com-mented that she was "a Democrat in Republican territory," and in 1979 she came home to Texas.

Immediately liberals and feminists began speculating on what role she would take in the political life of the state, but she confined her public engagements to speaking about her ex-periences and encouraging other women to take an active role in the politics of the state. Her legacy in Texas politics remains a controversial one. Many politicians feel that she deserted the state political force and that she failed to lend a hand to en-courage other women to follow her lead in politics. Others feel that the fact that Farenthold ran for statewide public office has paved the way for other women to make statewide races. Her campaign manager once said that when Farenthold ran for the governor's office in 1972, she often heard the refrain from men in the rural areas of Texas: "Well, I might as well vote for a woman in the 1970s, I voted for one in the 1920s." Many women are hoping that Farenthold's gubernatorial races, as well as her courageous stand for governmental reform, will provide the impetus to encourage more women to run for public office in the coming decades.

REFERENCES

Adams, Ruth. "Sissy Farenthold of Texas." *The London Guardian* (February 21, 1973): 1.

Coleman, Suzanne. *The Politics of Participation: The Emergent Journey of Farenthold, Frances.* Unpublished master's thesis. Arlington: The University of Texas at Arlington, 1973.

Crawford, Ann Fears. *From Ferguson to Farenthold: Texas Women in Politics.* Unpublished paper delivered at the Texas State Historical Association (San Antonio, 1978).

Daniels, Mary. "Sissy Farenthold." *Chicago Tribune.* (February 18, 1973): 22.

Deaton, Charles. *The Year They Threw the Rascals Out.* Austin: Shoal Creek Publishers, Inc., 1973.

Frances Farenthold. "Announcement for Governor, 1972." Copy in files of Ann Fears Crawford.

Frappolo, Elizabeth. "The Ticket That Might Have Been . . . Vice-President Farenthold." *Ms.* (January, 1973): 74-76, 116-120.

Ivins, Molly. "Rep. Frances Farenthold: A Melancholy Rebel." *Texas Observer* (April 9, 1971): 1-4.

Ivins, Molly. "The Dogged Ascent of Sissy Farenthold." *Viva* (October, 1974): 73-75.

Ivins, Molly. "Whistlestopping with Sissy: A tale of two train trips." *Texas Observer* (April 26, 1974): 3-5.

Katz, Harvey. *Shadow on the Alamo.* New York: Doubleday & Company, 1972.

Katz, Harvey. "The Amazing Grace of Sissy Farenthold." *Ramparts* (October, 1972): 10-11.

McCrory, James. "Mrs. Farenthold Sets Issues in Governor Race." San Antonio *Express-News* (March 3, 1974): 24.

Trillin, Calvin. "U.S. Journal: Texas Reformer." *The New Yorker* (June 17, 1972): 78-82.

Victirsin, Val. "The View from Texas." *National Review* (September 15, 1972): 1011-1029.

INTERVIEWS

Joe Bernal and Ann Fears Crawford. San Antonio, January 1976.

Suzanne Coleman and Ann Fears Crawford. Austin, July 1979.

Creekmore Fath and Ann Fears Crawford. Austin, February 1973.

Terence O'Rourke and Ann Fears Crawford. Austin, October 1976.

Ann Richards and Ann Fears Crawford. Austin, April 1978.

Sarah Weddington and Ann Fears Crawford. Austin, April 1977.

— *Photo by Lon Cooper, courtesy News and Information Service,*
The University of Texas at Austin.

Congresswoman From Texas

Barbara Jordan

In 1976 a cheering crowd at the Democratic National Convention held at New York's Madison Square Garden rose to its feet to greet the keynote speaker. It was the first time in the history of United States politics that a black woman had given a keynote address at a political convention, and Democrats gave Congresswoman Barbara Jordan a historic and rousing ovation. They applauded again when she announced in ringing tones:

> There is something different and special about this opening night. I, Barbara Jordan, am a keynote speaker, and notwithstanding the past, my presence before you is one additional bit of evidence that the American Dream need not forever be deferred.

"Different and special" are two words that Congresswoman Jordan may well have used to describe herself. She early declared, "I never intended to become a run-of-the-mill person." Born poor and black in the heart of Houston's Fifth Ward on February 26, 1936, she was the daughter of a Baptist preacher who often worked nights as a warehouse clerk to rear and educate his three daughters. A stern disciplinarian, B.M. Jordan instilled in Barbara, his youngest daughter, a strong sense of dignity and character.

A Christian upbringing was an integral part of her formative years, and as a member of Houston's Good Hope Baptist Church, she was influenced by the teaching of A. A. Lucas, a concerned pastor who brought politics into his church. Lucas, in his efforts to instill the pride of black citizenship in his congregation, began a local chapter of the National Association for the Advancement of Colored People, and initiated several class-action suits which set Supreme Court precedents that later helped pave the way for Barbara Jordan to run for the Texas Senate.

While attending E. O. Smith Junior High School and Phyllis Wheatly High School, she competed in speech and debate contests, winning honors in extemporaneous speaking. While in high school she heard Judge Edith Sampson speak and resolved that she would become a lawyer. However, her father disapproved, telling her teacher that law was not a profession for a woman.

When she completed high school, Jordan entered all-black Texas Southern University, winning more honors on the TSU debate team. Here she developed her characteristic oratorical style and delivery that became a part of her later political life.

After graduating from Texas Southern University with a bachelor of arts degree *magna cum laude* in political science, Jordan became the first woman to attend Boston University Law School. After she received her LLB degree in 1956, she returned to Houston and set up law practice at her family's kitchen table. Jordan returned to Boston University ten years after her graduation to receive an honorary doctor of laws degree.

The beginning of Barbara Jordan's legal career also marked her entry into politics, and her work with the Harris County Democrats led to an active part in the 1960 Kennedy-Johnson campaign. She began with the usual chores of stuffing envelopes and coordinating volunteer canvassers, but, when she was asked to substitute for a speaker at a rally, her speech was so impressive that she was immediately promoted to the speaking circuit.

Politics soon became a way of life, and Jordan was good enough in her jobs to be elected vice chair of the Harris County

Democrats. In 1962 she helped fight for the endorsement of gubernatorial candidate Don Yarborough by the Harris County Council of Organizations, a key black political group. When labor lawyer Chris Dixie suggested that she run for the Texas House of Representatives, Jordan began seriously to consider a career in politics.

Her campaign theme was "Retrenchment and Reform"; and although she gained twenty-three percent of the vote cast in the election when blacks in Houston composed only twenty percent of the electorate, she still lost. She wisely moved away from her emphasis as a black politician and concentrated on broadening her base of support to unite all voters. With additional financial support she ran again for the Texas House in 1964, gaining additional Anglo votes. She lost once again, however, and in addition suffered resounding political defeat when Governor John Connally vetoed her nomination to the State Democratic Executive Committee.

Jordan considered moving to another part of the United States where she would have a chance to win an election as a black woman. She determined, however, that her roots were in Texas and that her future was tied to the Texas political scene. In addition, two legal cases of the 1960s and 1970s had helped carve out a new senatorial district in Houston, with a representation that was thirty-eight percent black.

Reynolds v. Sims established the standard of "one man-vote," making this dictum applicable not only to states, but to their political subdivisions as well. Then the case of *Baker v. Carr* in 1976 held that federal courts must consider on their merits suits challenging the apportionment of state legislatures in violation of the Equal Protection Clause of the Fourteenth Amendment. In light of these decisions reapportionment of the Texas legislature followed, creating the Eleventh Senatorial District and carving out a seat that seemed destined for Jordan.

Resigning her job as executive assistant to Harris County Judge Bill Elliot, Jordan challenged the dean of the Houston delegation, State Representative J.C. Whitfield, in the Democratic primary. Her campaign tactics were based on an ap-

peal not only to the blacks within her district to whom she
mailed out 35,000 sample ballots showing them how to vote for
Barbara Jordan, but also included canvassing white districts and
gaining the support of Anglos by probing such basic reform
issues as the antiquated industrial accident laws, the inequities
in the state minimum wage, and the need for lower automobile
insurance rates.

Beating Whitfield in the Democratic primary, she won the
Senate seat without a Republican challenge to become the first
black to be elected to the Texas Senate since 1883, and the first
black woman ever to sit in the Texas legislature. From the beginning of her legislative career she determined that she would not
be labeled as a black nor as a woman but merely as a Democrat,
reflecting with political awareness that defending racial and
feminist issues would not get her where she was determined to
go.

During the three terms she served in the Texas Senate, she
gained the respect of the leadership, the Senate's few liberals,
and the conservative majority, reinforcing the political reality
that she would carry to the United States House of Representatives — work within the system. She studied and mastered
Senate procedures, and soon she was recognized by members of
the legislature as an expert on parliamentary procedure. She
sought out influential members and asked their advice, thereby
gaining their respect. "I had to get inside the club," she stated,
"not just inside the chamber."

Confidence, dignity, and an oratorical style that matched,
if not excelled, that of most of her male colleagues gave her
power that has not been challenged by any woman member of
the Texas legislature since. Her command of parliamentary procedure gained her an enviable record in passing legislation—out
of 150 bills introduced, almost half passed. In addition, she
chaired the Urban Affairs Committee, the Labor and Management Committee, and the prestigious State Affairs Committee.
At the end of her first term in the Sixtieth Texas Legislature her
fellow Senators passed a resolution unanimously praising her
service to the state and her conduct as a freshman Senator. Her

response to their accolades was pure Barbara Jordan: "When I came here, you were all strangers; there were perhaps mutual suspicions, tensions, and apprehensions. Now I believe they have been replaced by mutual respect."

Much of the mutual respect was earned by Senator Barbara Jordan's ability to tackle tough legislation. Shunning the typical woman's legislative issues — education and child-welfare — she took on the Texas business establishment, advocating and winning the fight to improve the Workmen's Compensation Act by increasing the maximum benefits for an injured worker, while also specifying a minimum twenty-five percent of damages to be paid to attorneys in workmen's compensation cases. Her fight for a minimum wage bill, the first for the state of Texas, as well as her sponsorship of a bill to establish a Texas Fair Employment Practices Commission also pitted her against the more conservative members of the Senate and the business lobby.

Her political techniques won her the admiration of the Senate "wheeler-dealers," and she was not adverse to a little political arm-twisting herself, calling in her political chips to stop a move to block voter registration by mail. She also added to her list of firsts by serving as the first freshman Senator assigned to the Texas Legislative Council, the research branch of the legislature.

On March 28, 1972 Senator Oscar Mauzy of Dallas nominated Barbara Jordan as president *pro tempore* of the Senate, and the nomination was seconded by every Senator. Thus she became the first black woman in American history to preside over a state legislative body. Following a longstanding tradition, on June 10, 1972 Governor Preston Smith and Lieutenant Governor Ben Barnes left the state so that Jordan could serve as acting governor for a day.

Although her service in the Texas Senate had been rewarding and Jordan had gained statewide recognition for her legislative service, she began to look for a greater challenge. It presented itself when, pursuant to the 1970 census, Harris County was again redistricted and gained a new congressional seat. Political bargaining on her part with Lieutenant Governor

Ben Barnes helped to establish the Eighteenth Congressional District, again constructed especially for Barbara Jordan. However, she gained the enmity of many people in the Eleventh Senatorial District by relinquishing her state Senate seat and by diluting her district to such a point that her black constituents felt that they had little representation in the state legislature.

In 1972 Jordan was elected to the United States House of Representatives, winning eighty-one percent of the votes cast in her district and becoming the first black woman from the South to occupy a seat in Congress. She extended her influence to the people throughout her district, telling them at her swearing-in ceremony: "If I fail you, do not talk about it at your churches, on buses, at beauty and barber shops, but call me. Call me anything you like, but call me."

The tactics and strategies that Jordan mastered in the Texas legislature carried over into her Congressional career. " 'I sought the power points,' " she once stated. " 'I knew if I were going to get anything done, they (Congressional and party leaders) would be the ones to help me get it done.' " Helping her most was longtime supporter President Lyndon Johnson. Jordan had worked hard during the 1969 Democratic Convention to bring the support of the Texas delegation behind a plank in the Democratic platform that supported Johnson's policies. Johnson had been supportive of her Congressional campaign, and, when the Congressional black caucus instructed her to seek a seat on the Armed Forces Committee, Johnson told her that instead she belonged on the Judiciary Committee. Johnson asserted his influence, and there she landed.

Her position on the Judiciary Committee brought her nationwide attention during the impeachment hearing of President Richard Nixon. Voting for every impeachment resolution, she made a most moving and impressive speech concerning her faith in the Constitution and the Democratic process.

> We, the people? I felt for many years that somehow George Washington and Alexander Hamilton just left me out by mistake. But through

the process of amendment, interpretation, and court decision, I have finally been included in 'We, the people.'

My faith in the Constitution is whole, it is complete, it is total. I am not going to sit here and be an idle spectator to the diminution, the subversion, and the destruction of the Constitution.

Her words brought her national acclaim seldom accorded a freshman member of Congress.

Following President Nixon's resignation Congresswoman Jordan participated in Vice-President Gerald Ford's confirmation hearings, criticizing his voting record on civil rights and anti-poverty legislation and claiming that he lacked the forthright leadership demanded by the American people. Her attitude mellowed somewhat after Ford's speech in his swearing-in ceremony, and she suggested that the American people should give him a chance.

While the Watergate hearings took up most of Jordan's freshman year, she was able to sponsor and co-sponsor several bills, as well as maintain a ninety-nine percent voting record in her first six months—higher than almost every other member of Congress.

Despite the recognition she gained as a freshman congresswoman, Jordan continued to be criticized by numbers of liberal groups for not advocating more liberal legislation. In addition, the black caucus and various women's groups criticized Jordan for failing to be more vocal on issues affecting blacks and women. Jordan defended her failure to be categorized as either a black politician or a woman politician by stating:

I do believe I can do more by quietly working my way in and seeing that change is brought about and that's solid change, not elusive or knee-jerk. I'm neither a black politician, nor a woman politician. Just a politician, a professional politician.

She further expressed her views on women's issues by explaining that every minute she was in her office she felt that she was dealing with issues that affected women.

A great deal of her time in the House was spent with the Texas delegation, attending the Wednesday luncheons of the group, although her main concern continued to be her constituents in Houston. She once said:

> I am here simply because all those people in the 18th District of Texas cannot get on planes and buses and come to Washington to speak for themselves. They have elected me as their spokesman, nothing else, and my only job is to speak for them.

The congresswoman from Texas spoke out loud and long in support of the rights of all citizens when the Voting Rights Act of 1965 came up for renewal by Congress. Her stand in favor of extending coverage of the act to many areas of the country, Texas included, found her aligned against Texas governor Dolph Briscoe, his secretary of state Mark White, and the majority of the Texas delegation.

The 1965 act had prohibited states or localities that were covered to change voting laws without advance approval of the United States attorney general. Jordan's amendments extended the pre-clearance requirement to any jurisdiction in which less than fifty percent of the eligible voters registered or voted in the 1972 presidential election. In addition, and of particular importance to Texas with its strong enclaves of Mexican Americans, it extended coverage to areas where voting materials were written solely in English, when more than five percent of the eligible voters had a "single mother tongue" other than English.

Despite criticism from liberal groups Jordan's voting record in the House of Representatives was more liberal than conservative, and in line with her votes in the Texas Senate. Her record reflected a concern for the poor, the disadvantaged, and the average consumer. With her sponsorship of the repeal of the Fair Trade Laws, enabling the practice of verbal price fixing by manufacturers, she gained a mark from consumer protection advocates. She also co-sponsored legislation establishing equal credit for women, an important breakthrough for single working women; a wider food commodities program for school lunch programs; freedom of information; emergency public service jobs; home rule for the District of Columbia; tax credits for low-income workers; and numerous health programs.

When Congresswoman Jordan announced on December 11, 1978 that she would not seek a fourth term in the House of Representatives, there was a great deal of speculation about her health. Jordan, however, countered that she did not want to be locked into her role as a legislator. "The longer you stay in Congress," she said, "the more difficult it is to leave. I don't want to wake up one fine morning and say there is nothing else in the world Barbara Jordan can do."

There was something else for her to do back in her native Texas. When her term was over, Barbara Jordan, former Texas Senator and former congresswoman from Texas, returned to build a home outside of Austin and to assume the Lyndon Baines Johnson public service professorship at the LBJ School of Public Affairs at The University of Texas. There she yearly holds two seminars, one on political values and ethics and one on intergovernmental relations. She continues to support the Democratic party and actively campaigned for President Jimmy Carter in both his campaigns for the presidency in 1976 and 1980. Her voice remains active in Democratic politics; but her strongest contribution may have been the door she opened for black women in the Texas legislature. Barbara Jordan proved the inspiration for other black women to take an active role in politics, in their communities, and to run for legislative seats. As one former legislator, Eddie Bernice Johnson, who served in the Texas House of Representatives from Dallas for three terms remarked: "Because Barbara was there first, it has been easier for all of us."

REFERENCES

"A Profile of Barbara Jordan." *Texas Observer* (November 3, 1972): 3.

Amen, Rhoda. "Congresswoman Jordan: 'gentle lady from Texas'." Austin *American-Statesman* (July 10, 1975): A-16.

Barta, Carolyn. "Barbara Jordan From There to Here." Dallas *Morning News* (February 18, 1979): B-7.

Broyles, William. "The Making of Barbara Jordan." *Texas Monthly* (October, 1976): 33-47.

Bryant, Ira B. *Barbara Charline Jordan — From the Ghetto To the Capitol. New York:* D. Armstrong Co., Inc., 1977.

Cleland, Jack. "Representative Jordan Looks to Judiciary Panel." Houston *Chronicle* (January 3, 1973): 14.

Curtis, Tom. "Johnson at Head of List Honoring Barbara Jordan." Houston *Chronicle* (December 12, 1971): 1.

Elliott, Karen. "Black Star Over Washington." *Texas Parade* (March, 1974).

Jordan, Barbara and Shelby Hearon. *Barbara Jordan: A Self-Portrait.* New York: Doubleday & Company, Inc., 1979.

Jordan, Barbara. "How I Got There." *Atlantic Monthly* Special Issue. (March, 1975).

Lowry, Candy. "A Legislative Day with Barbara Jordan." Austin *American-Statesman* (April 19, 1971): A-14.

Morehead, Richard. "Barbara, You've Come a Long Way." Dallas *Morning News* (February 13, 1975): A-1.

Sanders, Charles. "Barbara Jordan: Texan is New Power in Capitol." *Ebony* (February, 1976).

Tuma, Laura. "Politics to Professorship." *Daily Texan* (March 22, 1979).

Weddington, Sarah, *et al. Texas Women in Politics.* Austin: Foundation for Women's Resources, 1977.

INTERVIEWS

Eddie Bernice Johnson and Ann Fears Crawford, Dallas, July 1976.

Photo by Larry Murphy, courtesy News and Information Service,
The University of Texas at Austin.

Barbara Jordan and her students at the LBJ School of Public Affairs.

Adviser To
The President

 Sarah Ragle Weddington

When the Sixty-third session of the Texas legislature opened in January 1973, there were some decided changes in the
women members of the House and the Senate. The reform impetus in the House of Representatives led by Frances Farenthold
was in shambles, owing in part to Farenthold's defeat in her race
for the governor's office. Barbara Jordan had retired from the
Senate to run successfully for the U.S. Congress, and many
critics felt that women in the legislature would fail to provide
the leadership they had with a Farenthold in the House and a
Jordan in the Senate.

Nevertheless, when the session opened, the House of
Representatives held five women — the highest number ever. In
addition, a young woman who was to make her legislative career
a stepping stone to the national political scene came to the
House from Travis County's District 37-B. Few people would
have prophesied that a twenty-seven-year-old woman would
assume the mantle of leadership that Farenthold and Jordan had
laid down, become the dean of the Travis County delegation,
and eventually move into position as the senior adviser to the
president of the United States.

Women's issues propelled Sarah Ragle Weddington to the
Texas House of Representatives, and women's issues carried her

to the White House to serve as special assistant to President Jimmy Carter. The road to the White House began on February 5, 1945, when Sarah Ragle, the daughter of a Methodist minister, was born in Abilene, Texas. Graduating from high school at the age of sixteen, she attended McMurry College, majoring in speech and education.

Practice teaching convinced her that she didn't want to be a teacher and she settled on law school as her next career alternative. Even though the college counselor told her how difficult it had been for his son and that he thought it would be even more difficult for a woman, Sarah enrolled with five other women at The University of Texas Law School. She worked as a legal proofreader and typist in the House of Representatives, as well as working in a juvenile defender's program. In 1967 she and a classmate, Linda Coffee, were the only two women who graduated with their class. Both had become involved in the women's movement in Austin and both worked with the Problem Pregnancy Center, a special focus of the movement and the agency that served as counseling agent for women seeking abortions.

Weddington worked as an assistant to law professor John Sutton, helping to draft the Code of Ethics for Lawyers for the American Bar Association. Marriage to law student Ron Weddington took her to Fort Worth, where she became the first woman to serve as assistant city attorney for Fort Worth. Later the couple returned to Austin and opened a law office; they were divorced in 1974.

Early in 1970 her college classmate Linda Coffee, now practicing law in Dallas, introduced Sarah to a prospective client, who was to become famous in legal circles as "Jane Roe," and would serve as the client in the two lawyers's legal test case to get "declaratory relief" from the Texas abortion laws, which had remained virtually unchanged since 1854.

In March 1970 the two lawyers filed a suit entitled *Roe v. Wade* in the federal district court in Dallas. On behalf of "Jane Roe," they claimed that the Texas abortion laws were unconstitutional. This was Sarah Weddington's first appearance in court in a contested case. In June 1970 the court declared the Texas law unconstitutional, but refused to grant an injunction which would have given the plaintiff the right to a legal abortion in Texas.

Weddington and Coffee appealed the denial of the injunction, forcing the case before the United States Supreme Court. To gain financial support for the case, Weddington spoke to group after group about the antiquated abortion laws, and the James Madison Constitutional Law Institute provided both staff and financial assistance. Weddington quit her job to devote full time to preparing the case, and on December 13, 1971 a seven-judge court heard the case.

At this hearing and at a subsequent one before the nine-judge court on October 11, 1972 Weddington argued the case. Three months later, the decision of the court was handed down, and it was a momentous one. By a vote of seven to two, the Supreme Court had affirmed the right of a woman's doctor to perform an abortion during the first trimester of pregnancy and stated that during the second trimester a decision would depend upon state controls "reasonably related to the preservation and protection of maternal health." For the first time in the history of the United States women were able to have direct control over their bodies. In addition, Sarah Weddington had become the spokesperson for the abortion issue not only in Texas but across the nation.

While Weddington waited for the decision on the *Roe v. Wade* case, she filed as a candidate for the Texas legislature from Travis County. Her primary financial support came from a new entity on the Texas political scene, the Texas Women's Political Caucus, and her campaign staff was composed solely of women. One of her three male opponents referred to her as "that sweet little girl," and Weddington cites the fact that many people in the city joked about the fact that he spent over $30,000, only to be beaten by "that sweet little girl" spending only $15,000.

Overcoming her three opponents in the primary and winning the runoff election, Weddington became the first woman legislator elected from Travis County. High on her list of legislative priorities were family planning, women and credit, consumerism, legislation affecting children, and a displaced homemakers bill, along with a strong stand on the passage of an Equal Rights Amendment in Texas.

During her first session in the legislature, she gained appointments to committees on appropriations, insurance, and criminal jurisprudence, along with an appointment to the Special House Rules Revision Committee. She co-sponsored with Senator Charles Herring a kidney health-care act to provide life-saving procedures to terminal kidney patients and successfully passed House Bill 920, making it unlawful to deny credit or loans on the basis of sex. The bill served as an amendment to the Consumer Credit Code, applying to transactions where interest charged exceeds ten percent.

Although Weddington gained a reputation as an advocate for women's issues, sponsoring a number of bills dealing with equal rights protection and establishing a state Commission on the Status of Women, she also expanded her legislative interests to include public employees' salaries, health care, the preservation of historic structures, public kindergartens, and the veterans' land program.

Reelected to serve again in the Sixty-fourth Legislature, Weddington co-sponsored with Representative Kay Bailey House Bill 284, designed to provide greater protection for victims of sexual assault. The bill provided that in a rape case a victim's past sexual experiences would not be admissible evidence unless a judge determined it material to the case. Other provisions of the bill were the elimination of the definition of consent and the extension of the statute of limitation to three years.

Weddington took a strong stand against the so-called "Bentsen Bill," which would have provided a separate presidential primary for the state of Texas. She also sponsored legislation to benefit state and university employees, providing emergency pay raises, funding for merit raises, and increases in retirement benefits.

As a member of the legislature, she served as a delegate to the Constitutional Revision Convention, which sought to revise the Texas constitution. The people of Texas, however, turned down the proposed revisions, and Weddington expressed her disappointment at the time and energy wasted and the opportunities lost to bring the state constitution up-to-date.

The opening of the Sixty-fifth legislative session saw Weddington fighting anti-abortion efforts and a movement to rescind the Equal Rights Amendment in Texas. In addition, she expanded her legislative horizons to sponsor bills providing for a centralized state job agency, funding for the arts with an optional city tax of one percent on hotel and motel stays, and the bill creating the statewide Commission on the Status of Women. In the judicial field she sponsored legislation to create a new district court for Travis County and a bill providing for optional county home rule.

As an informed and active legislator, Weddington gained numerous awards for her legislative skills and her work on behalf of women across the state. She won praise as an expert on constitutional matters, and her colleagues from Travis County recognized her as dean of the Travis County delegation. She was named Woman of the Year by the Texas Women's Political Caucus in 1973, and in the same year, the Austin *American-Statesman* named her an "Outstanding Woman," stating that "she is an effective, hardworking legislator who listens when constituents and colleagues have something to say." The National Organization of Women granted her the Susan B. Anthony Award, and *Texas Monthly* named her as one of the ten best legislators of the Sixty-fourth legislative session.

The statewide magazine, however, was quick to admonish her when she left the Sixty-sixth session to travel to China, on a trip sponsored by the American Committee on U.S-China Relations, missing the last month of the legislative session. Weddington, however, defended her actions by stating that she had checked with the Speaker and her committee chairpersons and made certain that her legislation was in order. In addition, she had checked with each member of the Travis County delegation, and they agreed that she should go. Weddington was quite surprised when she returned to find the media had taken her to task for making the trip. She recalled:

> Part of the resentment on many people's part was that news leaked out while I was gone that I was being considered for a job in Washington. I had not meant for the news to be released while I was in China, and I think people were resentful that I was not here to tell them whether I was thinking of going to Washington or not.

The decision to accept a job in Washington was a difficult one for a woman whose personal and political roots were deep in Texas. Although Weddington was pleased with the direction her political career was taking in Texas, she was disheartened with the efforts of the legislature during her last session. When the position as general counsel to the United States Department of Agriculture was offered her by the newly-appointed head, Texan John White, Sarah resigned her seat in the legislature and accepted. She later remembered:

> I saw my future in Texas politics, and I was not really interested in going to Washington. However, I reevaluated the reasons I was staying in Texas. I was contemplating a statewide race, and I found that funding was going to be a problem. Then I went to Washington for an interview, and I found that they were not just looking for a 'token woman,' but they wanted someone who would be involved in policy and would be an integral part of the department.

A dedicated worker at whatever job she undertook, Weddington accepted the general counsel's job and expanded her administrative expertise by supervising a staff of some 350 people. Moreover, she aligned herself with Democrat John White, rapidly becoming a leader of the Democratic party on a national level, and solidified her position in the upper echelons of national party politics.

In September 1978 President Jimmy Carter appointed Weddington to replace Midge Costanza as special assistant to the president, concentrating on women's issues. Immediately the anti-abortionist forces opposed her appointment, but she stated that she would support the president's stand on the abortion issue. Other critics assailed her when President Carter fired Bella Abzug, head of the President's National Advisory Committee on Women. With Weddington working hard to bring the committee together after half the committee resigned in protest over Abzug's firing, columnist Ellen Goodman wrote:

> The one official now in charge of representing women's concerns in the administration is the raw recruit, Sarah Weddington. No one knows yet what she will be permitted to do or what she will be able to do. But all we've seen so far from the lady of Texas is a pair of velvet gloves.

Nevertheless, Weddington worked hard to bring women's issues into focus, keeping all choices available to women throughout the nation. Her speaking schedule was a difficult one, and she toured the country telling women that there was a need to blend women's issues with the broader issues facing the country. She headed the Task Force on Women, charged with investigating inflation, taxation, desegregation, welfare, federal employment, and other issues concerning women.

In addition, Weddington served as an effective spokesperson for the Carter administration, often pointing out that Carter's record on appointment of women to federal office was better than any other president. She also saw herself as the person designated to see that Carter's commitment to the passage of the Equal Rights Amendment to the Constitution was carried out.

Weddington's ability to work closely with the president and his administrative aides paid off when, on August 10, 1979 she moved even closer to the White House's political power. Hamilton Jordan told the president's special assistant that she had been chosen to replace Tim Kraft as senior adviser to the president. Once again, her top priority became passage of the ERA, and Weddington convinced the administration to put significant emphasis on the passage of the amendment. Moving about the country, she worked on a one-to-one basis with groups and legislators to convince them of the rightness of the issue and continued to work for more women appointees to federal agencies and offices.

Her loyalty to the Democratic administration and to Carter as president was paramount in her service to the administration, and Weddington was quoted as saying: "I'm here to reflect the administration's position, and a lot of what I do is behind the scenes. The person who should get the credit is the president." Failure to effect passage of the Equal Rights Amendment before Carter left office was only one of the disappointments that Weddington had to face in the election year 1980. When Carter was defeated for reelection by Republican Ronald Reagan, Weddington had to once again make a career choice. She had worked avidly for the president's reelection, and the president showed his concern for his special adviser by offering to help her with another job or position.

Weddington's attitude toward political roles and high office is reflected in an oft-repeated story that she likes to tell of "getting up in the morning, getting into my 1972 Texas Gremlin; driving down to the White House, and having the gates open. The guards salute, and I think, 'Now, that's power.' " As the president's special adviser, however, she was more than aware of the fact that someday she would drive out and the gates would no longer open in the same way. As far as her service in Washington is concerned she is proudest of the fact that women were appointed to offices at levels where they could affect every decision made in the federal government.

Where to go from the White House? Many of her friends speculated that she would go into the corporate legal field; others felt she would once again like to work for an agency of the federal government. Texas politicians argued that the former legislator's roots in Texas were so strong that she would once again contemplate a statewide race in Texas. Many agreed that her greatest desire is to serve her state in the attorney general's office — if the money were available for a woman candidate.

Weddington, however, chose to take some time to "unwind, reflect, and explore some of the things I have long wanted to do." Her role as visiting professor of government at Wheaton College in Massachusetts and as political editor of *Glamor* magazine gave her time to explore and investigate the next step for the young woman from Texas who had served as adviser to a president.

REFERENCES

Bell, Joseph N. "A Landmark Decision." *Good Housekeeping* (July 1973): 77-79; 148-152.

Brown, Cathy. "Women Fight Abortion Bills." *Daily Texan* (April 30, 1975): 2.

Cobler, Sharon. "Women's Rights Battles Not Finished." Dallas *Morning News* (April 27, 1974): 22.

Crawford, Ann Fears. *The Good Old Girls — Women in the Texas Legislature 1973-1979.* Unpublished paper delivered at the American Studies of Texas Association meeting (Denton, 1979).

Dudley, Mary. "The Odyssey of Sarah Weddington." *Texas Woman* (November, 1979): 25-31.

Dudley, Mary. " 'Women to Gain Legislative Clout,' Weddington Says." Austin *American-Statesman* (September 16, 1976): 2.

Green, LaVerne. "Rep. Weddington Advocates Abortion Availability Here." Austin *American-Statesman* (October 18, 1973): C-5.

Griffith, Dotty. "Woman Lawyer Outspoken." *Daily Texan* (December 2, 1971): 4.

Kaighin, Abby. "Weddington Fears Success Fading Quickly." Austin *American-Statesman* (June 1977): C-1.

Putzel, Henry Jr. "Roe v. Wade." *U.S. Reports — Cases Adjudged in the Supreme Court.* Washington: U.S. Printing Office, 1974.

Richardson, Barbara. "Legislator Sees Effort to Curtail Women's Rights." Dallas *Times-Herald* (April 30, 1974): 1.

Smith, Alison. "Weddington Leads Women's Battle." *Daily Texan* (May 11, 1973): 3.

"This Right of Privacy." *Texas Observer* (February 16, 1973): 1-5.

Tolchin, Susan and Martin. *Clout: Womanpower and Politics*. New York: Coward, McCann, and Geohegan, Inc., 1975.

Turboff, Marilyn. "Weddington Advises More Action on Abortion Ruling Anniversary." *Daily Texan* (January 23, 1975).

Weddington, Sarah. *A Session of Accomplishments: The 64th Legislative Session*. Austin: Texas House of Representatives, 1964.

Weddington, Sarah. *A Study on the Status of Women in Insurance and Comments on Proposed Regulation*. Austin: Texas House of Representatives, n.d.

Weddington, Sarah. "Court Abortion Victory Not Enough." *Daily Texan* (February 1, 1973): 1.

Weddington, Sarah. *Legislative Session: 63rd. Legislature*. Austin: Texas House of Representatives, 1963.

Weddington, Sarah. *Legislative Session. 64th Legislature*. Austin: Texas House of Representatives, 1964.

Weddington, Sarah, *et al. Texas Women in Politics*. Austin: Foundation for Women's Resources, 1977.

Wood, Susan. "The Weddington Way." Washington *Post* magazine (February 11, 1979): 6-11.

INTERVIEWS

Ann Richards and Ann Fears Crawford, Austin, April 1977.

Sarah Weddington and Ann Fears Crawford. Austin, January 1978.

Sarah Weddington visits with President Jimmy Carter at a Washington reception.

Worker For Women

Lupe Anguiano

In December 1980 CBS's famed television news show *60 Minutes* focused on a San Antonio project sponsored by the National Women's Program Development Corporation. The corporation's goal was to assist women heads of families on welfare to become self-supporting, and the executive director of the program was Chicana activist Lupe Anguiano, who had spent a decade fighting for Chicana rights across the United States.

So forceful was Lupe's role as an innovative worker for women on welfare that when *Ms.* magazine cited the "Women to Watch in the 1980s," the one woman from Texas the magazine named was Lupe Anguiano. "I have a great desire to go out into the world and work for and among people," Lupe wrote in a personal letter to Pope Paul IV on June 8, 1964. With the Pope's permission, Guadalupe Anguiano left the Victory Noll Convent and began an odyssey that would take her from farm workers' marches to working with welfare women on San Antonio's impoverished south side.

No one understood the problems of poverty and welfare better than Lupe, for she had grown up in migrant farmworker camps and had experienced as a child the humiliation of not being able to speak English and of being segregated from her classmates who regularly attended school in her hometown. Born March 12, 1929 in La Junta, Colorado, the fourth child of

Rosaria and Jose Anguiano, Lupe moved with her family from California to Colorado, where her father sought a job with the railroad. Needing a more reliable income, her mother took the children back to California to enter the migrant stream of agricultural workers, and for the first thirteen years of her life Lupe and her family followed seasonal work from harvest to harvest.

Her early years were filled with exposures to severe injustices which existed both in the migrant-worker system and in the public-school system. She found that she was punished for speaking Spanish, her native language, and in many instances Anglos and Mexican-Americans were required to attend separate schools. "That was the worst part of my life," she recalled of those years.

Despite the poverty of the migrant camps, where rain often poured through the roofs of the huts and where there often was not enough to eat, Rosaria served as teacher and comforter to her children. No holiday went without a reminder that God was good. "I still get excited at Christmas," says Lupe. "I remember that Mother always decorated the house and set up the creche. It was wonderful."

Life, however, was not always wonderful for the migrants, and her brothers soon became involved in efforts to organize a union among the farmworkers. Lupe, who was elected president of the student body in the eighth grade, still remembers the taunts of her schoolmates: "Lemon picker! Lemon picker!" they would call after her. Another heartbreak was the death of her mother, who left a legacy of strength and faith to all her children.

After graduating from high school and junior college in Ventura, California, Aguiano entered the Victory Noll Convent in Huntington, Indiana. She took her final vows in 1958 and spent several years as a teacher. She loved working with young people, but felt a need to build a better society for everyone in the United States. Experiencing a sense of disillusionment with the church when she attempted to concern herself with community problems, she left the convent in 1964.

Immediately Lupe became involved in a wide variety of activities, working as a counselor for a youth program in East Los Angeles and serving as a coordinator for a federal poverty program designed to provide aid to both Anglos and blacks. Anguiano had to learn to get along with all of them, and they had to learn to accept her, a Chicana, in her emerging role as an activist.

For her work in the community the League of Mexican American Women honored her as "Key Woman of 1966." When President Lyndon B. Johnson invited her to attend a White House conference dealing with problems of education, unemployment, poverty, and farm workers, Anguiano was enthusiastic, as she felt she understood these problems better than most people for they had always been an integral part of her life.

After the conference Vice-President Hubert Humphrey invited her to join the Department of Health, Education, and Welfare. Serving as an education specialist, Anguiano was charged with writing the greater part of the Bilingual Education Act. When the bill was finally passed, however, she found that she had been excluded from the task force set up to develop the federal guidelines. "I felt that I was passed over because I was a woman, and I knew that my ideas on preserving native language were good ones," she recalled.

Discouraged, she left HEW and went to work with Cesar Chavez in the organization of the first Coachella Valley strike in California and was delegated director of the grape boycott in Cleveland, Ohio. Working in Michigan, she was successful in gaining the support of Detroit Mayor Cavanaugh and United Auto Workers President Walter Reuther on behalf of the farmworkers in their campaign to have table grapes boycotted in the U.S. In reflecting on her work with Chavez, the famed California farmworker organizer, Anguiano recalls, "He was the first person I worked with who really accepted my capabilities and gave me full responsibility."

Working with the National Association for the Advancement of Colored People, helping the Pueblo Indians in New Mexico, and a term as a civil rights specialist with HEW preceded her work with the Women's Task Force at HEW. Her work with the task force convinced her that women could save the world and that the Mexican-American woman needed to become active in politics, her community, and ethnic affairs. "Now is the time for 'las mujeres' not to stand behind their man, but to take their places beside them," she said.

As executive director of the Southwest Regional Office for the Spanish-speaking, a project of the National Council of Catholic Churches, Anguiano toured the southwestern states developing programs to aid Mexican-Americans. She spoke out for Mexican-American rights, expressing her feeling that there was a real lack of understanding by Anglos of what Chicanos were trying to accomplish. "The Southwest is different from other immigrant societies," she found. "The Chicano's roots are here. The culture of the Southwest has been determined by Mexicans, as well as by Anglos."

With exposure to Mexican-Americans in a variety of jobs throughout the Southwest, Anguiano came to the realization that many Chicanas were women locked into several generations of a welfare society and were wasting their skills and talents as unemployed persons while collecting their welfare checks. She recalled:

> Many of the women wanted to get off welfare, but they felt they were dependent on men. Eighty percent of the welfare recipients were women heads of households, and many lacked educational qualifications to get jobs to support their families.

Winning her one-woman war on welfare became a full-time job for Lupe. She applied for permission to rent an apartment in a welfare housing project, but found that her salary prohibited her from qualifying. In order to gain insights into the needs of women living in poverty environments, she lived with families headed by women dependent on welfare. The six months she spent with these families in substandard living conditions proved to be a frustrating experience for her. Accompanying the women on their daily rounds often meant spending entire days in food-stamp lines, welfare offices, and doctors' waiting rooms. Hostile treatment by agency personnel was merely one of the humiliations these women had to endure. Transportation and child care were ever-present problems, and many times hunger was a reality when the families simply ran out of food. Living in their poor surroundings in excessive heat in the summer and extreme cold in the winter was a way of life — a way of life that could produce only desolation and despair among the women and children. While Anguiano lived in the project six women attempted suicide. Four succeeded.

At the end of six months Anguiano left the welfare housing project with a case of rheumatic fever, but with an ever-increasing desire to aid these women on welfare. In time welfare reform became her goal, and she found that the problems of these women on welfare were not understood by the welfare department or by the women themselves. "Welfare should serve as a transition to help a woman become a productive, self-sufficient member of society," she came to believe, as she began pounding doors of community agencies and banks to get money to help women set up businesses and to find independence through self-supporting jobs.

Two Chicana women turned their cooking talents into the Stinson Field Cafe, providing home-cooked meals near one of San Antonio's airfields. In addition, Anguiano worked to provide scholarship money for vocational training. She secured transportation and child-care facilities, and manged to help some five hundred women get off the welfare rolls.

Former welfare recipients enrolled in cash register courses given at San Antonio College, nurses' aid training, typing courses, and general employment training. These jobs, however, all paid minimum wages, and, despite the initial optimism among the women, the cost of transportation and child care together with medical expenses made the individual ventures hopeless. Although a sense of freedom and productivity proved an exhilarating experience for these women, most were unable to support themselves and their families on minimum wages. Lack of mobility and resources also prevented the women from realizing their potential and seeking to improve their employment skills. As Anguiano testified before the Welfare Reform Subcommittee of the U.S. House of Representatives: "I cannot describe the extreme frustration of this experience."

Anguiano decided that if she were going to make any inroads into the welfare system that she had to start on the state level by working through the legislative process. With state legislators she designed and helped to pass legislation to set up a pilot program allowing the State Department of Public Welfare to sponsor training programs for women heads of households who could apply for Aid to Families with Dependent Children. Anguiano found that in the state of Texas there were some 94,000 Texas families who were under the AFDC welfare program; 96 percent of these families were headed by women; 86 percent of these women were members of a minority group.

The program that Anguiano designed passed the legislature in 1977, providing training to women in non-traditional occupations. In addition, it provided for welfare benefits to be extended to AFDC women until they become self-sufficient. Then through her corporation, the National Women's Program Development, Inc. of San Antonio, Anguiano obtained a grant to work on individualized job-training preparation for women on welfare.

Invited by the Carter administration to work on welfare reform at the national level, Anguiano was instrumental in the changing of welfare laws to enable mothers of children over seven to work outside the home. She reasoned that if welfare laws stipulated that a woman on welfare had to work until her children reached the age of eighteen, the program would result in additional displaced homemakers. To Anguiano, the welfare program presented another example of institutionalized sexism in government. In hearings before the Welfare Reform Committee of the Department of Health, Education, and Welfare, she stated:

Perhaps no other program so clearly exemplifies the deep-rooted, harmful, and dehumanizing effects of institutionalized sexism as does the current AFDC program.

To Anguiano government makes the mistake of viewing women only in terms of caring for children rather than as providing for children. Thus women heads of households continue to be victims within the welfare system.

In addition to working with women on welfare Anguiano served as a participant in the first national leadership conference of Rural American Women in 1978. Rural women who attended the conference heard Anguiano speak out in favor of adequate day care, pointing out that her own day care as an infant was a fruit box in the field. Then she was appointed by President Jimmy Carter to serve on the continuing committee for the International Women's Year.

Joining actress Jean Stapleton and humanist Coretta Scott King, Anguiano read the "Declaration of American Women" at the Houston IWY conference in November 1977. The declaration, a statement drafted by various women's groups across the nation, served as the cornerstone for the National Plan of Action for American Women that the group presented to President Carter. According to Anguiano, her favorite part of the declaration read:

> We are part of a worldwide movement of women who believe that only by bringing women into full partnership with men and respecting our rights as half the human race can we hope to achieve a world in which the whole human race — men, women, and children — can live in peace and security.

Numerous awards have come to Lupe Anguiano during her years as a concerned Chicana working for the rights of all women. In 1977 she was given an achievement award by the Texas Women's Political Caucus, for which she chairs the welfare reform caucus; and in 1978, she was named recipient of the Public Endeavor Award by Women in Communications. But one of the happiest days of her life was the day that she returned to California, where members of her family still live, to help Cesar Chavez arrange financing for the United Farm Workers Union to purchase eighty houses located in the camp of the lemon pickers, the place she had lived as a child.

For a woman who speaks with a soft voice, Lupe Anguiano's impact on women's issues has been a forceful one. She cites her role models as Chavez, Gloria Steinem, and Texas's Liz Carpenter, but for many Chicana women, Lupe Anguiano herself has become a role model. She remains one of the Mexican-American women in the Southwest who has fulfilled her role as an active Chicana. Anguiano feels her heritage is a rich one and that her life is centered in the Southwest, saying:

> I am not confused, discouraged, or alienated from society. I feel deeply that I am part of La Raza, and I feel deeply my role as a woman. It's a very exciting adventure that we're into, and my history is here.

REFERENCES

"Anguiano fights to reshape American Society." San Antonio *Express* (August 31, 1975): 24.

Anguiano, Lupe. *Testimony before Welfare Subcommittee, U.S. House of Representatives.* Washington: U.S. House of Representatives, October 31, 1977. Reprinted by National Women's Political Caucus, 1977.

Anguiano, Lupe. *Welfare Reform Hearings, Department of Health, Education and Welfare.* Washington, Department of Health, Education, and Welfare, March 10, 1977. Reprinted by National Women's Political Caucus, 1977.

"Assistance Grant OK'd." San Antonio *Express* (February 26, 1978): 16.

"Bill Would Aid AFDC Women." San Antonio *Express* (March 16, 1978): 9.

Clarke, Newlon. "Lupe Anguiano." *Famous Mexican-Americans.* New York: Dodd, Mead and Company, 1972.

Crawford, Ann Fears. "Mujer." Unpublished manuscript submitted to *Ms.* magazine, 1976.

Crawford, Ann Fears. "News release — National Women's Conference." (November 14-18, 1977).

Crawford, Ann Fears and Pedro Chapa, Jr. "Active Chicana — Lupe Anguiano." *¡Viva! Famous Mexican Americans.* Austin: Steck-Vaughn Company, 1976.

"500 Women Attend Jobs Seminar Here." Wichita Falls *Times* (March 5, 1978): 1.

"Meditation in Modern Attire." *The Christian Science Monitor* (January 26, 1978). Reprinted by National Peace Academy Campaign.

"More Delays in Welfare Reform." Texas Women's Political *Times*, Volume VII, No. 1.

Report on Welfare Resolution passed at IWY Conference to International Women's Years Commissioners. San Antonio: National Women's Political Caucus, December 9, 1977.

"Rural Women with 'Stories to Tell,' Gather in Capitol." New York *Times* (February 25, 1978): 32.

INTERVIEWS

Lupe Anguiano and Ann Fears Crawford. San Antonio, March 1975.

Lupe Anguiano and Ann Fears Crawford. San Antonio, November 1977.

Lupe Anguiano and Ann Fears Crawford. Austin, April 1979.

First Chicana Legislator

Irma Rangel

With the opening of the Sixty-fifth session of the Texas legislature in January 1977, the first Mexican-American woman ever to serve in the Texas legislature took her seat in the House of Representatives. Kingsville attorney Irma Rangel, with no more prior political experience than one successful race for county chair of the Democratic party in her area, successfully challenged two men and one woman to win her legislative seat.

The road to the state legislature began for Rangel in 1975 when she attended a Women in Public Life Conference in Austin. "I could see black women and Anglo women on the program," she recalls, "but no Mexican-American women." This disturbing observation, as well as her desire to see that people in her district were adequately represented in the legislature led her to enter the race for the House of Representatives.

Her victory, along with all the accomplishments and victories in her life, she is quick to credit to her family. Born May 15, 1931 in Kingsville, Texas, Rangel grew up in the town, one of three daughters of Presiliano Rangel and his wife Herminia. Both her parents were field workers with little education. Her father was determined to be a success in the world, became a barber's apprentice, and soon he owned the shop. Then he expanded his interests into owning land and solidified his position as one of the most successful Mexican-American business and political leaders in the community. Rangel's mother owned a dress shop, and she and their father instilled in their three daughters a sense of duty and service to those less fortunate than they. All three daughters entered the arena of public service. One sister became a schoolteacher, and Minnie, the other, became a pharmacist, often dispensing medicines without charge to the poor who could not pay. Irma was determined to become a schoolteacher also, but her parents strongly urged her to study business administration at Texas A & I Rangel, however, knew that the business world was not for her.

Achieving success in South Texas as a Mexican American young woman was not all that easy. Rangel and her sisters had watched their parents struggle as equal partners to gain their position in the business community. "We grew up so accustomed to racial discrimination, I don't think it ever occurred to us to think that we were also being discriminated against as women," she recalls.

A graduate of A & I, armed with her Texas teaching certificate, she taught in nearby Robstown and Alice before accepting a job teaching children of Americans and Venezuelans employed by oil companies in South America. In 1964 she returned to the United States and taught in Menlo Park, California. There she authored her book, *How to Teach Spanish in the Elementary Grades.*

Rangel returned to Venezuela in the summer of 1965 to teach modern math to South American educators, and while there she made her decision to enroll at St. Mary's Law School in San Antonio. Attending law school had long been her dream, and she had the financial support of her family to help her through the difficult years as a student. It was at St. Mary's that she began to realize how important it was for Chicanos to be interested and involved in the betterment of society.

As a law clerk for Judge Adrian Spears in San Antonio Rangel gained valuable experience, but she felt isolated from the political arena. When she was offered a position as assistant district attorney in Corpus Christi, she refused until they offered a salary equal to her male counterparts. She became active on the boards of the Corpus Christi Y.W.C.A. and Family Counseling Services. Her legal and board work made her keenly aware of the difficulties young women experienced with abortion. Often suicide was the only alternative for many; others went through the tortures of illegal abortions. She also found that juvenile delinquency in South Texas was often caused in part by a lack of respect for families on welfare. All of these experiences took root and helped form convictions that later manifested themselves in legislation she introduced in the House of Representatives.

The young attorney worked for a time with the Canales and Garza law firm in Corpus Christi and then returned to Kingsville to form the firm of Garcia and Rangel. She realized that the move would inevitably involve her in politics, but when she was asked to run for Democratic county chairperson, Rangel felt she didn't have a chance of winning. However, she hadn't counted on the influence of her family. "I hadn't lived in Kingsville for seventeen years," she recalled. "My victory was a matter of identification with my father, mother, and sister,who were well loved in our community."

The victory over her opponent by 500 votes was cause for celebration by Rangel and her family, but the decision to run for the Democratic House seat from District 49 was a difficult one. Although the absence of Chicanas at the LBJ School for Public Affairs's Conference on Women in Public Life convinced her that Mexican-American women should be more involved, she had very little campaign money. Estimating that she would need from $20,000 to $30,000 to make an effective race, she received a seed-money contribution of $1,750 from the Texas Women's Political Caucus and announced her candidacy. Working at the grass-roots level, she often walked from house to house in her district, talking to the voters on a person-to-person basis, asking about their needs and their problems.

With a district primarily composed of Mexican Americans, Rangel realized that the prime problem in her area was poverty, and that a large portion of her constituency was composed of migrant workers. Although many people told her that migrants wouldn't work in a political campaign because they had no stake in government, she found that much of her support came from migrant women who donated to her campaign before leaving the state traveling the migrant stream harvesting field crops. Rangel gives these women a great amount of credit for her victory in a hard-fought race. "They knew I had been involved with the farm workers' march in 1966 and that I was compassionate toward their problems and their concerns," she recalled.

Incumbent State Representative Greg Montoya was defeated in the primary, but then Rangel had to face Jean K. Hines of Rivera in a June runoff. Hines was running with strong support and financial backing from the influential South Texas King Ranch political faction. Engraved announcements were sent out from the ranch soliciting support for Hines, and King Ranch employees campaigned on her behalf. Rangel realized that her father's political opposition to the ranch faction would be an additional detriment to her campaign.

When election day came around, however, she found her grass-roots support paid off, and she won a close but satisfying victory over Hines. Facing no Republican opposition in the November general election, she was on her way to the statehouse. "I suddenly realized what a great responsibility I had assumed," she recalled. "The people of my district had the confidence in me to work for my election and to vote for me. I was very pleased and proud. That moment of happiness is different from any other experience."

For a freshman legislator she took a strong stand in the House during the Sixty-fifth legislative session. She opposed bills dealing with abortion and county-ordinance powers, as well as Governor Dolph Briscoe's bill designed to finance the state highway system. In addition she successfully introduced legislation designed to simplify and extend the absentee voting system. House Bill 1845 was of particular importance to her district with its migrant population.

Irma Rangel considers one of her greatest achievements the introduction of House Bill 1755 designed to provide employment and educational programs for mothers with dependent children. Many of these women were on welfare, and Rangel visualized the program proposed in House Bill 1755 as a long-range one that would eventually help remove families from the welfare roles. She stated:

> Welfare is an inherited way of life. In my district there are grandchildren and great-grandchildren still living on welfare. Essentially, they have inherited a welfare life. Aid to Families with Dependent Children helps mothers become working mothers or educated mothers. We need to get them off the welfare rolls.

The original bill would have provided assistance to AFDC recipients in obtaining employment experience and skills training from vocational institutions, community colleges, universities, skills centers, and through the facilities of C.E.T.A., the Federal Comprehensive Employment and Training Act. One important aspect of the original bill was a provision for the continuation of welfare services to a project participant until the person became totally self-sufficient.

The ability to get along with a number of factions and to maintain a close relationship with her constituents brought Irma Rangel back to the legislature for additional terms. Although one of the precepts for legislative success is the ability to get along with the Speaker of the House's team, Rangel often opposed legislation favored by the team. She has remained an effective voice in the Mexican-American caucus and often works with other women in the legislature on behalf of legislation that affects women in Texas.

Serving in the legislature has not been without its disappointments to her. During her first session in the House she saw the costly highway bill, priority legislation for Governor Briscoe, absorb much of the funding that Rangel would liked to have seen spent on education, employment, and aid to families with dependent children. In subsequent sessions she saw her bill devoted to employment and education suffer the fate of many bills dealing with women — the important funding for the bill was cut.

Education and employment — especially among women and minorities — remain high on her list of priorities. She also feels that health, bilingual education, and the plight of the elderly in Texas are problems that the legislature must confront. She is a shrewd enough politician, however, to realize that funding for many programs will be hard to obtain during the 1980s.

Providing food for needy elderly people was one of her concerns during the Sixty-seventh legislative session. Rangel introduced House Bill 1629, the Good Faith Donor Act, designed to exempt retailers and manufacturers from liability when food was donated to the needy. While people in South Texas went hungry some twelve million tons of edible food, much of it merely bruised or discolored, was destroyed in the state during 1980, and Rangel believes that the food would have been better used to supply the nutritional needs of the elderly.

With proposed cuts in federal programs threatening to cut off many of the food sources for the needy elderly, alternative sources for food were needed, and Rangel argued that it was imperative that there be some means of assuring donors that they would not be liable for damage or injury to consumers caused by donated food. Testifying before the Judiciary Committee of the Texas House of Representatives on March 31, 1981, Rangel stressed that the food under consideration was not readily marketable because of its appearance, and stressed that food banks across the country were struggling to get food donated to meet the needs of the poor. With representatives of wholesalers, retail grocers, and charitable organizations testifying in favor of the bill, the legislature passed the measure, and Governor Bill Clements signed it into law effective July 1981.

With her continuing focus on issues relating to women and Mexican-Americans, Rangel hopes to serve as a role model and inspiration to other Mexican-American women. She realizes that one of the reasons that she was elected and that she is able to serve in the House is that she is a lawyer and unmarried. Having the supportive family and the able office staff that she has also aids her in her personal life and in performing her legislative duties. She deplores the fact that more Mexican-American women do not seek to go to law school and to make careers for themselves in the political and professional fields. There are, however, barriers to Mexican-American women seeking a career in a profession or in politics, and Rangel is quick to admit that

> The Mexican-American woman is just as qualified to enter politics as any other woman. Now that the barrier is broken, I hope that they will have a greater awareness of their abilities. However, Mexican-American women have been trained to have a greater dedication to their families. The current economic situation and the attitudes of many Mexican-American men also built this sense of dedication into their consciousness.

Wherever she goes Irma Rangel continues to encourage the Mexican-American women of Texas to speak out, and to step out of their traditional role and explore the fields of politics, law, and medicine. The fact that she has gone to the legislature and served as an able legislator from her South Texas district sets her apart as a model to all Chicanas across her native state. Rangel hopes that in the near future she can look back and say, "I was only the first."

REFERENCES

A Bill Relating to Application Forms for Applying For an Absentee Ballot and to Procedures for Conducting the Absentee Voting. House Bill 1845. Austin: Texas House of Representatives, 65th Legislative Session. 1977.

A Bill Relating to Educational Opportunities and Assistance in Obtaining Employment for Persons Receiving Certain Public Assistance. House Bill 1755. Austin: Texas House of Representatives, 65th Legislative Session. 1977.

Cobler, Sharon. "Issues Not Isolated." Dallas *Morning News* (August 9, 1976): 3.

Denny, Leisa. "Bill would help food situation." *Daily Texan* (April 6, 1981): 8.

Hightower, Jim and Jo Clifton. "Key Votes." *Texas Observer* (June 17, 1977): 10.

McIntosh, Prudence. "The Good Old Girls." *Texas Monthly* (January 1978): 149-152.

Newton, Billy. "Rangel — Area Needs to Draw New Industry." Corpus Christi *Caller* (December 26, 1976): 1.

Phaup. J.D. "Ms. Rangel Goes to Austin: The Education of a Legislator." In Maxwell, William Earl and Ernest Crain *et al. Texas Politics Today*. St. Paul: West Publishing Company, 1978.

Rangel, Irma. *Letter* to Ann Fears Crawford. (May 31, 1981).

Saavedra-Vela, Pilar. "Irma Rangel — Breaking Down Barriers in Texas." *Agenda* (January-February 1978): 35.

INTERVIEWS

Irma Rangel and Ann Fears Crawford. Austin, February 1981.

Irma Rangel and Ann Fears Crawford. Austin, July 30, 1981.

Courtesy House Media Services, Texas House of Representatives

Irma Rangel is shown on the floor of the Texas House of Representatives with friends. Left to right are Senfronia Thompson, State Representative from Houston; Chris Miller, former State Representative from Fort Worth; Irma Rangel, and Anita Hill, State Representative from Garland.

Courtesy John Jefferson, Photographer.

The Right Woman
In The Right Place
At The Right Time

Dr. Lorene Lane Rogers

When Dr. Lorene Lane Rogers retired as the first woman president of The University of Texas at Austin, the Austin *American-Statesman* editorialized: "When Rogers retires Friday, she leaves a university that is better for having had her as president. That is no mean accomplishment."

Accomplishment had always been a way of life for Lorene Rogers, and serving as the first woman president of a major coeducational university in the United States was the capstone of her career. She was born on April 3, 1914 in the tiny town of Prosper, Texas. Her upbringing in this small town in northeast Texas is readily apparent in her voice and demeanor. Texas is strong in her speech, and her erect posture and carefully folded hands bespeak her careful training and Texas heritage. Her strong sense of independence, which many of her critics labeled as "hardheadedness," she attributes to growing up as an individual in a small town.

After earning the honor of being selected the valedictorian of her high school class she enrolled at North Texas State Teachers College in Denton, now North Texas State University. Her years at North Texas were years of expanding horizons for the capable and talented young girl from Prosper. During her college years she attended her first symphony orchestra performance and heard both Robert Frost and Carl Sandburg read their poetry when they came to visit the college campus. Her love of language and writing led her to choose to take her bachelor's degree in English literature, and her stamina and strong-mindedness were apparent when she gained her degree without taking a single note in her classes.

North Texas is also the place where she met and married a fellow student, Burl Gordon Rogers. She accompanied him to New Jersey to make their home. When he was killed in a laboratory explosion at the chemical plant where he was working, Rogers found herself widowed at the age of twenty-seven.

These were difficult years for her, and she recalls that she felt as many women do who lose their husband — completely lost and terribly alone. However, her husband had left her a most valuable professional legacy — an abiding interest in the field of chemistry. She had become fascinated through the years with all the chemistry talk between him and his colleagues, and in 1942, without a single college credit in chemistry on her transcript, she enrolled at The University of Texas to major in the field. Five years later, with great single-mindedness, she received a master's degree in organic chemistry and had completed the requirements for a Ph.D., finishing all the experimental work for her doctorate in biochemistry in one year.

Her first teaching assignment was at Sam Houston State University in Huntsville, but her ultimate goal was to join the UT faculty. When she applied for a job in the chemistry department as a teaching assistant, she first experienced discrimination in the teaching profession. Although she got the job, she was offered one-half a man's salary for the same job. For the first time she demonstrated her legendary "hard-headedness" — she turned down the job.

In 1949 she did accept a position at UT, but not in the chemistry department. The all-male chemistry faculty voted against having a woman as part of their staff, and Rogers joined the home economics department to teach nutrition courses for the next fifteen years.

Her academic focus, however, remained on chemistry, and she made significant studies in the effects of nutrition on mental retardation. Moreover, her teaching was excellent as were her relationships with her students, with many members of her classes recalling: "She was the best teacher I ever had."

Through her affiliation with the home economics department Rogers attained the position of full professor, a rank she might never have reached had the chemistry faculty voted to give her tenure. She also broke an all-male barrier by becoming assistant director of the University's Clayton Foundation Biochemical Institute, serving in that position from 1957 to 1964.

In the 1960s when university faculty and staff positions were first being scrutinized for their lack of female members, Lorene Rogers was one of the first to be singled out for an administrative position. She was appointed associate dean of UT's graduate school, and she credits her five years in that position as being the training ground she needed to handle the job as president of the university.

In 1971 Lorene Rogers took another step forward. With the clamor for women in administrative positions within the university community growing, UT President Stephen Spurr named Rogers vice president and charged her with bringing the university's affirmative action program into line with federal guidelines. Her efforts to develop the plan were met with controversy, and federal officials turned down the first drafts of the finished program, finally approving a third.

Rogers knew that her vice presidency was the highest position that any woman had ever held within the university system, but she also knew that it was time for a rest. She had made all the arrangements for her sabbatical when UT-System Chancellor Charles A LeMaistre fired President Spurr, long a controversial figure. LeMaistre asked Rogers to assume the position of president *ad interim*, and Rogers accepted, fully expecting to serve only until a permanent president could be found.

Immediately members of the faculty of an institution that had often been labeled "basically male chauvinistic" began a not so subtle campaign against Rogers. During the year she was acting president a number of men on the teaching staff commented — and these comments came to her — "Surely we can get somebody other than a woman to run the university."

Many people failed to take into consideration her long tenure with the university, or the fact that in her own quiet way she had fought the admitted discrimination against women holding fulltime faculty positions. During the time she served in an advisory position to review the management and operations of the military academies in the United States, she visited the new Air Force Academy at Colorado Springs only to be informed that she could not join her male colleagues in eating with the cadets. Instead a special place was set for her on the balcony overlooking the dining hall. Although Rogers protested, the officials stood firm. In typical Lorene Rogers fashion, she packed her bags, walked out, and came home to Texas.

From the beginning of her work at UT-Austin, few persons outside the university community understood her longtime and total commitment. One of the reasons that she accepted the job as president of the university, over the protests of a number of the faculty and students, was her firm conviction that The University of Texas should continue to grow, and that she could bring peace to a campus that had been strife-torn during the 1960s.

There was no town too small or too far away for her to venture to speak on the problems of the university and to muster support for the school. While many university presidents remained aloof from the students, faculty, and alumni groups, Rogers betook herself about the state to a number of college campuses, speaking to many such groups.

In her first address before the University's alumni, keynoting the Distinguished Alumnus Award on October 18, 1974 she told the audience:

> There are many ways of measuring the quality and worth of a university . . . But no measure is more telling and more accurate than the quality of the alumni who go from these halls.

If we look at the quality of the distinguished
men and women who have crossed the stage tonight,
as well as the many other distinguished alumni of this
institution scattered throughout the nation and the
world . . . then this university must be considered
great by anyone's standards.

After the controversy surrounding her appointment to the
president's chair Rogers realized that she had to establish a sym-
pathetic atmosphere between herself and the students, if she
wanted to be an effective president. She invited a random selection of students to her office every five or six weeks for informal
chats. The students sat around the floor, drinking Cokes and
talking. Much like a dormitory counselor, Rogers would make a
few remarks, and then the students would ask questions on any
topic they wanted to talk about.

Rogers never faltered in answering the question of why she
accepted the job as president of the university, when, according
to many, nobody wanted her. She told students and press alike
that she had been asked repeatedly by the regents if she wanted
the position of president on a permanent basis; each time she
told them: "I do not!"

Each time she meant it. "If the position had come to me at
fifty, instead of sixty, I might have been interested," she said.
"But I knew how hard a job it was, and I knew myself well
enough to know how much of myself I would put into the job."

Chairman of the Board of Regents Allan Shivers had much
to do with her selection. Overlooking the recommendations of a
university-appointed advisory committee, Shivers convinced
Rogers that these two committees, both making recommendations from a selection of presidential candidates, would never
agree and that the regents felt she was the best person for the
job.

When her selection was formally announced students and
faculty immediately opposed her, and the university campus
was in turmoil. Students demonstrated outside her office window, faculty members met to discuss ways of boycotting classes

to bring the university to a standstill, and drag vendors hawked T-shirts emblazoned with the caption ''Buck Rogers.'' Her inherent good humor came to the forefront when she donned one of the T-shirts herself.

She even had to endure the taunts of feminists, who had expected a woman president to appoint an avalanche of women to administrative positions. Many felt that Rogers did less than an effective job in recruiting women within The University of Texas's system. Among the faculty at UT-Austin women held an appallingly low twenty percent of the positions; even the affirmative action plan that Rogers helped draft had done little to recruit women faculty into many departments.

Rogers, however, could cite a number of women brought in to hold administrative positions: Peggy Kruger, equal opportunity officer; Elspeth Rostow, head of the LBJ School of Public Affairs; Billie Brown, head of the nursing school; Wareen Spirduoso, chair of the department of health and physical education; and Donna Lopiano, director of intercollegiate athletics for women. In addition, she appointed two women Ashbel Smith professors, Dr. Joanne Ravel in chemistry and Dr. Janet Spence in psychology. Prior to the appointments she made, the longtime Ashbel Smith professorships had been held by men only.

Among the numerous innovations she instated, however, she was proudest of reestablishing the College of Liberal Arts, which had previously been split into three colleges and a division. The split had proved unwieldy, and the decision to reconstitute the College of Liberal Arts seemed a wise and logical one to Rogers. She could also point to other high marks of her administration: increased funding for student scholarships; recruitment of a number of outstanding scholars to the faculty; increased minority recruitment; expansion of the holdings of the school's libraries; and a smooth transition between presidents at the university. When she announced that she planned to resign as president in September 1980, she gave the regents ample time to choose her successor. In addition, she met with the new president, Dr. Peter Flawn, during the weeks before her resignation took effect.

However, in the transition period controversy arose over her appointment of John Sutton as law school dean, over the objections of the law school faculty and wthout the recommendation of the faculty-student committee that had interviewed him. While the Austin *American-Statesman* queried, "Why not the best?" one law school alumnus wrote to the paper congratulating Rogers on "her excellent sense of perspective and her unwillingness to be intimidated."

Even with her retirement a reality people still expressed opinions about Rogers, some claiming that with Rogers's retirement the university had had its "token woman" president, and that the system could settle back now with a male president who could "get the job done right." Others applauded her for her typical woman's job of cleaning house — a house that was in dire need of a good cleaning, including a few skeletons in the proverbial closets of academe. Many pointed to the case when the regents wanted the scandal surrounding the Humanities Research Center hushed up. Instead, Rogers pushed ahead with her typical "hard-headedness" to uncover missing papers, books, and thefts that had occurred in the holdings of the enormous UT rare books collection.

Early in her administration she removed the dean of the extension division, and later he was indicted by the Travis County grand jury for misappropriation of university funds. Then, in what one critic terms a "hatchet job," she eliminated the entire extension division system and instituted a new department of continuing education, appointing a dean to report directly to the vice president for academic affairs.

Like a well-organized housewife, she had reordered the running of her house. Each person within the system reported directly to someone else, and she added two new vice presidents, one for research and one for administration. Still her critics claimed that "Queen Lorene," as she was often called, insulated herself against the advice of longtime university officials and faculty.

The regents, however, were more than a little pleased with her performance. "She did a good job and she should be commended," recalled former regent Edward Clark. "She brought a spirit of harmony to the campus and proved that all Texans are not the rough and tumble folks as many think of us. The university should be proud of its woman president."

Colleagues also pointed out that Rogers served as "ambassador-at-large" for the university, acting as liaison between the school and the citizens of Texas. She proved that the university could be first class, giving first class service to the taxpayers. Because Lorene Rogers was such an active president future presidents will be less inclined to lock themselves in an "ivory tower."

Her loyalty to the university she served was no more apparent than in December, 1978, when she went to Houston's M. D. Anderson Hospital for an operation. Although her physician counseled that she needed rest after major surgery, she made a bargain with him that she be allowed to go to Dallas, where the university was hosting Notre Dame at the Cotton Bowl, but not to attend the game.

One week after her surgery she hosted the dinner before the game, gave a welcoming speech to the Notre Dame players, and then talked to the UT football players, telling them that for the first time in a number of years she would not be at the game in person to watch them. Afterwards she flew home to Austin to rest and watched her favorite football team on television.

With her retirement, Lorene Rogers could put behind her problems that had been apparent during her administration. No longer did she have to serve as two persons, the president of the university and the "president's wife." She once commented to a member of the board of regents: "What I need is a wife. A woman president still has to do a number of things that a woman does. I don't have a wife to entertain for me or to make out a Christmas card list."

One example of this double duty occurred when the university wives met at the president's house. The day of their meeting was also the day when the president met in executive council with her officers. Rogers dutifully met with her vice presidents and assistants for an executive session that took more than the average work day, and then announced: "Gentlemen, now I must go be the president's wife." She then went home to stand for several more hours in a reception line greeting faculty and administrators' wives. For Lorene Rogers, one duty was just as important as the other.

Although she has retired quietly to her home in Austin's Westlake Hills, she has continued to serve actively in many posts, including one as the first woman elected to the board of Texaco Oil Corporation. With her she took a full quota of memories, including that of students serenading her each year in April on her birthday. One of the most pleasant memories is of an event at the time of the announcement of her retirement. Leon Green, a former member of the UT Law School faculty, sent her a letter applauding her as "the right person at the right time" for the University of Texas. For Dr. Lorene Rogers, those words summed up her long service to the university she loved — a job well done.

REFERENCES

Bibliography files. "Lorene Rogers." Austin-Travis County Collection. Austin Public Library, Austin, Texas.

"Chemist Heats UT-Austin." *Alcalde* (November-December 1974): 6-7.

Crawford, Ann Fears. "Dr. Lorene Rogers." *Texas Woman* (October 1979): 31-39.

Evans, Derro. "Lorene Rogers, Lorene Rogers." *Texas Parade* (June 1976): 52-54.

Gegenheimer, Greg. " 'Gang of Four' unsuited for UT law dean post." Austin *American-Statesman* (July 8, 1979): B-4.

"Lorene Rogers' term successful." Austin *American-Statesman* (July 7, 1979): A-6.

Michaels, Marguerite. "Woman Power is Deep in the Heart of Texas." *Parade* (March 5, 1979): 9.

"Playing politics at UT law school." Austin *American-Statesman* (July 7, 1979): A-6.

Reaves, Gayle. "Faculty protests nomination." Austin *American-Statesman* (July 22, 1979): A-1.

Reaves, Gayle. "Sutton accepts UT law dean post." Austin *American-Statesman* (July 24, 1979): B-1.

INTERVIEWS

The Honorable Edward Clark and Ann Fears Crawford, Austin, July 1979.

Dr. Ira Iscoe and Ann Fears Crawford, Austin, July 1979.

Dr. Joanne Ravel and Ann Fears Crawford, Austin, July 1979.

Dr. Lorene Rogers and Ann Fears Crawford, Austin, July 1979.

Courtesy John Jefferson, Photographer

A Woman
Of Words

Liz Carpenter

When President Jimmy Carter established the United States Department of Education as a separate entity on October 17, 1979, he appointed former federal judge Shirley Hufstedler to head the new department. One of Hufstedler's first priorities was a telephone call to Texas to Liz Carpenter. "I need you! America needs you!" she said to Lady Bird Johnson's former press secretary, imploring Carpenter to return to Washington to serve as assistant secretary of education for public affairs. Carpenter accepted Hufstedler's challenge and now laughs at questions asking "Why Liz Carpenter?" "I know why I got the call," she says. "I was the one woman who knew how to cut through Washington bureaucratic red tape."

Although Carpenter couldn't resist the temptation of helping to put together a new department, she admits that returning to Washington after having lived there for thirty-five years filled her with uncertainty and doubt. She had gone to the nation's capital as a young reporter in the 1940s, married and reared her children there, and worked in partnership with her husband Leslie in their news bureau. Taking a leave of absence in 1960 to campaign for John F. Kennedy and Lyndon Johnson, she had worked closely with both Lyndon and Lady Bird throughout the Johnson years in the White House. For her, Washington held memories of her husband, her family, and the Johnsons. Even with the Democrats in office, it was difficult to imagine working again in a Washington filled with those memories.

Liz Carpenter had made one nostalgic journey — back to Texas in the late 1970s. She laughingly recalls that when Johnson's term as president of the United States was over, she was removed from the White House "kicking and screaming," and then accepted a position as vice president of Hill and Knowlton, a Washington international public relations firm. In 1976 she told Claire Crawford of *People* magazine: "I think I'm used up, as far as Washington is concerned. I've had a crash course in everything from FDR to Elizabeth Ray. Now I want to think more and laugh more."

She does her thinking and laughing, surrounded by friends and family, high in the hills overlooking Lake Austin, in a house that is every writer's retirement dream. "Grassroots," with its sweeping vistas and hand-painted Texas wildflowers adorning the walls, is a house for laughter, but tranquility is seldom present when Carpenter is in residence. The telephone never stops ringing with requests for her to speak or head yet another writer's group. Or perhaps a group of Central Texas women is meeting, summoned to a Saturday summit to plan strategy for the last big push for passage of the Equal Rights Amendment, or simply to discuss an upcoming political campaign.

Despite the Washington years and her term as assistant secretary for the Department of Education, "Grassroots" is home for Carpenter, a place where she can plan another book, schedule her speaking engagements, and reflect on what her thirty years of service in the public arena mean. No one is more aware of her Texas roots than Carpenter, who was once quoted as saying: "Salado [Texas] is fixed and immovable in my life," and she is fond of citing the Texas ancestors who gave strength and purpose to her life.

The one time that Mary Elizabeth Sutherland was late for an historic occasion was at her birth, September 1, 1920, in Salado. She missed by six days being born on the day that women were given the right to vote. Suffrage had great meaning to her family and she often tells of one of her great-aunts who went to Washington to lobby for the vote and paid for advertisements promoting women's suffrage in her hometown newspaper. She grew up surrounded by family, the daughter of Thomas Shelton Sutherland and his wife Mary Elizabeth Paterson Sutherland, and from her early years Liz, as she has always been known, could recite the five generations of Texans who make up her heritage.

One of the more illustrious of these Texans was the empresario Sterling C. Robertson, who came from Tennessee to settle families around the Brazos River Basin northwest of Stephen F. Austin's grant. A signer of the Texas Declaration of Independence, he served in the First Congress of the Republic. Still another ancestor was George C. Childress, who wrote the fiery declaration and went to Washington to fight for recognition of the Texas republic, and still another, Hulon P. Robertson, served as speaker of the Texas House of Representatives.

The women in the Robertson and Sutherland families were equal to the men, and one of Carpenter's great-grandmothers reared her twelve children and managed a plantation and some thirty slaves. Liz Carpenter points proudly to the fact that she was named for this indomitable Southern woman. Fighting for suffrage and equality for women was nothing new to her family, as her great-aunt Luella Robertson addressed Salado College alumni on the subject of equal education for women as early as 1875, and another aunt was in the forefront of the suffrage marches in Washington before women were granted the right to vote. Young Mary Elizabeth grew up listening to stories of women's fight for suffrage, encouraged by a mother who wrote poetry and short stories and instilled in her daughters a sense that marriage was not the only career they could pursue.

Although the centuries-old Robertson mansion in Salado offered a secure sense of history, when her son Thomas graduated from Belton High School, Liz's mother moved her five children to Austin to live in the shadow of The University of Texas. Liz entered the second grade at Wooldridge school, writing the school song when she was confined to bed with scarlet fever. There was a constant coming and going of relatives who attended the university, and the Sutherland dinner table was the gathering spot where everyone discussed the events of the day. "We were a family of words, talkative Sutherlands," she later recalled, and with one sister serving as editor of the Belton high school newspaper, Liz never worried about a career. She followed family tradition by being editor of her high-school newspaper, The Austin *Maroon*, and during these years she met Leslie Carpenter, whom she married in 1944.

The Depression years live in her memory, and she recalls her mother's cooking the plain and simple fare that had to feed the entire family, plus any friends who happened to wander in at mealtimes. Especially memorable were the whirlwind trips her father made to Austin from West Texas, where he worked as a highway contractor. Tom Sutherland would always bring a steak or oysters for an oyster stew for the family. Her vivid memory of the out-of-work men and the deprivations of the Depression made her an enthusiastic advocate of President Johnson's programs, such as Head Start, designed to serve below-poverty-level families. In 1981 she still mentions in each of her speeches the necessity for education to be the top priority of the nation, calling for the education of youth to be considered a "national purpose." She rants against the Reagan administration's materialistic concerns and feels that the Republicans are putting education "on the back burner." "They're interested in bigger bombs and smaller Head Start programs," she states.

Working during summer vacations on the Austin *American-Statesman* Liz found that newspaper work fascinated her. She was also exposed to a concern for good writing in the newsroom. Her first political assignment was to interview Clara Driscoll, then serving as a Democratic committeewoman from Texas at a time when President Franklin Roosevelt and Alben Barkley were differing over political questions. She interviewed Driscoll at the Driskill Hotel, where Driscoll and Frank Scofield, the head of the IRS in Travis County, were discussing the Roosevelt-Barkley split. Although she had never been in a hotel room in her life, Liz Sutherland made the decision that covering politics in smoke-filled rooms was a career worth pursuing. "I want to live that way all my life," she decided. "That's a great life!"

She furthered her journalism training at The University of Texas and gained political experience by running for vice president of the student assembly. In her announcement speech she asked students not to vote for her merely because she was a girl nor in spite of it, but because she would make the most effective officer. She won the election, becoming the first woman vice president of the student body and then went on to become the first woman editor of the *Daily Texan*, the campus newspaper. In a nostalgic article written in 1975 for the *Alcalde*, the magazine of The University of Texas Ex-Student's Association, Carpenter reflected on her undergraduate days at the university. She reminisced, "We walked in sunshine there and afterwards grew beyond all our young expectations. Now alone, I still reach and hunger for more. Perhaps that itself is life and learning."

Graduating in 1942 with a bachelor of journalism degree, she and fellow student Leslie Carpenter went to Washington. With her journalism degree in hand she went from bureau to bureau in the National Press Building looking for employment, and when she landed a job as a reporter for UPI, she married Leslie Carpenter on June 17, 1944. She attended her first press conference when Franklin Delano Roosevelt was in office. The new reporter stood at the back of the room, and, being short, all she could see of the president was his cigarette holder and the jaunty angle of his head. At the end of the conference all the new reporters got to shake FDR's hand.

Carpenter was impressed with Eleanor Roosevelt and her fight for the social equality of women in the United States. When Carpenter was press secretary for Lady Bird Johnson many writers compared the president's wife to Eleanor Roosevelt, although Lady Bird was never an outspoken exponent of women's rights. Many people credit Liz Carpenter with helping to focus Lady Bird Johnson's concern for education and social progress.

Liz and her husband organized their own news bureau in the nation's capital, and Carpenter went on to gain honors in the capital city, including being elected president of the Women's National Press Club. She lent her typical Texas touch to the installation ceremony by providing tamales and *chili con queso* for the entire group, but as only women were allowed at the ceremony, her husband had to watch her installation from behind the balcony curtains.

Raising two children, Scott and Christy, while covering Washington politics for a dozen newspapers, filled Carpenter's time until 1960. Then, after campaigning for the Kennedy-Johnson ticket, she became the first woman to serve as an executive assistant to a vice president of the United States. Having known the Johnsons for some twenty years, Liz Carpenter knew the hectic hours and the exhausting schedule she would be subjected to. Among her nonpolitical duties were managing the weddings of the Johnson daughters, making all the arrangements for the visit of Bashir Ahmed, the camel driver from Pakistan whom Lyndon Johnson invited to the LBJ ranch, and accompanying the vice president on his official travels.

Working for Johnson was not always a joyful experience. On one occasion the vice president called her to tell her that if she didn't keep her mouth shut, he fully intended to give her to the Johnson City Foundation. Having gained a reputation as the "wittiest woman in the Great Society," Carpenter quipped, "It's a nice place to visit, but I wouldn't want to live there." Her most memorable experience, however, was riding in the motorcade on the Dallas morning when President Kennedy was assassinated and LBJ took the oath of office as president of the United States. Another event to remember was being honored by Theta Sigma Phi, the woman's honorary journalism society, with its Headliner award in 1962.

Liz Carpenter later said of Johnson's years as president, "They were a crash course in everything. You regretted any moment you slept and any invitation you turned down." One of the crash courses she profited from was the educational programs advanced by the Great Society. Both Johnson and

Carpenter lived through the Depression years in Texas, and they observed the neglect of education throughout the state. To both of them, furthering the education of the youth of the United States was a project endowed with a sense of mission, and Carpenter's ideas concerning education are rooted strongly in the LBJ philosophy.

Another area where a sense of mission is readily apparent is the beautification programs that Lady Bird Johnson fostered during her years as First Lady. To Carpenter the land is a part of her heritage, and both she and Mrs. Johnson were active participants on press trips through the Big Bend or on a jaunt down the Snake River. When Texas celebrated HemisFair '68 Lady Bird Johnson helped promote the state's tourist industry by arranging tours for the foreign news media, personally escorting them through the fairgrounds and on to Johnson City. Arranging such travel jaunts was Carpenter's responsibility, as she served as Lady Bird's press secretary and staff director from 1963 until the time that the Johnsons left the White House.

Leading a group of Washington reporters through the Big Bend National Park was another media event, scheduled for Lady Bird's program of rediscovering America, and Carpenter was determined that everyone would share in the experience in wilderness living. Stringing eighty miles of telephone wire from Alpine, Texas to a makeshift pressroom was only the first of many problems which Carpenter was called on to solve, and when the pilots had to buzz the West Texas airfields to scare off a herd of Texas antelope, *Time* magazine claimed that the First Lady's press secretary might just have arranged that frontier event. Carpenter did arrange cowboy breakfasts and sundown margarita parties, served by eager West Texans, but the highlight of the wilderness adventure was a flotilla of reporters, Secret Service men, the First Lady, Secretary of the Interior Stewart Udall and his wife, and the indefatigable Liz merrily rafting down the Rio Grande River. Another rafting adventure down Wyoming's Snake River was designed to show the news media the breathtaking beauty of America's wilderness unhampered by unsightly billboards. Although the group was deluged by a downpour, humorist Art Buchwald kept the participants amused with his lively comments.

Not all Lady Bird's beautification projects met with the wholehearted support of every group. When the First Lady arranged for yellow tulips to be planted around a memorial commemorating the United States infantry, a veteran's organization protested that the yellow tulips were a reflection on the courage of the soldiers. Next year the beautification program provided red tulips.

Both Lady Bird and Liz Carpenter lobbied Congress on behalf of the highway beautification bill, and when President Johnson signed it into law on October 22, 1968 both women could point with pride to the thousands of miles they had traveled, the numbers of poverty neighborhoods they had toured, and the hours spent bringing the cause of beautification to the media and the people. Carpenter feels that Lady Bird Johnson's greatest contribution lies in "creating a new climate of opinion and a new awareness of how we are desecrating our country."

With wit and wry good humor Carpenter also describes the multitudinous arrangements required for the weddings of the Johnson daughters. Prior to Luci Baines Johnson's wedding Carpenter quipped to her office staff: "It's going to be a long, hot summer with rioting in the East Wing." Not since the day when Alice Roosevelt married Nicholas Longworth had there been such a hectic time in the White House. Providing day-by-day details concerning wedding dresses, satisfying labor leaders who clamored for gowns made only in union shops, managing the press and photographers, and releasing recipes for wedding cakes all came within the province of Carpenter's office. When one woman reporter inquired as to the number of raisins to be used in Lynda Bird's wedding cake, Liz solved the problem with her customary wit by assigning the reporter to count each and every raisin.

When Lyndon Johnson announced that he would not seek reelection to the presidency, Carpenter arranged for Lady Bird's "last hurrah," a coast-to-coast tour winding up in California's

Redwood National Park, where the press serenaded the first lady with "Auld Lang Syne." Hectic months of packing and final arrangements ended in January 1969, when Richard Nixon moved into the White House and the Johnsons flew home to the LBJ ranch. Knowing the pain that leaving the White House caused her, Leslie Carpenter brought champagne for them to share, and Liz toasted the Johnsons with a "Here's to the Great Society!" "Here's to a girl from Salado, Texas!" her husband replied.

The death of her husband was a sorrowful time in her life, but Liz Carpenter soon found herself deeply involved with another mission — working for women's rights and the passage of the Equal Rights Amendment. Her work began in 1971 when, at the request of Shana Alexander and Betty Friedan, she helped organize the National Women's Political Caucus to recruit women into the political arena. As cochairperson of ERAmerica, she feels that she was in a unique position to relate to many women's groups that more militant women failed to reach.

With other feminists, including Friedan and Gloria Steinem, she began touring the country speaking for the passage of ERA, and her fiery speeches gained headlines for the women's movement. She minced no words in dealing with women who failed to work actively for the passage of the amendment; many women, she felt, believed in equal pay for equal work, but their support of ERA went no further. She was quick to admonish them:

> They betray their ignorance and they betray their sex . . . They're acting like house servants on the plantation. They're standing around handing Massa a drink while the rest of us are out in the fields pickin' cotton.

She was also known to take a male politician or two to task if she believed they had strayed too far from Johnsonian ideals and programs. When Texan John Connally, LBJ's protege, deserted the Democrats to support Republican Richard Nixon for president of the United States, Carpenter quipped: "If John Connally had been at the Alamo, he would have organized Texans for Santa Anna."

Her support of the Democratic party, even in times of trouble, remains strong, and she denounces President Ronald Reagan for demolishing the Department of Education that she helped build. She is heartened by signs of rebuilding among the Democrats and feels that the way of progress lies solely with the Democratic party. "We've got to fight back," she exclaims, and speaks out strongly in favor of a return to the ideals and programs Democrats represent. She is also quick to cite President Jimmy Carter's appointment of over four hundred women to government positions as giving impetus to the move of women into policy-making positions in government.

After serving with the Department of Education, she returned to Texas, dividing her time between writing, speaking on public issues and in support of the ERA, and serving as a consultant to the LBJ library. Her determination and convictions about ERA are as strong as ever, and she laughingly declares that she would tour the country speaking for free in support of the amendment, but feels that "Money keeps you warmer than love." To her the passage of ERA remains the prime need of women in American life.

Although opposition from right-wing opponents of the amendment has received much media attention, Carpenter feels that opponents of ERA are "losing their steam, and that their focus on single-issue politics has weakened their cause." She adheres firmly to the "old LBJ school of politics" and declares that she refuses to give up the fight for an Equal Rights Amendment until the last vote is counted. In January 1982 she will be counting every vote, gearing up for a drive among targeted legislatures in Illinois, North Carolina, Florida, Missouri, and Georgia. She mentions the ERA in every speech she gives, no matter in which part of the country, and is heartened by such women as those in Georgia, who are making the ERA their personal crusade.

Carpenter is cognizant of the opposition that she will be encountering in the final push for equal rights. She detects some decided changes in the focus of the women's movement, however, but a backlash against the progress that women have made since the 1970s fails to weaken her determination: "You can stall or you can stymie the woman's movement, but you can't turn back the march of human rights." The focus in her speeches is always on pushing forward, noting that networking among women's groups has helped the new professional woman rise in corporations and industry. She cites the young woman lawyer as one notable instance of women giving direction to many of the programs that women are striving for; no longer are the women who are merely "visibly safe" the only ones who are making strides. "Gutsy determination is what brought the new woman to the forefront of the movement," she says, "and it's what will continue her rise upward."

Although her salty comments and wry remarks make her much in demand as a speaker, Carpenter sets aside what time she can to pursue her own personal project, a book of informal essays tentatively entitled *Moments*. Concentrating on what she refers to as "parts and pieces of my life," the essays will focus on her activism in the women's movement and her life in Washington. Planned as an addition to her popular *Ruffles and Flourishes*, Carpenter's new book will be a summing up of her life. "What did it all mean is what I hope the book will put forth," she says.

Some of the essays in *Moments* are planned to recapture her sense of her own roots in Texas; those roots are both deep and meaningful to her. "Texas walks with an air of success," she feels, "and this sense of purpose and success is strong in the state's women." She cites the pioneer influence and the fact that Texas is still a relatively young state as reasons for the sense of activity and purpose among its people:

> Texas women have a memory of their history, and the pioneer influence helps them feel that they are never helpless. There's a great deal of 'get up and go' spirit

among Texas women, and they've always been good neighbors — they had to be on the frontier. . . .

No one exemplifies the Texas woman's 'get up and go' spirit more than "the girl from Salado," Liz Carpenter. She is fond of citing an old Chinese proverb, "May you live in interesting times," and where Liz Carpenter is, the times have always been, and will continue to be, exceedingly interesting.

REFERENCES

Bengston, Carolyn. "Liz Carpenter: After 34 years in Washington, she's back home." Austin *Citizen* (January 21, 1977): 3.

Carpenter, Liz. "'A Simple-Girl Who Found Adventure in the White House'," Austin *American-Statesman* (February 1, 1970): F-12.

Carpenter, Liz. "How to Sell a Book." *Parade* (February 28, 1971): 4.

Carpenter, Liz (editor). *LBJ: images of a vibrant life.* Austin: Friends of the LBJ Library, 1973.

Carpenter, Liz. "Looking Over My Shoulder." *Alcalde* (September-October 1975): 13-16.

Carpenter, Liz. *Ruffles and Flourishes.* New York: Doubleday & Company, 1970.

Carpenter, Liz. "What Is the Future of the Republic? Loving Life & Living It with Strength." *Vital Speeches of the Day.* (Speech delivered to the Texas Philosophical Society, San Antonio, December 6, 1980).

Crawford, Claire. "Liz Carpenter Reflects on 34 Years in Washington, Then Heads Home for Texas." *People* (December 6, 1976): 8.

"Ex-Austin Woman Elected National Press Club Prexy." Austin *American* (June 2, 1954): 11.

Fawcett, Ruth. "The Wisdom and Wit of Liz Carpenter." *Texas Woman* (January 1980): 24.

"First Lady Visit Hinted at Salado." Austin *American-Statesman* (August 25, 1967): 1.

Lide, Frances. "Texans Predominate at Inaugural Party." Washington *Evening Star* (July 1, 1954): 7.

"Liz Carpenter will join UT journalism faculty." *Daily Texan* (December 10, 1976): 1.

Mackintosh, Prudence. "The Good Old Girls." *Texas Monthly* (January 1978): 22.

Maguire, Pat. "First Lady's First Lady Due Roundup Honors." Austin *Statesman* (November 10, 1970): 19.

McBee, Sue Brandt. "An evening on Liz's hilltop." *Austin Homes and Gardens* (March 1980): 11.

Newton, Julie. "'I'm Liz Carpenter and I'm running for educator'." *On Campus,* The University of Texas (February 14, 1977).

Potts, Diana. "Austin's most powerful women." Austin *Sun* (September 9, 1977): B-6.

"Witty Author Grew Up in Austin." Austin *American-Statesman* (February 1, 1970): F-12.

"Women's Caucus Hears Unity Plans." Austin *Statesman* (November 21, 1971): 13.

INTERVIEWS

Liz Carpenter and Ann Fears Crawford. Austin, September 15, 1981.

Liz Carpenter and Shirley Prud'homme (cassette). Austin, December 13, 1978. (Typed transcript and cassette in The Austin-Travis County Collection, Austin Public Library).

— *Photo by Frank Wolfe*

First Lady

Lady Bird Johnson

On January 22, 1973 former President Lyndon Baines Johnson died at his ranch near Stonewall, Texas, and was buried in the Texas Hill Country where he had been born and reared. Many people wondered how his widow, Lady Bird, the woman who had been his constant companion since the days he had worked as a young administrative aide to Congressman Richard Kleberg, would now occupy her time and whether she would ever surmount the feelings of loneliness and desolation that her husband's death was sure to bring. "I've had thirty-eight wonderful years; what more could I ask?" She told reporter Helen Thomas, and Thomas commented, "She always did her husband proud in his lifetime. In his death, she was magnificent."

Observers who had noted Lady Bird's demeanor and her devotion to her husband throughout his political career had often commented on how magnificent a companion and supporter she was, and some close friends cited Lady Bird's East Texas background as the source of her strength and determination. She was born in Karnack, Texas on December 12, 1912, the daughter of Thomas Jefferson Taylor, a farmer and merchant who advertised himself as "T.J. Taylor, Dealer in Everything," and his aristocratic wife, Minnie Lee Patillo Taylor. The Taylor and Patillo families had been neighbors in

Alabama, and Minnie Lee married Thomas Jefferson Taylor much against her parents' wishes, as they considered him to be nothing but a dirt farmer. Minnie Lee, however, rebelled against the stratified society into which she had been born, married Taylor, and came with him to Texas. In Karnack she was considered somewhat of an eccentric, for she adopted vegetarianism, advocated women's suffrage, read books, and traveled to New York each season for the opera.

Minnie named her daughter, the third of her children, Claudia Alta for her brother Claude, but one of the black nurses who cared for the infant commented, "She's as pretty as a lady bird," and the name stuck, shortened to "Bird" by her friends. Lady Bird remembers her mother as a rather ethereal figure who read Greek myths to her when she was quite young. However, her mother died when she was five years old, and "Bird" grew up under the watchful supervision of her Aunt Effie, who came from Alabama to care for her. Aunt Effie introduced Bird to the wonders of nature in the East Texas piney woods, and the two often wandered there for hours, Aunt Effie telling stories to encourage her young ward's romantic imagination. The Southern values that were Bird's heritage were also instilled in her by her aunt; many people commented in later years on the traces of Southern background so noticeable in her demeanor and speech.

From the first to the seventh grades she attended a one-room school, delighting in memorizing patriotic songs and poems throughout her school years. During the summers Lady Bird and Aunt Effie traveled to Colorado or to visit relatives in Alabama. Uncle Claude Patillo, realizing that Lady Bird would one day inherit large tracts of Alabama timberland and a sizeable amount of money from her mother's estate, dreamed of his niece attending the Harvard School of Business. So he saw that she was schooled in finance, and taught her to read the stock-market reports. The Southern romanticism and idealism that she inherited from Aunt Effie, together with the acute business sense instilled by her Uncle Claude, have characterized Lady Bird Johnson throughout her lifetime.

At the age of fifteen she graduated, a "straight A" student and third in her class, from Marshall High School. She attended St. Mary's Episcopal School in Dallas, and then enrolled in The University of Texas. She arrived at the university with a Buick convertible, a Neiman-Marcus charge account, a practical sense of the business world that led her to take both typing and short-hand, and a longing for the cultural enrichment that the university offered. She never missed a play put on by the Curtain Club, and although she had earlier made up her mind to be a teacher, she resolved to become a dramatic critic on a New York newspaper. After receiving her undergraduate degree, she remained at the university for another year to study journalism, submitting feature stories to the *Daily Texan* and trying her hand at writing short stories. She joined Theta Sigma Phi, the honorary journalism society, serving as secretary of the group. She also was elected publicity manager of The University of Texas Sports Association, and was rushed by Alpha Phi, a social sorority. T.J. Taylor, however, put his foot down on her affiliation with the group, feeling that sororities were undemocratic.

Graduating with a second degree in journalism in 1934, Lady Bird Taylor was ready to become a teacher, a secretary, or a practicing journalist when her friend Gene Boehringer introduced her to Lyndon Johnson. Johnson invited her to breakfast, and their whirlwind romance began with Lyndon, "a young man in a hurry," telling her the entire story of his life and hurrying her off to Corpus Christi to meet his boss and the entire Kleberg family. When he proposed on their second date, Lady Bird thought that he was joking. She took him to Karnack, however, to meet her father, who was impressed with Lyndon and assured his daughter that some of the best trades he had ever made were made in a hurry.

When Lady Bird said "yes," a jubilant Lyndon called a friend to make all the arrangements for the marriage at St. Mark's Episcopal Church in San Antonio. Lady Bird asked her college roommate to be her attendant, and the young couple left for San Antonio. When Lyndon forgot to buy his bride a ring, the ceremony was held up while best man Dan Quill selected an assortment from a nearby store, and with a $2.98 ring Lyndon Johnson and Claudia Alta Taylor were married. Thirty-six years later President Johnson asked his wife why she had waited so long to replace the inexpensive ring with a nicer one, and Lady Bird replied: "Why, darling, I was waiting to see if the marriage lasted."

Lady Bird's management skills served the young couple well, for Lyndon's salary was less than three hundred dollars a month. Lady Bird managed the household finances, saved enough to buy a savings bond each month, and entertained Texas friends such as Congressman and Mrs. Maury Maverick with Southern home cooking. Even in those days Lyndon Johnson would bring friends and fellow workers home for Lady Bird's good cooking and a chance for good political talk.

On February 22, 1937 Texas Congressman James P. Buchanan died, and Lyndon Johnson decided to enter the race to name his successor. Lady Bird conferred with Texas politician Alvin Wirtz, determined with him that to make a creditable showing in the race Johnson would need ten thousand dollars, and then arranged with her father to borrow that amount against her share of her mother's estate. Proudly boasting his support of President Franklin D. Roosevelt and aided by Texas governor Jimmy Allred's endorsement of his candidacy, Johnson won the election and then joined FDR on the presidential train barnstorming through the West.

Johnson solidified his political support in Washington through his close relationship with Speaker of the House Sam Rayburn. When Senator Morris Sheppard died in 1941, Lyndon Johnson filed for his seat, but on the campaign trail the young congressman was challenged by that master of political huckstering, W. Lee O'Daniel, and his hillbilly band. "Pappy" O'Daniel lent a carnival air to Texas campaigning and Johnson countered with two bands and two singers, plus a pageant depicting the history of the United States. Although President Franklin Roosevelt poured telegrams into Texas in support of the ardent New Dealer, Johnson lost to O'Daniel by a slim margin. Lady Bird later said how much courage it took for her husband to accept this defeat. Lyndon Johnson himself resolved never to lose another political race.

In 1941, when the United States declared war on Japan, Lyndon Johnson was the first member of Congress to enter the armed forces. While her husband was serving in the Navy in Australia, Lady Bird moved in with John Connally's wife Nellie and took over the running of Johnson's congressional office. Not only did Lady Bird manage office affairs, she also acted as liaison with members of Congress and Johnson's constituents in the Tenth District, increasing her understanding of her husband's legislative duties and developing political skills that served her husband throughout his career in public office. Later a proud Lyndon Johnson said of his wife: "Bird ran my office so well that I was reelected. The Tenth District would happily have elected her over me, if she had run."

When Congressman Johnson returned to Washington, he and his wife began looking for a business base in Texas. The Austin radio station KTBC was desperately in need of financial support, and Lady Bird used the money from the sale of her Alabama timberland and the inheritance from her mother to buy the station. Noticing how rundown and dirty the station was, Lady Bird went to work with her broom and mop and cleaned it up. Throughout the years that Lyndon Johnson remained in public life, Lady Bird paid the monthly checks for the station's expenses, worked with the management in directing the station, and today remains the chairwoman of the board of the LBJ Company, which operates KLBJ-AM and FM radio stations in Austin.

After years of living in rented apartments and houses in Washington, Lady Bird found the perfect home for the Johnsons to buy, and rushed to tell her husband of her discovery. Johnson was involved in a political discussion with John Connally at the time and paid little attention to his wife's pleas. Finally an exasperated Lady Bird said, "I want that house," and slammed out of the room, leaving an amazed Johnson. "I think I'd buy that house," Connally advised his friend. With money from her

Aunt Effie, Lady Bird purchased the house she dreamed of, and after ten years of trying to have a child, she gave birth to Lynda Bird on March 19, 1944. Lucy Baines followed on July 2, 1947, and Lyndon Johnson was delighted with the continuation of his LBJ initials, commenting: "It's cheaper this way. We can all use the same luggage!"

In 1948 Lyndon Johnson faced his most serious political competition when he chose to challenge former governor Coke Stevenson for the Senate seat held by O'Daniel. The race was such a hard-fought one that it has become legendary in the annals of Texas politics. In a campaign that Lady Bird later called "an endurance contest of the spirit," she traveled about the state giving speeches and encouraging voters to support her husband. With Marietta Brooks she organized coffees that helped to bring more women into the campaign as workers, and once when the two women were traveling in Central Texas their car turned over. Lying by the side of the road, all Lady Bird could think of was that she wished she had voted absentee. As soon as she was judged fit to travel, however, in typical Lady Bird Johnson style she changed her clothes, shook hands at a reception in Seguin, and continued to San Antonio to make a statewide radio broadcast, neglecting to mention the accident to her husband until he noticed her bruises.

The result of the election remained in doubt for days, as totals seesawed back and forth, first giving Stevenson a plurality and then Johnson. Lady Bird watched anxiously until the results declared Johnson a winner by eighty-seven votes, winning for her husband the nickname "Landslide Lyndon." Then she waited anxiously while the State Democratic Executive Committee, meeting in Fort Worth, certified him as the Democratic candidate by a vote of twenty-nine to twenty-eight. Johnson stated that his heart was "so full of gratitude there is no room for bitterness," and went on to defeat the Republican candidate by an overwhelming majority.

The years that Johnson served in the United States Senate, rising from freshman senator to majority leader, were active growing ones for Lady Bird also. With her friend "Scooter" Miller she enrolled in the Capital Speakers' Club series, polishing the public speaking skills that she needed for her husband's campaigns. She redecorated their Washington home, and when Johnson bought the family ranch in Johnson City, she undertook the job of refurbishing and adding on to the old stone ranchhouse, finding it a restorative retreat when the Johnsons came home to Texas.

While she was redecorating their homes Johnson decided to redecorate his wife, often traveling to Neiman-Marcus and returning with boxes of clothes for her. He encouraged her to cut her hair and to wear high-heeled shoes. His admonition that "I can't stand muley colors!" changed her fashion outlook, and throughout her later life she has worn the bright reds, corals, and yellows that he loved. He was expansive with gifts to both his wife and their daughters, often arriving home with a pet dog for Lucy or elegant gowns for each of them. Lady Bird's fashion philosophy became serviceable clothes that pleased Lyndon, commenting, "I begrudge making a career out of clothes, but Lyndon likes bright colors and dramatic styles that do the most for one's figure, and I try to please him."

Pleasing Lyndon became the foremost concern of her life, and she took an active role in his campaigns, often leaving their children in the care of friends and staff members. "You are loved," she assured her children before leaving for the numerous receptions she attended with her husband or the business trips she made between Austin and Washington. She valued the time that she spent with her children, and her husband often commented that he had the best wife and the nicest daughters that a man could have. When the Johnsons moved into the White House Lady Bird was fully cognizant of the numerous sacrifices and changes that each of her daughters would be required to make. In her practical way she cautioned them: "You can adjust or you can adjust!"

On July 2, 1955, Lucy Baines Johnson's eighth birthday, her father suffered a massive heart attack at the Virginia estate of his Texas political supporter George Brown. Lady Bird remained at his side during the hospital days and later while he convalesced at the ranch. She worked with their cook, Zephyr Wright, to prepare low-calorie menus for her husband and superintended the construction of a swimming pool where he could exercise. Although Lyndon Johnson was far from the ideal patient, he did spend more time with his wife and daughters, often demanding to know where Lady Bird was at any given moment. "Here I am, darling!" was her constant response.

Increasingly, Lyndon Johnson depended on his wife's advice and counsel, and he could also count on her where his wishes and needs were concerned. When he wanted music in every room of their house, she installed it; when he demanded a new lawn for a party planned for only three weeks in the future, Lady Bird saw that it was picture perfect by party time. In six months's time Johnson was anxious to return to work and from 1956 until 1960 he increased his stature in the Senate by his role in the passage of a civil rights bill, and by his leadership in bringing both Alaska and Hawaii into the United States.

As the election year of 1960 approached, Johnson was increasingly mentioned as a possible presidential candidate, and when he announced that he would seek the presidency there was no more ardent supporter than his wife. Commenting on how she felt about the upcoming campaign, she told reporters that her husband depended on people who were both "wise and knowlegeable," and that he often sought her advice. She mentioned that she looked forward to an "interesting and exhilarating" campaign, adding that she felt it was important for her to be with her husband. "I think people can assess a man better when they know what kind of wife and family he has," she added.

On July 8, 1960 Lyndon and Lady Bird Johnson arrived in Los Angeles to make a final bid for the Democratic nomination for the presidency of the United States. "Ladies for Lyndon" campaigned fervently for Johnson, and amidst clanging Texas cowbells and marching trombone players, delegates passed out pennants reading "All the Way with LBJ." When John F. Kennedy won the Democratic presidential nomination, Lyndon Johnson accepted second place on the ballot. Lady Bird took her husband's loss with good grace, commenting to reporters, "I wouldn't be saying what is true if I didn't say that I'm disappointed for my country. Lyndon would have made a noble president."

Lady Bird was so active a campaigner on behalf of the Kennedy-Johnson ticket that Republicans called her the Democrats' secret weapon, but she had to leave the campaign to sit beside her ailing father, who died on October 22. Soon after the funeral she was back on the campaign trail, substituting for her husband on the *Today* program, when he developed a sore throat. The Johnsons met active opposition to their campaign in downtown Dallas, where crowds carrying placards labeled "Traitor" screamed and spat at them. Women wearing Nixon buttons tore at Lady Bird's hair, but the Johnsons moved through the screaming crowd in an orderly, calm fashion. "I couldn't believe this was Texas," Lady Bird commented. "I couldn't believe this was home, where I had gone to school as a girl." In November the Democrats were triumphant, and Lady Bird's campaign efforts won her an accolade from President Kennedy's brother Robert, who admitted, "Lady Bird carried Texas for us."

The Kennedys visited the ranch, and the Johnsons visited the First Family at their home at Hyannisport. Then it was off to Washington where once again Lady Bird began establishing a new home for her family. The Johnsons purchased Perle Mesta's chateau "Les Ormes," and Bird renamed it in American style simply "The Elms." She remodeled the kitchen, moved in some simple, homey furniture, and hung the paintings by Texan Porfirio Salinas that they had collected over the years. The Johnson dog, Little Beagle, was joined by two others, Him and Her, and Lady Bird immediately began planning for possible world travels by taking a course in intensive conversational Spanish.

Lyndon Johnson was determined to be an active vice president, and the Johnsons traveled around the world on behalf of the United States, celebrating the independence of Jamaica in that country and the commonwealth anniversary of Puerto Rico there, then visiting Greece, Iceland, and the Scandinavian countries. But the real highlight of Johnson's vice presidency was the "flying carpet" visit of the Pakistani camel driver Bashir Ahmed to the United States. Invited by Johnson in an impetuous moment in his native country, Ahmed was a reporter's delight. He charmed the Johnson girls, relished the State Fair of Texas, and enjoyed a typical LBJ barbecue at the ranch.

Living in Perle Mesta's home inspired Lady Bird to entertain, and during the Johnson vice presidency she received as guests numerous foreign dignitaries, including Ayub Khan, the chief of state of Pakistan, Empress Farah of Iran, and Indira Gandhi of India. Lady Bird's schedule was always a hectic one; she toured coal mines much in the manner of Eleanor Roosevelt, concerned herself with the economy of many of the less wealthy states, cut ribbons to open historic events and buildings, and delivered speeches to women's groups. Often she was called on to share the speaker's platform with her husband, and she was the one person who could halt Johnson when he tended to speak for too long a time. Once when he talked until his voice began to sound husky, Lady Bird passed him a note that read, "It's time to stop." Lyndon did.

Lady Bird, the girl from East Texas who dreamed of romantic adventures, traveled 120,000 miles visiting thirty foreign countries during her husband's vice presidency, and she never failed to find in each place a sense of excitement and adventure. "I have an omnivorous curiosity about the wide, wide world," she told reporter Ruth Montgomery. " . . . My life is a wonderful kaleidoscope of interesting things. I love to see America, too. I see the faces of America spread out before me as I travel through the land, and I never tire of it."

Nothing excited her more than the anticipated trip of the Kennedys to Texas in November 1963. Elaborate preparations had been made for the Kennedy's overnight stay at the ranch after scheduled speaking stops in Houston, Fort Worth, Dallas, and Austin. On that fateful day in Dallas Lady Bird was seated in the third car in the motorcade between her husband and Senator Ralph Yarborough. It was a clear, sunshiny day and she was filled with elation and excitement over the Kennedy's reception by Texans when shots rang out, and Secret Service man Rufus Youngblood pushed Lyndon Johnson to the floor of the car. Throughout the nightmare ride to Parkland Hospital, the agonizing time there, and the terrible realization that President Kennedy had been assassinated and Governor Connally wounded, Lady Bird felt a sense of sorrow and helplessness. Later on Air Force One, while Judge Sarah Hughes swore in Lyndon Johnson as president of the United States, Lady Bird's sense of history came alive. She later recalled:

> I felt that I was stalking the stage in a Greek tragedy; just putting one foot before the other. There was a sense of unreality and nightmare and great tragedy; yet there was also a sense of wanting to take in, and remember, everything that was going on . . .

During the next few weeks, including the time of President Kennedy's funeral, Lady Bird was solicitous of Jacqueline Kennedy's comfort, waiting to move into the White House until the Kennedy family had finished packing and moving. She told reporters, "I wish to heaven I could serve Mrs. Kennedy's happiness. I can at least serve her convenience." She was also well aware of the changes that would affect her daughters. Secret Service men were assigned to follow Lynda Bird to classes and on dates at The University of Texas, and Lucy's girlhood took on all the aspects of a major media event. To keep her mindful of her heritage and a sense of family closeness, at Christmas that year Lyndon Johnson presented his wife with a photograph of himself, inscribed with the same words he had written on the first photograph he had given her when they met: "For Bird, a girl of principles, ideals, and refinement, from her admirer, Lyndon."

During the Johnson years in the White House Lyndon Johnson found much to admire in his wife. Lady Bird's strong qualities were never more in evidence than as First Lady of the United States, when she brought to the White House a sense of Texas warmth and hospitality. There were many "acts of grace if not delight" that she described in her *A White House Diary*, and she was always beside her husband, seeing that he appeared in the best light under even the most grueling circumstances. Once when he complained of the crowded schedule Lady Bird had accepted for him, grumbling to publisher Katherine Graham about an engagement his wife had accepted, Graham told him, "She also got you where you are today."

The woman whom her press secretary Liz Carpenter once described as "a touch of velvet, with the stamina of steel," needed all the strength she could muster for the whistlestop tour through the South during Johnson's 1964 campaign. Numerous Southern leaders differed with President Johnson over his civil rights bill and refused to be part of Lady Bird's barnstorming effort on her husband's behalf. She often found hostile crowds and signs saying, "Fly Home, Lady Bird," even in the state of Alabama where she had numerous relatives and childhood friends.

When her daughter Lucy changed the spelling of her name to "Luci," Lady Bird refused to become excited, but Luci's conversion to Catholicism on her eighteenth birthday was another time of adjustment. Lady Bird took pride in her daughters's toleration of the media and their acceptance of all the activities that surrounded the First Lady. Lady Bird relished the rush of parties when Luci married Patrick Nugent and when Lynda Bird wed Charles Robb in the White House. The birth of her first grandchild, Patrick Lyndon, when the Johnsons were in the White House was another source of happiness and fulfillment to her.

Instead of following a political program set by her husband or a cultural one to rival Jacqueline Kennedy's sponsorship of the arts, Lady Bird pioneered a nationwide beautification program that gained her recognition from organizations ranging from the Sierra Club to the Industrial Designers Society of America. In 1965 she organized the Committee for a More Beautiful Capital in Washington, leading the effort in planting thousands of spring flowers such as tulips, azaleas, and daffodils throughout the district. The girlhood years spent exploring nature with Aunt Effie were inspiration for her concern with beautification, and she often recalled her joy in "walking through the piney woods of East Texas listening to the wind sighing, or along the banks of Caddo Lake with gnarled cypresses, trees heavy with moss . . . ."

She set her goal as First Lady to be a doer rather than a talker, and Lady Bird Johnson seemed to be everywhere, planting pansies on Washington's mall, a dogwood on Interstate 95, and two cherry trees, gifts of the Japanese government, at the Tidal Basin during the opening of the 1965 National Cherry Blossom Festival. When daughter Luci quipped, "My mother really digs those trees," Lady Bird laughed that she would settle for a simple epitaph for her life: "She planted three trees."

No place in the United States was too remote for Lady Bird Johnson to explore in order to help better the environment. Secretary of the Interior Stewart Udall and Mary Lasker, head of the Lasker Foundation, convinced her that her support was needed in behalf of beautification, and in February 1965 President Johnson sent a Message of National Beauty to Congress. The White House Conference on National Beauty followed, with numerous organizations and officials lending their support to the First Lady's beautification program. When President Johnson signed the highway beautification bill into law on October 22, 1965, much of the credit for the passage of the bill went to Lady Bird, who had successfully lobbied members of Congress and had written letters to editors of thousands of newspapers.

Whether rafting down the Rio Grande, exploring blighted neighborhoods, or leading a group through a western canyon, Lady Bird remained at the forefront of the beautification effort.

One Republican stated that Lady Bird had done so much for beautification that he felt guilty every time he planted a geranium. In addition to her activities on behalf of the environment, Lady Bird took an active role in promoting the president's education program, including Head Start. When the Johnsons left the White House Lady Bird had well earned the comparisons that people made between her and Eleanor Roosevelt as active, socially-concerned First Ladies.

The final months of Lyndon Johnson's presidency were marred by the escalation of the war in Vietnam, rioting at the 1968 Democratic convention, and an increasing hostility toward the president by many people. When Lyndon Johnson announced in March 1968 that he would neither seek nor accept his party's nomination for another term as president, Lady Bird shared in his anxiety and frustrations about Vietnam and in his sad decision that it was time to step down as president. In January 1969, when President Richard Nixon was inaugurated, the Johnsons ate lunch with Washington friends and then flew home to Texas. As their airplane landed at Bergstrom Air Force Base near Austin, they saw signs reading, "Welcome Home, Mr. President," and heard the U. T. Longhorn band playing "The Eyes of Texas." Warmed by their welcome, they flew on to the ranch, where aides dumped their luggage in one large pile. "The chariot has turned into a pumpkin, and all the mice have run away!" Lady Bird laughed.

In the months before her husband's death Lady Bird stayed busy helping with the plans for the LBJ Library and the School of Public Affairs at The University of Texas at Austin. Named a distinguished alumna of the university, the second woman so named, she was appointed to the university's board of regents by Governor Preston Smith in January 1971. Her appointment came as a surprise to members of the Texas press, as she had refused the first time that Smith asked her to serve. Then she reconsidered, after reflecting on the number of people she had observed who had refused positions for which she felt they were qualified. Many critics of the political control that has often dominated the university looked to her to dilute the power of Regent Chairman Frank C. Erwin, Jr., but she was an acquiescent regent and disappointed feminists by failing to work for leadership roles for women on the male-dominated UT faculty.

After her husband's death, Lady Bird busied herself with business and family interests, continuing to superintend the affairs of the LBJ Company, serving on the National Park Advisory Board, actively selling off the cattle and some of the LBJ ranchland, and continuing her work for beautification of the countryside. The Austin City Council named the park she helped landscape beside Town Lake in her honor, and wherever she spoke out for beautification she gained more friends dedicated to the preservation of the environment.

Her later years have given her time to catch up on the "mothering" she missed when her children were growing up. In 1977, when Lynda Bird's husband Charles Robb ran for lieutenant governor of Virginia, Lady Bird lent her support to the campaign by helping to care for the couple's children. She travels with her children and grandchildren, enjoying a vacation in Greece with her daughters and snorkeling with her grandchildren in the Virgin Islands. She spends a great deal of time at the LBJ ranch, enjoying the peacefulness of the countryside, often inviting guests at symposia at the LBJ Library to visit there. In her seventies she remains vibrant and active, a serenely handsome woman who has deservedly earned the respect of everyone who has known her or her husband. Many never admired her more than the day of her husband's funeral, as she stood under the spreading oak trees at the LBJ ranch, greeting visitors with a soft smile and thanking them for coming to pay their last respects to her husband. "Lady Bird never loses a friend," Lyndon Johnson once commented, and to many of his aides and supporters Lady Bird will always remain Lyndon Johnson's "right-hand woman."

REFERENCES

Bell, Jack. *The Johnson Treatment*. New York: Harper and Row, 1965.

Bengston, Carolyn Seay. "Lady Bird: America's First Lady." Austin *American-Statesman* (December 1, 1963): F-8.

Brandon, Henry. "Lady Bird Johnson Tells About Life With LBJ." New York *Times* magazine (September 10, 1967): 147-149.

Carpenter, Liz. *Ruffles and Flourishes*. Garden City: Doubleday and Company, 1970.

Christian, George. *The President Steps Down*. New York: Macmillan Company, 1970.

Foreman, Norma Holly. *The First Lady as a Leader of Public Opinion: A Study of the Role and Press Relations of Lady Bird Johnson* (Unpublished doctoral dissertation). The University of Texas at Austin.

Goldman, Eric F. *The Tragedy of Lyndon Johnson*. New York: Alfred A Knopf, 1969.

Hall, Gordon Langley. *Lady Bird & her daughters*. Philadelphia: Macrae Smith Company, 1967.

Johnson, Lady Bird. *A White House Diary*. New York: Holt, Rinehart and Winston, 1970.

Johnson, Lady Bird. "The Pioneer Spirit." *McCall's* magazine. (April 1976): 74.

Johnson, Rebekah Baines. *A Family Album*. New York: McGraw-Hill Book Company, 1965.

Kearns, Doris. *Lyndon Johnson and the American Dream*. New York: Harper and Row, 1964.

King, C. Richard. "seven who served." *Alcalde* (March-April 1979): 12.

Klinefelter, Karen. "Lady Bird Looks Both Ways." Dallas *Morning News* (January 12, 1969): E-1.

Leighton, Frances Spatz. "First Lady's First Day." *This Week* magazine (March 1, 1964): 6-12.

Lewine, Frances. "Family, Projects Ease Loneliness." Austin *American-Statesman* (May 20, 1973): C-1.

Lewine, Frances. "The Nation's Lady Bird." Austin *American-Statesman* (January 5,1964): D-1.

Means, Marianne. *The Woman in the White House*. New York: Random House, 1963.

Miller, Merle. *Lyndon*. New York: Putnam, 1979.

Montgomery, Linda. "The Johnson Women: Then and Now." *Texas Woman* (July 1979): 23-31.

Montgomery, Ruth. *Mrs. LBJ*. New York: Holt, Rinehart and Winston, 1970.

Mooney, Booth. *LBJ: An Irreverent Chronicle*. New York: T.Y. Crowell, 1976.

Mooney, Booth. *The Lyndon Johnson Story*. New York: Farrar, Straus and Company, 1956.

"Mrs. Johnson Honored for Environmental Work." Austin *American-Statesman* (October 29, 1972): 15.

"Mrs. LBJ Country." *Look* (July 12, 1966): 35-39.

"Mrs. LBJ Is Among UT Regent Appointees." Austin *American-Statesman* (January 9, 1971): 1.

Newlon, Clarke. *LBJ: The Man from Johnson City*. New York: Dodd, Mead and Company, 1964.

Sadler, Christine. "Our Very Busy First Lady." *McCall's* magazine (March 1954): 72.

Schreiber, Flora Rheta. "The Personal Story of the First Family." *Family Weekly* magazine (February 2, 1964): 4.

Taylor, Leslie. "Mrs. LBJ Said 'No' First Time to Regent Seat." Austin *American-Statesman* (February 27, 1971): 1.

"The Doors of the World Swung Open." *Alcalde* (November 1964): 18.

"The First Lady Bird." *Time* magazine (August 28, 1964): 36.

Thomas, Helen. "'What More Could I Ask?'" Dallas *Morning News* (January 26. 1973): 1.

"Ways to Beautify America." *U.S. News & World Report* (February 22, 1965): 72-77.

Index

Clara Driscoll ● Louise Ervendberg ● Oveta Culp Hobby ● Babe
● Sarah Hughes ● Elisabet Ney ● Barbara Jordan ● Henriet
Lizzie Johnson Williams ● Lupe Anguiano ● Adina De Zavala ●
Lady Bird Johnson ● Jane Long ● Annie Webb Blanton ● Mary
Jane Long ● Annie Webb Blanton ● Mary Austin Holley ● Mi
Clara Driscoll ● Louise Ervendberg ● Oveta Culp Hobby ● Babe
● Sarah Hughes ● Elisabet Ney ● Barbara Jordan ● Henriet
Lizzie Johnson Williams ● Lupe Anguiano ● Adina De Zavala ●
Lady Bird Johnson ● Jane Long ● Annie Webb Blanton ● Mary
Jane Long ● Annie Webb Blanton ● Mary Austin Holley ● Mi
Clara Driscoll ● Louise Ervendberg ● Oveta Culp Hobby ● Babe
● Sarah Hughes ● Elisabet Ney ● Barbara Jordan ● Henriet
Lizzie Johnson Williams ● Lupe Anguiano ● Adina De Zavala ●
Lady Bird Johnson ● Jane Long ● Annie Webb Blanton ● Mary
Jane Long ● Annie Webb Blanton ● Mary Austin Holley ● Mi
Clara Driscoll ● Louise Ervendberg ● Oveta Culp Hobby ● Babe
● Sarah Hughes ● Elisabet Ney ● Barbara Jordan ● Henriet
Lizzie Johnson Williams ● Lupe Anguiano ● Adina De Zavala ●
Jane Long ● Annie Webb Blanton ● Mary Austin Holley ● Mi
Clara Driscoll ● Louise Ervendberg ● Oveta Culp Hobby ● Babe
● Sarah Hughes ● Elisabet Ney ● Barbara Jordan ● Henriet
Lizzie Johnson Williams ● Lupe Anguiano ● Adina De Zavala ●
Lady Bird Johnson ● Jane Long ● Annie Webb Blanton ● Mary
Jane Long ● Annie Webb Blanton ● Mary Austin Holley ● Mi
Clara Driscoll ● Louise Ervendberg ● Oveta Culp Hobby ● Babe
● Sarah Hughes ● Elisabet Ney ● Barbara Jordan ● Henriet
Lizzie Johnson Williams ● Lupe Anguiano ● Adina De Zavala ●
Lady Bird Johnson ● Jane Long ● Annie Webb Blanton ● Mary
Jane Long ● Annie Webb Blanton ● Mary Austin Holley ● Mi
Clara Driscoll ● Louise Ervendberg ● Oveta Culp Hobby ● Babe
● Sarah Hughes ● Elisabet Ney ● Barbara Jordan ● Henrie
Lizzie Johnson Williams ● Lupe Anguiano ● Adina De Zavala ●